Low Cholesterol Diet Cookbook
for Beginners

160+ Easy and Delicious Recipes to Support Heart Health
and Overall Wellness | Includes a 45-Day Meal Plan for
Effective Cardiovascular Improvement

Olivia Robbins

Disclaimer

The content of this book, including all recipes, meal plans, and health advice, is intended for informational and educational purposes only and should not be considered a substitute for professional medical advice, diagnosis, or treatment. Always consult your physician or a qualified healthcare provider before making changes to your diet, especially if you have a medical condition or are taking any medications. The author and publisher disclaim any liability for any adverse effects arising from using or applying the information contained herein.

The nutritional values of recipes in this book are estimates and may vary based on specific ingredients and methods of preparation. The information provided in this cookbook is not intended to diagnose, treat, cure, or prevent any disease.

Table of contents

Introduction

What is the Low Cholesterol Diet?

The Low Cholesterol Diet Cookbook for Beginners is more than just a collection of recipes or eating plan — it's a way of eating that prioritizes heart health, longevity, and overall wellness. As more people become aware of the risks associated with high cholesterol, this diet offers a proactive way to manage those risks through mindful, nutritious eating; by focusing on reducing harmful fats and embracing foods that naturally lower cholesterol, the Low Cholesterol Diet provides a sustainable, long-term approach to health.

As you embark on this path with our Low Cholesterol Diet Cookbook for Beginners, it's essential to understand the role cholesterol plays in your body and how managing it can significantly impact your overall health.

The waxy substance in your blood, cholesterol, is essential for developing healthy cells. Your body produces all the cholesterol it needs, but it also comes from specific meals. Two primary forms of cholesterol circulate in your bloodstream: LDL (bad cholesterol) and HDL (good cholesterol).

Here are the core components of the diet:

Rich in Fibre Products: Foods such as fruits, vegetables, cereals, barley, beans, oats, and lentils are high in soluble fiber and help lower blood cholesterol absorption.

Emphasis on Healthy Fats: Unsaturated fats found in olive oil, avocados, nuts, seeds, and fatty fish (like salmon and mackerel) help improve cholesterol levels by lowering LDL and raising HDL cholesterol.

Minimal in Trans and Saturated Fats: The diet minimizes the consumption of red meat, full-fat dairy, and processed foods, often high in saturated and trans fats that raise LDL cholesterol.

Plant-Based Focus: While lean meats and fish are allowed in moderation, plant-based proteins like beans, legumes, and tofu are heavily encouraged.

These ideas support cardiovascular health by providing a natural, food-based method of managing cholesterol without prescription drugs.

Nutritional Information for Recipes

Understanding the nutritional content of your meals is essential for managing cholesterol levels. We've provided detailed nutritional information for each recipe in this cookbook, including calories, total fat, saturated fat, cholesterol, sodium, and protein. This allows you to make informed decisions and track your daily intake, ensuring that you stay within the recommended heart-healthy diet guidelines.

By referencing this information, you can balance your meals and snacks throughout the day to meet your dietary goals without compromising flavor or satisfaction.

The Low Cholesterol Diet's Health Benefits

The Low Cholesterol Diet's ability to lower the risk of cardiovascular diseases, including heart attacks and strokes, is one of its key benefits. But its benefits go far beyond that:

Improved Heart Health: Reducing low-density lipoprotein cholesterol lowers the risk of artery blockages and enhances circulation by preventing plaque development in the arteries.

Weight Management: The diet encourages nutrient-dense meals high in fiber and other nutrients but low in calories. This kind of eating can help you manage weight more healthily without feeling deprived.

Enhanced Longevity: Individuals can reduce inflammation and oxidative stress linked to aging and chronic diseases by eating whole foods and healthy fats.

Better Blood Pressure Control: A diet focused on whole grains, fruits, and vegetables—all high in potassium and magnesium—can help control blood pressure.

Improved Mood and Cognitive Function: A diet rich in vitamins, antioxidants, and omega-3 fatty acids enhances cognitive function and promotes brain health. Studies suggest that omega-3s, in particular, can help improve mood and reduce symptoms of depression.

Better Sleep: Many people experience improved sleep patterns by avoiding heavy, fatty foods and focusing on lighter, more balanced meals. Better-quality sleep can be achieved by controlling the hormones that contribute to sleep with lean proteins and healthy fats.

Increased Energy Levels: If you swap out processed foods for nutrient-dense whole foods, you won't have to worry about feeling lethargic after consuming high-fat, high-sugar meals. This will give your body the nutrition to maintain energy levels throughout the day.

Embracing the Low Cholesterol Diet Cookbook means adopting a lifestyle that values health, mindfulness, and connection. Regular physical activity — whether a daily walk, yoga, or strength training — synergizes with the diet to promote heart health.

When you approach food with intention and purpose, you're more likely to make healthier choices and savor your meals. Over time, these habits impact your well-being, helping you live a longer, healthier, and more fulfilling life.

How This Cookbook Can Help

Transitioning to a low-cholesterol diet doesn't mean you have to compromise on flavor or satisfaction. This cookbook will help you adopt a heart-healthy lifestyle by guiding you through delicious, nutritious, yet straightforward-to-make meals.

These dietary changes can improve your cholesterol levels and enhance your overall well-being. Remember, every small change counts, and your journey toward heart health is personal.

Myths and Facts about Cholesterol

Myth 1: You Should Avoid All Cholesterol

Fact: Cholesterol is a vital substance that your body needs. It is necessary to produce cell membranes and synthesize vitamin D and hormones like estrogen and testosterone. The body makes all the cholesterol it requires, and it becomes problematic only when levels in the blood become too high due to dietary intake.

Myth 2: You Don't Need to Worry About Cholesterol Until You're Older

Fact: High cholesterol can affect individuals of all ages, including children and young adults. The two significant health hazards for people of any age are eating poorly and not exercising. Early lifestyle choices can set the foundation for future health, making it essential to adopt heart-healthy habits sooner rather than later.

Myth 3: Thin People Don't Have High Cholesterol

Fact: High cholesterol can affect everyone, regardless of weight. It's a common misconception that only overweight or obese individuals are at risk for high cholesterol. In reality, cholesterol levels are influenced by various factors, including genetics, diet, and lifestyle. Being thin doesn't guarantee low cholesterol, as even those who appear outwardly healthy can have elevated LDL (bad) cholesterol levels, which increases the risk of heart disease.

Myth 4: Eating Cholesterol-Rich Foods Raises Blood Cholesterol Levels

Fact: Dietary cholesterol has a more minor impact on blood cholesterol levels than once believed. Saturated and trans fats found in meals like processed snacks, full-fat dairy products, and red meat are the main offenders.

Myth 5: All Fats are Bad for Cholesterol Levels

Fact: Not all fats are created equal. Unsaturated fats can raise HDL cholesterol and lower LDL cholesterol. Examples of these fats include almonds, avocados, olive oil, and fatty seafood like salmon.

Myth 6: Only Medication Can Lower High Cholesterol

Fact: Lifestyle changes can significantly impact cholesterol levels. Effective tactics include:

- Eating a diet low in trans and saturated fats.
- Exercising frequently.
- Keeping a healthy weight.
- Abstaining from tobacco use.

Such changes can reduce LDL cholesterol by up to 20-30%, which may sometimes eliminate the need for medication.

Myth 7: Children Don't Need to Have Their Cholesterol Checked

Fact: A genetic condition known as familial hypercholesterolemia results in high cholesterol from a young age. Early identification can assist in minimizing the dangers associated with this condition.

Myth 8: High Cholesterol Always Shows Symptoms

Fact: High cholesterol typically has no symptoms and is often called a "silent" condition. Many people are unaware they have high cholesterol until they experience a severe event like a heart attack or stroke. Frequent screening is essential for managing and detecting problems early.

Myth 9: Switching to "Cholesterol-Free" Foods is Enough

Fact: Foods labeled "cholesterol-free" can still be high in saturated and trans fats, raising LDL cholesterol levels. It's important to read nutrition labels carefully and focus on overall nutrient content rather than just cholesterol claims.

Myth 10: If You Have High HDL, High LDL Doesn't Matter

Fact: While high HDL cholesterol is beneficial, it doesn't negate the risks associated with high LDL cholesterol. Both levels need to be within healthy ranges to reduce the risk of cardiovascular diseases.

Understanding the myths and facts about cholesterol is the first step toward taking control of your heart health.

Ingredients to Embrace

The Low Cholesterol Diet emphasizes nutrient-dense, fiber-rich, and heart-healthy foods that support optimal cholesterol levels while promoting satiety, energy, and long-term health. Here's a breakdown of foods you should aim to include:

Fruits and Vegetables

Why They're Recommended: Fruits and vegetables are high in fiber, vitamins, and antioxidants, all of which help lower LDL cholesterol and reduce inflammation. Fiber, particularly soluble fiber, helps remove cholesterol from the bloodstream by binding to it and facilitating its excretion.

Examples: Apples, berries, oranges, spinach, kale, broccoli, carrots, and tomatoes.

Practical Tips: Aim for various colors to ensure a broad intake of nutrients. Add vegetables to soups, salads, or stir-fries, and enjoy fruits as snacks or desserts. Opt for fresh, frozen, or unsweetened dried varieties to avoid added sugars and preservatives.

Whole Grains

Why They're Recommended: Brown rice, barley, and oats are examples of whole grains that are good providers of soluble fiber, which lowers blood cholesterol absorption.

Examples: Oats, quinoa, barley, brown rice, whole wheat bread, and whole grain pasta.

Practical Tips: Start your day with a bowl of oatmeal topped with fruit, or swap white bread for whole-grain options. Incorporate grains like quinoa or barley into salads or side dishes to boost fiber intake.

Healthy Fats

Why They're Recommended: Healthy fats, especially unsaturated fats, help raise HDL (good) cholesterol while lowering LDL cholesterol. They also provide essential fatty acids like omega-3s, which support heart health and reduce inflammation.

Examples: Olive oil, avocados, nuts, seeds (flaxseeds, chia seeds), and fatty fish (salmon, mackerel, sardines).

Practical Tips: Use olive oil to cook and dress salads. As a snack, grab some almonds or sunflower seeds. Include fatty fish in your meals at least twice a week to increase heart-healthy omega-3 fatty acids.

Legumes and Plant-Based Proteins

Why They're Recommended: Beans, lentils, chickpeas, and other legumes are high in fiber and low in fat. They offer plant-based protein and can be an excellent substitute for red meat, which is high in saturated fat.

Examples: Lentils, black beans, kidney beans, chickpeas, tofu, and tempeh.

Practical Tips: Add beans to soups, salads, or casseroles for a nutrient boost. Try plant-based proteins like tofu in stir-fries or tempeh in sandwiches as a meat substitute.

Lean Proteins

Why They're Recommended: Selecting lean protein sources like fish and chicken can help lower saturated fat intake, which is connected to elevated levels of low-density lipoprotein (LDL) cholesterol.

Examples: Skinless chicken, turkey, and fish like salmon, tuna, and trout.

Practical Tips: Grill, bake, or steam lean proteins instead of frying them. Try marinating chicken or fish in herbs and spices for added flavor without extra fat.

Ingredients to Avoid

Certain foods can raise LDL cholesterol levels, contribute to plaque buildup in arteries, and hinder the overall health goals of the Low Cholesterol Diet. Here's what to avoid or limit:

Saturated Fats

Why They're Restricted: Saturated fats increase LDL cholesterol, contributing to cardiovascular disease development. These fats are found in high amounts in animal products and processed foods.

Examples: Red meat, pork, lamb, full-fat dairy products (cheese, butter, cream), coconut oil, and palm oil.

Challenges: Many people find it difficult to reduce their intake of red meat and full-fat dairy, staples in traditional diets.

Tips to Overcome: Substitute red meat with lean poultry or plant-based proteins. Swap full-fat dairy with low-fat or non-fat versions. Use olive oil instead of butter for baking and cooking.

Trans Fats

Why They're Restricted: Trans fats raise LDL cholesterol and lower HDL cholesterol, making them one of the most harmful types of fat for heart health. They are found in partially hydrogenated oils and processed foods.

Examples: Packaged snacks, baked goods (cakes, cookies, pastries), fried foods, and margarine.

Challenges: Trans fats can be hidden in many processed foods, even those marketed as "low-fat" or "healthy."

Tips to Overcome: Always check food labels for "partially hydrogenated oils" and avoid these products. Opt for homemade snacks and baked goods where you control the ingredients.

Refined Grains and Sugary Foods

Why They're Restricted: Refined grains and added sugars contribute to weight gain, negatively affecting cholesterol levels and overall heart health. They also lack the fiber in whole grains, which is essential for lowering cholesterol.

Examples: White bread, white rice, sugary cereals, pastries, candy, and sugary drinks (soda, sweetened teas).

Challenges: Sugar cravings can make it hard to avoid these foods.

Tips to Overcome: Choose whole-grain alternatives like whole-wheat bread or brown rice. Choose fruits or homemade desserts made with natural sweeteners like honey or maple syrup for sweets.

Cooking Methods: Enhance Flavor Without the Extra Fat

One of the best ways to follow the Low Cholesterol Diet is to use cooking methods that enhance flavor without adding unwanted calories or unhealthy fats.

Healthier Cooking Techniques

- Grilling or Broiling: These methods allow fat to drip away from the food, making them great for cooking lean proteins like chicken or fish.
- Baking or Roasting: Baking vegetables or fish enhances their natural flavors without needing extra oil. Utilize spices and herbs to give the food more flavor.
- Steaming: Steaming is ideal for retaining vegetable nutrients without adding fat. You can enhance the flavor with herbs, lemon juice, or vinegar.
- Sautéing: Use a small amount of olive oil to sauté vegetables or lean proteins. For an even lighter option, sauté with vegetable broth.

Enhance Flavor with Herbs and Spices

To enhance the flavor of your food, use herbs and spices rather than heavy sauces: garlic, onion, ginger, and turmeric are anti-inflammatory and help reduce cholesterol.

Fresh herbs like basil, parsley, cilantro, and thyme add freshness and zest to any meal without extra calories.

How to Incorporate the Low Cholesterol Diet into Your Life

To make it easier to follow the Low Cholesterol Diet, consider these practical steps:

Meal Planning: Meal planning is the key to successfully following the Low Cholesterol Diet. It ensures you're prepared with nutritious options, reducing the temptation to reach for unhealthy alternatives. Plan your meals for the week ahead, focusing on balanced recipes that include a variety of vegetables, lean proteins, and whole grains. Incorporate heart-healthy snacks like carrot sticks and hummus or a handful of nuts to keep you satisfied between meals.

Shopping Smart: When grocery shopping, stick to the store's perimeter, where fresh produce, lean meats, and whole grains are typically found. Avoid processed foods in the center aisles, which often contain hidden trans fats and added sugars.

Cooking Techniques: Instead of frying, opt for grilling, baking, steaming, or sautéing. These techniques allow you to add healthy fats without sacrificing the nutritional content of your products.

Batch Cooking: Prepare large quantities of critical components, like roasted vegetables or cooked grains, for multiple weekly meals. This step saves time and ensures you always have healthy options available.

Prep Snacks: Having healthy snacks like cut veggies, hummus, or a handful of nuts ready to go can help avoid reaching for processed snacks.

Use Tools and Apps: Numerous tools and apps help with meal planning and food tracking. Such apps offer recipe suggestions, grocery lists, and calorie tracking to ensure you stick to your diet goals. They can also help you monitor your intake of saturated fat and cholesterol.

Taking small steps like these will make adopting the Low Cholesterol Diet manageable and enjoyable.

Dining Out: Staying on Track While Enjoying Social Settings

Eating out or attending social gatherings can be difficult, but you can follow the Low Cholesterol Diet without experiencing any restrictions if you know a few tricks.

Dining at Restaurants

When eating out, it's vital to choose dishes that align with the **Low Cholesterol Diet** principles:

- Review the Menu in Advance: Many restaurants post their menus online, so take a few minutes to look for heart-healthy options before you arrive.
- Request Adjustments: Ask your server to make changes, such as grilling rather than frying or serving with dressing on the side. Eating places usually happily accommodate dietary restrictions.
- Select Simple, Whole Foods: Try to find recipes that include salads, steamed veggies, or grilled chicken or fish. Avoid fried foods, creamy sauces, and heavy cheese or butter dishes.

Handling Social Events

Social events can present temptations, but with a bit of planning, you can still enjoy yourself while staying true to your goals:

- Eat Before You Go: Have a light, healthy snack before attending a party or event. This approach will help curb hunger and reduce the temptation to overindulge in unhealthy options.
- Bring a Dish: If appropriate, offer a dish that fits your dietary needs. This step ensures there will be something for you to eat, and it's a great way to share heart-healthy food with others.
- Practice Mindful Eating: If you're at a buffet or dinner party, practice portion control and mindful eating. Focus on the company and conversation rather than the food.

Troubleshooting Common Challenges

Even with the best intentions, there will be challenges along the way. Here's how to overcome common obstacles:

Dealing with Cravings

Cravings for unhealthy foods can strike, but there are ways to manage them:

- Healthy Substitutes: Grab a handful of almonds or a little fruit if you want something sweet. For salty cravings, try air-popped popcorn or roasted chickpeas.
- Hydration: Sometimes, cravings can be mistaken for hunger or thirst. Sip a glass of water to see if the urge goes away after ten minutes.

Handling Slip-Ups

No one is perfect, and dietary slip-ups are bound to happen. Don't let one indulgence derail your progress:

- Get Back on Track: If you've strayed from the Low Cholesterol Diet, resume your healthy eating habits at the next meal. One mistake doesn't undo all your progress.
- Reflect and Adjust: Think about why the slip-up occurred. Were you too hungry, or did you need to have healthy snacks available? Use the experience to refine your strategy moving forward.

Discovering New Flavors, Health, and Confidence

Making the shift to a Low Cholesterol Diet can feel overwhelming at first, but with the proper knowledge and approach, it becomes easier to adopt these healthier habits. Start by adding more recommended foods to your diet rather than feeling restricted by what you can't have. Experiment with flavors and recipes until you find heart-healthy meals you love eating.

Making educated decisions, experimenting with new foods, and adhering to sensible meal planning and shopping techniques will enable you to confidently start your road toward lower cholesterol and a healthy lifestyle.

Celebrate Your Progress and Stay Motivated

The Low Cholesterol Diet is a lifestyle change that requires effort, but the rewards for your heart and overall health are well worth it.

Celebrate small victories, whether trying a new heart-healthy recipe or making it through a challenging social event without derailing your progress. Stay motivated by remembering your goals, and keep experimenting with new flavors and dishes that align with the diet's principles. You're on the right track, and with these pointers and strategies, you may successfully and self-assuredly incorporate the Low Cholesterol Diet into your daily routine.

Let's get cooking for a healthier heart!

Breakfast Recipes

Creamy Avocado Toast with Tomato and Basil

Yield: 2 servings | **Preparation Time:** 10 minutes | **Cooking Time:** 5 minutes

Calories: 295 kcal | Carbohydrates: 34g | Total Fat: 18g | Saturated Fat: 2.5g | Cholesterol: 0mg | Protein: 6g | Sodium: 170mg
(per serving)

Ingredients:

- 2 pieces of sprouted or whole grain bread (preferably unsweetened and low-sodium)
- 1 ripe avocado (about 150g)
- 1 medium tomato (about 100g), thinly sliced
- 1 tbsp (2.5g) fresh basil, chopped
- 1 tsp (5 ml) extra virgin olive oil (optional for drizzling)
- ½ tsp (2.5 ml) fresh lemon juice
- 1 garlic (optional)
- Salt to taste (preferably a heart-friendly variety, such as sea salt or low-sodium salt)
- Freshly ground black pepper to taste
- 1 tbsp (10 g) hemp seeds or flaxseeds (optional)

Instructions:

Remove the pit from the avocado, cut it in half, and scoop the flesh into a small bowl. Mash the avocado with a fork until smooth but with some small chunks for texture. Incorporate the newly squeezed lemon juice, a small amount of salt, and pepper, blending thoroughly.

Slices of whole grain bread should be gently toasted in a skillet or toaster until golden and crispy.

If you like a subtle garlic flavor, gently rub the halved garlic clove over the warm toast after toasting. This adds an aromatic layer of flavor without needing extra fats.

Assemble the toast. Spread an even layer of the mashed avocado mixture onto each slice of toasted bread.

Place the thinly sliced tomatoes over the layer of avocados. Sprinkle the fresh basil evenly over the tomatoes.

Drizzle extra virgin olive oil over the toast if desired for additional richness. At the end, add optional hemp or flaxseeds for more texture and nutrients. Season with a little more salt and pepper to taste.

Serve immediately and enjoy the toast fresh to maintain the bread's crunch and the ingredients' freshness.

Berry and Spinach Smoothie Bowl with Chia Seeds

Yield: 2 servings | **Preparation Time:** 10 minutes | **Cooking Time:** None

Calories: 285 kcal | Carbohydrates: 42g | Total Fat: 9g | Saturated Fat: 1g | Cholesterol: 0mg | Protein: 9g | Sodium: 80mg
(per serving)

Ingredients:

- 1 cup (150g) frozen mixed berries, including strawberries, raspberries, and blueberries
- 1 banana, sliced
- 1 cup (30g) fresh spinach
- ½ cup (120 ml) unsweetened almond milk or milk from any plant
- ½ cup (120 ml) plain unsweetened Greek yogurt or non-dairy yogurt
- 1 tbsp (12g) chia seeds
- ½ tsp (2.5 ml) vanilla extract (optional)
- 1 tbsp (16g) almond butter (optional for creaminess and added protein)

Toppings (customizable):

- 2 tbsp (24g) chia seeds (for garnish)
- 2 tbsp (28g) granola (low-sugar)
- 1 tbsp (10g) flaxseeds or hemp seeds
- Fresh berries (blueberries, raspberries, strawberries, etc.)
- Coconut flakes (unsweetened)
- Sliced almonds or pumpkin seeds

Instructions:

Blend the base ingredients:

Combine the frozen mixed berries, banana, spinach, almond milk, Greek yogurt, chia seeds, optional vanilla extract, and almond butter in a blender. Blend until creamy and smooth. If the smoothie is too thick, add almond milk, 1 tablespoon at a time, until it reaches the right consistency.

Divide the smoothie evenly between two bowls.

Add toppings: Top each bowl with your choice of toppings. For texture and extra nutrition, you can sprinkle chia seeds, granola, fresh berries, banana slices, flaxseeds, coconut flakes, and/or nuts.

Serve immediately, as the vibrant ingredients are best consumed right after preparation to maintain flavor and texture.

Oatmeal with Almond Butter and Fresh Banana

Yield: 2 servings   **Preparation Time:** 5 minutes   **Cooking Time:** 10 minutes

Calories: 295 kcal | Carbohydrates: 34g | Total Fat: 18g | Saturated Fat: 2.5g | Cholesterol: 0mg | Protein: 6g | Sodium: 170mg
(per serving)

Ingredients:

- 1 cup (90g) old-fashioned rolled oats
- 2 cups (480 ml) water (or unsweetened almond milk for creamier oatmeal)
- 1 medium banana, sliced
- 2 tbsp (32g) almond butter (unsweetened)
- 1 tsp (2.5g) ground cinnamon (optional)
- 1 tsp (5 ml) vanilla extract (optional)
- 1 tsp (4g) chia seeds
- Pinch of salt (0.5g) optional, preferably a low-sodium variety

Customizable Ingredients/Garnishes:

- Fresh berries (blueberries, strawberries, or raspberries)
- Sliced almonds or walnuts (for extra crunch)
- Hemp seeds or flaxseeds
- Unsweetened coconut flakes
- Maple syrup (or honey, if desired, for sweetness)
- Cacao nibs (for a chocolatey touch)

Instructions:

Place the two cups of water (or almond milk) in a medium pot and bring to a boil. Once boiling, stir in the rolled oats. After lowering the heat to low, simmer the oats for 5-7 minutes, stirring now and again, or until they have absorbed most of the liquid and thickened to your preferred consistency.

Once the oats are cooked, stir in the optional ground cinnamon, vanilla extract, and a pinch of salt to enhance the flavor. You can also add the chia seeds for additional fiber and nutrients at this stage.

Divide the cooked oats into two bowls. Top each bowl with 1 tablespoon of almond butter, swirling it into the oats for a creamy texture.

Arrange the sliced banana evenly on top of the oatmeal. Depending on your preferences, you can sprinkle additional toppings like fresh berries, seeds, nuts, or coconut flakes.

Enjoy your oatmeal warm. If you want it a little sweeter, drizzle some honey or maple syrup on top.

For a heartier breakfast, include nuts or berries to increase the fiber and antioxidant value.

Fluffy Egg White and Veggie Omelet

Yield: 2 servings   **Preparation Time:** 10 minutes   **Cooking Time:** 10 minutes

Calories: 150 kcal | Carbohydrates: 7g | Total Fat: 6g | Saturated Fat: 1g | Cholesterol: 0mg | Protein: 15g | Sodium: 210mg
(per serving)

Ingredients:

- 6 large egg whites
- ½ cup (15g) spinach, roughly chopped
- ¼ cup (40g) bell pepper, diced (any color)
- ¼ cup (40g) cherry tomatoes, halved
- ¼ cup (20g) mushrooms, sliced
- 1 small onion, finely chopped
- 1 tbsp (15 ml) olive oil (or a cooking spray for a lower-fat option)
- 1 tbsp (4g) fresh parsley, chopped
- Salt to taste (preferably low-sodium)
- Freshly ground black pepper to taste
- ½ tsp (0.5g) dried oregano (optional)
- 2 tbsp (30g) feta cheese (optional for a creamy texture)
- Cooking spray (optional for lower-fat cooking)

Customizable Ingredients/Garnishes:

- Avocado slices for healthy fats
- Chopped cilantro or fresh basil for garnish
- Sliced olives for added flavor
- Hot sauce or salsa for spice

Instructions:

Heat 1 tablespoon of olive oil (or use cooking spray for a lower-fat option) in a non-stick skillet over medium heat. Add the chopped onion and sauté for 2-3 minutes until it softens. After that, add the cherry tomatoes, chopped bell peppers, and mushrooms. Cook for 2-3 minutes or until all the vegetables are soft. After adding the spinach, simmer for another minute or until it wilts. Arrange the veggies on a plate and season with salt and pepper.

Lightly whisk the egg whites in a medium-sized dish with a dash of salt, black pepper, and oregano (if using) until foamy. This helps incorporate air into the whites, making the omelet fluffier.

Wipe the skillet clean and spray it with cooking spray or add olive oil. Pour in the whisked egg whites and cook over medium-low heat. Allow the eggs to set on the bottom while gently pushing the edges inward to allow uncooked egg whites to flow to the edges of the pan.

When the egg whites are mostly set but still slightly runny on top (about 3-4 minutes), spoon the cooked veggies onto one half of the omelet. If using feta cheese, sprinkle it over the vegetables at this point. Using a spatula, fold the omelet in half, then continue cooking until it is fully set, about 1 more minute.

Carefully slide the omelet onto a plate and garnish with fresh parsley, avocado slices, or other desired toppings.

Serve this omelet with whole-grain toast or a small bowl of mixed fruit for added fiber and nutrients.

Chia Seed Pudding with Coconut and Mango

Yield: 2 servings   **Preparation Time:** 10 minutes   **Chilling Time:** 4 hours (or overnight)

Calories: 260 kcal | Carbohydrates: 27g | Total Fat: 15g | Saturated Fat: 10g | Cholesterol: 0mg | Protein: 5g | Sodium: 20mg
(per serving)

Ingredients:
- ¼ cup (45 g) chia seeds
- 1 cup (240 ml) unsweetened coconut milk (from a carton, not canned)
- 1 tbsp (15 ml) maple syrup (or honey, if desired for sweetness)
- ½ tsp (2.5 ml) vanilla extract (optional)
- 1 ripe mango, peeled and diced
- 2 tbsp (10g) unsweetened shredded coconut (for garnish)

Customizable Ingredients/Garnishes:
- Fresh berries (such as blueberries or raspberries)
- Sliced almonds or chopped walnuts (for crunch)
- Coconut flakes (for added texture)
- Mint leaves for a refreshing garnish
- Lime zest for extra zing

Instructions:
Whisk together the chia seeds, unsweetened coconut milk, maple syrup (if using), and vanilla extract in a medium bowl. Stir well to ensure the chia seeds are evenly distributed and not clumping together.

Cover the bowl and refrigerate for at least 4 hours or overnight. During this time, the chia seeds absorb the liquid and thicken into a pudding-like consistency. Stir the mixture once after the first 30 minutes to help the chia seeds distribute evenly.

While the chia pudding is setting, peel and dice the mango into small cubes. Set aside until ready to assemble.

Once the chia pudding has thickened, give it a quick stir. Divide the pudding between two bowls or glasses. Top each serving with half of the diced mango.

Top each dish with 1 tablespoon of shredded coconut for an added taste and texture. Optionally, add any other garnishes like fresh berries, mint leaves, or lime zest to taste.

Serve the chia pudding chilled. You can also keep it in the fridge for up to 2 days, making it a great meal prep option.

Pair this pudding with a handful of raw almonds or walnuts for a heartier meal or snack for added protein and healthy fats.

Layer the chia pudding and mango with granola to create a parfait-style dessert or breakfast.

Whole Wheat Pancakes with Blueberries

Yield: 4 servings (8 pancakes)   **Preparation Time:** 10 minutes   **Cooking Time:** 10 minutes

Calories: 220 kcal | Carbohydrates: 36g | Total Fat: 6g | Saturated Fat: 1g | Cholesterol: 0mg | Protein: 6g | Sodium: 210mg
(per serving)

Ingredients:
- 1 cup (120g) whole wheat flour
- 1 tbsp baking powder
- 1 tbsp (12 g) ground flaxseed (optional for added fiber and omega-3s)
- 1 tbsp (15 ml) maple syrup or honey
- 1 large egg white or ¼ cup (60 ml) unsweetened applesauce
- 1 cup (240g) of unsweetened almond milk or milk from any plant
- 1 tsp (5 ml) vanilla extract
- 1 tbsp (15 ml) of heated coconut oil or olive oil
- ½ cup (75g) fresh or frozen blueberries
- Cooking spray

Customizable Ingredients/Garnishes:
- Fresh blueberries, strawberries, or raspberries (for serving)
- Sliced almonds or chopped walnuts
- Maple syrup (for drizzling)
- Greek yogurt (or plant-based yogurt for topping)
- Cinnamon or nutmeg (for added flavor)

Instructions:
In a large mixing bowl, whisk together the whole wheat flour, baking powder, and ground flaxseed (if using). In a separate bowl, combine the almond milk, egg white (or applesauce for a vegan option), maple syrup, vanilla extract, and olive oil. Whisk until smooth and well combined.

Gradually whisk the dry ingredients with the liquid. Be careful not to overmix—lumps are okay! Add the blueberries.

Cooking spray or a small quantity of oil can gently lubricate a non-stick skillet or griddle before heating it over medium heat.

Cook the pancakes:

For each pancake, pour about ¼ cup of batter onto the skillet. Cook for 2-3 minutes or until bubbles form on the surface and the edges look set. After flipping, cook for a further 1-2 minutes or until golden brown and cooked through.

Cook the remaining batter while transferring the pancakes to a platter and covering them to keep them warm. Serve the pancakes topped with additional fresh blueberries, nuts, and a drizzle of maple syrup, if desired.

Top with a dollop of Greek yogurt or your favorite plant-based yogurt for added protein.

Serve these pancakes as a heart-healthy breakfast alongside some fresh fruit, such as strawberries or banana slices.

Savory Quinoa Breakfast Bowl with Spinach and Feta

Yield: 2 servings   **Preparation Time:** 5 minutes   **Cooking Time:** 15 minutes

Calories: 280 kcal | Carbohydrates: 34g | Total Fat: 11g | Saturated Fat: 2.5g | Cholesterol: 15mg | Protein: 10g | Sodium: 220mg
(per serving)

Ingredients:
- 1 cup (170g) quinoa, rinsed
- 2 cups (480 ml) water or low-sodium vegetable broth
- 1 tbsp (15 ml) olive oil
- 2 cups (60g) fresh spinach, roughly chopped
- ¼ cup (60g) feta cheese, crumbled
- 1 small clove garlic, minced
- 1 tbsp (4g) of freshly chopped parsley (optional for garnish)
- Salt to taste (preferably low-sodium)
- Freshly ground black pepper to taste
- ¼ tsp (0.5g) red pepper flakes (optional)
- 1 tbsp (15 ml) lemon juice

Customizable Ingredients/Garnishes:
- Sliced avocado for added healthy fats
- Cherry tomatoes, halved
- Poached or soft-boiled egg (optional for additional protein)
- Chopped seeds or nuts (for crunch, try pumpkin or sunflower seeds)
- Sliced cucumber or radish for extra veggies

Instructions:
In a medium saucepan, combine the washed quinoa with water (or veggie broth). Heat the mixture to a boil over medium heat. After the saucepan reaches a boil, lower the heat, cover it, and let the quinoa cook for 12-15 minutes, or until it is fluffy and has absorbed all the liquid. After turning off the heat, use a fork to fluff the quinoa and set it aside.

Heat one tablespoon of olive oil in a medium pan over medium heat. Add the minced garlic and sauté for 1 minute until fragrant. Cook the chopped spinach for two to three minutes or until it wilts. For a bit of heat, add some optional red pepper flakes and a touch of salt and pepper for seasoning.

Once the spinach is cooked, stir it into the cooked quinoa. Mix well to combine all the flavors.

Divide the quinoa-spinach mixture between two bowls. Sprinkle each bowl with two tablespoons of crumbled feta cheese and drizzle with fresh lemon juice. Taste and add more salt and pepper to the seasoning if needed.

Add fresh parsley and other desired toppings, such as sliced avocado, cherry tomatoes, or almonds, to the top of each dish.

To increase protein, consider adding a poached or soft-boiled egg. You can also keep it vegan by skipping the feta and adding extra veggies or a drizzle of tahini.

Greek Yogurt Salad with Berries and Mixed Nuts

Yield: 2 servings   **Preparation Time:** 5 minutes   **Cooking Time:** None

Calories: 280 kcal | Carbohydrates: 32g | Total Fat: 10g | Saturated Fat: 1g | Cholesterol: 5mg | Protein: 15g | Sodium: 60mg

Ingredients:
- 1 cup (240 ml) plain non-fat Greek yogurt (or plant-based yogurt for a vegan option)
- ½ cup (70g) mixed fresh berries (blueberries, strawberries, raspberries, or blackberries)
- 1 tbsp (15 ml) maple syrup or honey
- ¼ cup (35g) mixed nuts, roughly chopped (such as almonds, walnuts, or pistachios)
- 2 tbsp (18g) old-fashioned rolled oats or granola (choose a low-sugar)
- 1 tbsp (12g) chia seeds or flaxseeds
- ¼ tsp (0.65g) cinnamon (optional)

Customizable Ingredients/Garnishes:
- Sliced banana or kiwi for extra fruit
- Cacao nibs for a chocolatey crunch
- Coconut flakes (unsweetened)
- Nut butter (drizzled for additional creaminess)
- Mint leaves for garnish

Instructions:
Divide the plain Greek yogurt evenly between two bowls or glasses as the base layer of the parfait.

In each serving, layer the mixed fresh berries on top of the yogurt. You can mix the berries or keep them separate for visual appeal.

Sprinkle the chopped mixed nuts evenly over the berries in both bowls. If using chia seeds or flaxseeds, sprinkle them on top as well.

Add a tablespoon of rolled oats or granola to each serving for added texture and fiber. If you prefer a touch of sweetness, drizzle ½ tablespoons of honey or maple syrup over the parfait.

Optionally, sprinkle a dash of cinnamon over the top of each parfait for extra flavor. Serve right away, garnished with mint leaves if preferred.

For a more substantial breakfast, pair this parfait with whole-grain toast or an additional serving of fruit.

Poached Eggs with Sweet Potato and Kale Hash

Yield: 2 servings	**Preparation Time:** 10 minutes	**Cooking Time:** 20 minutes

Calories: 320 kcal | Carbohydrates: 38g | Total Fat: 14g | Saturated Fat: 2g | Cholesterol: 180mg | Protein: 11g | Sodium: 250mg
(per serving)

Ingredients:

- 2 medium sweet potatoes (about 300g), peeled and diced
- 1 tbsp (15 ml) olive oil (extra virgin)
- 1 small red onion, diced
- 1 bell pepper (any color), diced
- 2 cups (140g) fresh kale, roughly chopped, stems removed
- 2 big eggs (for a lower-cholesterol alternative, use egg whites)
- 1 clove garlic, minced
- ½ tsp (1.5g) smoked paprika (optional)
- ½ tsp (1.4g) ground cumin (optional)
- Salt to taste (low-sodium variety)
- Freshly ground black pepper to taste
- 1 tbsp (4g) of freshly chopped parsley (optional for garnish)
- 1 tbsp (15 ml) apple cider vinegar (for poaching eggs)

Customizable Ingredients/Garnishes:

- Avocado slices for healthy fats
- Hot sauce or salsa for extra flavor
- Pumpkin seeds or sunflower seeds for crunch
- Cherry tomatoes

Instructions:

Warm 1 tablespoon of olive oil in a big skillet over medium heat. Add the chopped sweet potatoes and season with salt and pepper. Cook, stirring occasionally, until they soften and become golden brown, approximately 8-10 minutes.

Add the bell pepper, garlic, and chopped red onion to the pan with the sweet potatoes. Simmer the onions for 3-4 minutes or until they are transparent and tender.

Add the chopped kale and stir; simmer for 2-3 minutes, until the kale wilts and turns bright green. Add smoked paprika and cumin (if using), then add salt and pepper to taste as necessary. Remove from heat and set aside while you poach the eggs.

Fill a medium saucepan with water, then bring it to a simmer. Add a teaspoon of apple cider vinegar to the water. Gently crack each egg into a small dish and place it into the simmering water. The eggs should be poached for 3-4 minutes. Remove the eggs gently using a slotted spoon and set aside to drain on a dish covered with paper towels.

For a lower cholesterol option, use only the egg whites for poaching.

Divide the sweet potato and kale hash between two plates. Top each portion with a poached egg. Sprinkle with freshly chopped parsley or garnishes like avocado slices or hot sauce.

Overnight Oats with Apples and Cinnamon

Yield: 2 servings	**Preparation Time:** 5 minutes	**Chilling Time:** 4 hours (or overnight)

Calories: 280 kcal | Carbohydrates: 46g | Total Fat: 7g | Saturated Fat: 0.5g | Cholesterol: 0mg | Protein: 6g | Sodium: 60mg
(per serving)

Ingredients:

- 1 cup (80g) old-fashioned rolled oats
- 1 cup (240) unsweetened almond milk or milk from any plant
- 1 small apple, diced
- 1 tbsp (12g) chia seeds (optional)
- 1 tbsp (15 ml) maple syrup (or honey, if desired for sweetness)
- 1 tsp (2.6g) ground cinnamon
- ¼ tsp (1.25 ml) vanilla extract (optional)
- 1 tbsp (7g) ground flaxseeds (optional)
- Pinch (0.5g) of salt (optional)

Customizable Ingredients/Garnishes:

- Chopped walnuts or sliced almonds for crunch
- Raisins or dried cranberries for extra sweetness
- Fresh berries for a tart balance
- Coconut flakes (unsweetened)
- Greek yogurt (for extra protein)

Instructions:

In a medium-sized dish or jar, combine the rolled oats, honey, almond milk, diced apple, chia seeds, maple syrup (if using), cinnamon, vanilla extract (if using), and a pinch of salt. Give it a good stir to ensure all ingredients are mixed equally.

Place a lid or plastic wrap over the bowl or jar and place it in the refrigerator for at least 4 hours or overnight. The oats and chia seeds will soak up the liquid during this time and become tender and creamy.

In the morning, stir the oats well. If they are too thick, add a little almond milk to loosen them up. Divide the mixture into two bowls or jars.

Top each serving with desired garnishes, such as sliced almonds, raisins, or extra fruit. If preferred, serve cold or warm in the microwave.

Banana-Walnut Muffins with Whole Grain Flour

Yield: 12 muffins	**Preparation Time:** 10 minutes	**Cooking Time:** 20 minutes

Calories: 190 kcal | Carbohydrates: 22g | Total Fat: 10g | Saturated Fat: 1g | Cholesterol: 15mg | Protein: 4g | Sodium: 110mg
(per serving)

Ingredients:

- 1 ½ cups (180g) whole wheat flour
- 1 tsp (6g) baking soda
- ½ tsp (2g) baking powder
- ¼ tsp (1.5g) salt (preferably low-sodium)
- ½ tsp (1.3g) ground cinnamon
- ¼ cup (60 ml) olive oil or coconut oil (melted)
- ¼ tbsp (3,5 ml) maple syrup or honey (if desired for sweetness)
- 2 large ripe bananas, mashed
- 1 large egg (or 1 flax egg for a vegan option)
- ½ cup of unsweetened almond milk or milk from any plant
- 1 tsp vanilla extract
- ½ cup (120 ml) chopped walnuts (plus extra for garnish)

Customizable Ingredients/Garnishes:

- Chopped dark chocolate
- Coconut flakes (unsweetened) for texture
- Chopped dried fruit like raisins or dates
- Pumpkin seeds or sunflower seeds for crunch

Instructions:

Adjust the oven's temperature to 175°C/350°F. Line a 12-cup muffin tray with paper liners or gently oil the cups.

Whisk the whole wheat flour, baking powder, ground cinnamon, salt, and baking soda in a large mixing bowl.

Mash the ripe bananas till smooth in a different dish. Add the olive oil, honey (or maple syrup), egg (or flax egg), almond milk, and vanilla extract. Whisk until well combined.

Combine the wet and dry components gradually, stirring until combined. Be careful not to overmix, as this can make the muffins dense. Fold in the chopped walnuts.

Pour the same quantity of batter into each muffin cup, filling each about ¾ full. Sprinkle a few extra walnuts on top of each muffin for garnish.

After 18-20 minutes of baking in the preheated oven, a toothpick should come out clean in the middle of the muffins. After 5 minutes of cooling in the muffin tray, move the muffins to a wire rack to finish cooling.

For a balanced breakfast, serve these muffins with fresh fruit or a petite yogurt parfait.

Tofu Scramble with Bell Peppers and Onions

Yield: 2 servings	**Preparation Time:** 10 minutes	**Cooking Time:** 10 minutes

Calories: 250 kcal | Carbohydrates: 12g | Total Fat: 17g | Saturated Fat: 2g | Cholesterol: 0mg | Protein: 15g | Sodium: 180mg
(per serving)

Ingredients:

- 1 block (450g) firm or extra-firm tofu, drained and crumbled
- 1 tbsp (15 ml) olive oil (or avocado oil)
- 1 small onion, diced
- 1 bell pepper (any color), diced
- 1 clove garlic, minced
- 1 tsp (2.5g) ground turmeric (for color)
- ½ tsp (1.3g) ground cumin (optional)
- ½ tsp (1.1g) smoked paprika (optional)
- Salt to taste (preferably a low-sodium)
- Freshly ground black pepper to taste
- 1 tbsp (8g) nutritional yeast
- ¼ cup (5g) fresh parsley, chopped

Customizable Ingredients/Garnishes:

- Sliced avocado for healthy fats
- Hot sauce or salsa for extra flavor
- Fresh spinach (add to the scramble)
- Chopped tomatoes for added freshness
- Whole grain toast (serve on the side)

Instructions:

Drain the tofu and squeeze out any extra water using paper. Crumble the tofu into small pieces. Set aside.

Heat the olive oil in a big skillet over medium heat. Add the diced onion and cook for 2-3 minutes or until the chopped onion is tender. Add the minced garlic and bell pepper, then sauté for another 2-3 minutes until the vegetables are tender.

After pushing the veggies to one side of the pan, place the crumbled tofu in the middle. Sprinkle the turmeric, cumin, smoked paprika, salt, and pepper over the tofu. Stir often for 4-5 minutes while cooking the tofu or until it is cooked through and has a light brown color. Stir the tofu to coat it evenly with the spices.

For a cheesy flavor, stir in 1 tablespoon of nutritional yeast at the end of cooking. Mix it into the tofu scramble until well combined.

Once the tofu scramble is cooked, remove it from the heat and divide it between two plates. Garnish with fresh parsley or other toppings like avocado or hot sauce.

Serve this tofu scramble with whole grain toast or whole grain tortillas for added fiber and whole grains, which help lower cholesterol levels.

Quinoa and Berry Breakfast Bake

Yield: 6 servings   **Preparation Time:** 10 minutes   **Cooking Time:** 40 minutes

Calories: 210 kcal | Carbohydrates: 32g | Total Fat: 7g | Saturated Fat: 0.5g | Cholesterol: 30mg | Protein: 7g | Sodium: 80mg
(per serving)

Ingredients:

- 1 cup (170g) quinoa, uncooked (rinsed and drained)
- 1 ½ cup (360 ml) of unsweetened almond milk
- 2 large eggs (or ½ cup (125g) unsweetened applesauce)
- 2 tbsp (30 ml) maple syrup or honey (optional for sweetness)
- 1 tsp (5 ml) vanilla extract
- 1 tsp (2.5g) ground cinnamon
- ½ tsp (2g) baking powder
- 1 cup (140g) of mixed berries, defrosted or fresh (blueberries, raspberries, strawberries, or blackberries)
- ¼ cup (30g) finely chopped almonds or walnuts
- 1 tbsp (12g) chia seeds (optional)
- Pinch of salt (optional, preferably a low-sodium variety)

Customizable Ingredients/Garnishes:

- Sliced banana for extra sweetness
- Coconut flakes (unsweetened)
- Nut butter (such as almond butter)
- Pumpkin seeds or sunflower seeds

Instructions:

Preheat your oven to 350°F (175°C) and lightly grease an 8x8-inch baking dish or line it with parchment paper.

In a large bowl, whisk together the almond milk, eggs (or applesauce if vegan), maple syrup, vanilla extract, cinnamon, baking powder, and a pinch of salt if using. Stir in the rinsed quinoa and mix until everything is combined.

Fold in the mixed berries and chopped walnuts or almonds. You may use frozen or fresh berries; if you use frozen, there's no need to defrost them beforehand.

Transfer the quinoa mixture to the preheated baking dish and level it out. Bake for 35-40 minutes until the mixture is set and lightly golden on top. As it cools, the bake will get firmer.

Cool and serve:

Before slicing into squares or serving, let the quinoa and berry breakfast bake to cool for five to ten minutes. If desired, garnish with additional toppings like chia seeds, banana slices, or nut butter.

Serve this Quinoa and Berry Breakfast Bake warm, topped with a dollop of yogurt (Greek or plant-based) for added protein or drizzled with a little almond butter for extra healthy fats.

Almond Flour Pancakes with Maple Syrup

Yield: 4 servings (8 pancakes)   **Preparation Time:** 5 minutes   **Cooking Time:** 10 minutes

Calories: 240 kcal | Carbohydrates: 10g | Total Fat: 19g | Saturated Fat: 2g | Cholesterol: 55mg | Protein: 8g | Sodium: 185mg
(per serving)

Ingredients:

- 1 ½ cups (140g) almond flour
- 1 tsp (4g) baking powder
- ¼ tsp (1.5g) salt (preferably low-sodium variety)
- 2 large eggs (or 4 tbsp (60 ml) aquafaba for a vegan option)
- ¼ cup (60 ml) of unsweetened almond milk or milk from any plant
- 1 tsp (5 ml) vanilla extract
- 1 tbsp (15 ml) maple syrup (optional)
- 1 tbsp (15 ml) olive oil or frying spray

Customizable Ingredients/Garnishes:

- Fresh berries (blueberries, strawberries, raspberries)
- Sliced banana
- Chopped walnuts or sliced almonds
- Coconut flakes (unsweetened)
- Cinnamon or nutmeg for flavor

Instructions:

In a larger basin, whisk together almond flour, baking powder, and salt.

Whisk the almond milk, vanilla extract, eggs (or aquafaba for a vegan alternative), and 1 tablespoon of maple syrup (if using) in a separate dish. Mix until well combined.

Stir gently until the batter is smooth, and gradually add the wet components to the dry ingredients. Even though this batter is thicker than regular pancake batter, pouring it should not be difficult. If it seems too thick, add a tablespoon of additional almond milk at a time to get the right consistency.

Grease a non-stick skillet or griddle with cooking spray or olive oil and heat it over medium heat. Transfer around ¼ cup of batter onto the skillet for each pancake. Cook for 2-3 minutes on one side until bubbles form on the surface, then flip and cook for another 2 minutes until golden brown and cooked through.

While preparing the remaining batter, move the pancakes to a platter and keep warm. Serve the pancakes with fresh berries, banana slices, and a drizzle of pure maple syrup.

Add a cinnamon sprinkle or an almond butter drizzle for a more decadent topping.

Fresh Fruit Salad with Lime and Mint

Yield: 4 servings	**Preparation Time:** 10 minutes	**Cooking Time:** None

Calories: 90 kcal | Carbohydrates: 22g | Total Fat: 0.5g | Saturated Fat: 0g | Cholesterol: 0mg | Protein: 1g | Sodium: 5mg
(per serving)

Ingredients:
- 1 cup (150g) strawberries, hulled and halved
- 1 cup (150g) blueberries
- 1 cup (160g) pineapple, diced
- 1 kiwi, peeled and sliced
- 1 mango, peeled and diced
- 1 small orange, peeled and sectioned
- 2 tbsp (4g) fresh mint leaves, finely chopped
- 1 tbsp (15 ml) fresh lime juice (about half a lime)
- 1 tbsp (15 ml) maple syrup or honey
- Zest of 1 lime (optional for extra zing)

Customizable Ingredients/Garnishes:
- Sliced banana
- Chopped apple or pear
- Pomegranate seeds for added texture
- Chia seeds for a nutritional boost
- Coconut flakes (unsweetened) for added texture

Instructions:

Combine the strawberries, blueberries, pineapple, kiwi, mango, and orange in a large bowl. Toss gently to mix the fruits evenly.

Combine the chopped mint, honey, and fresh lime juice (if using) in a small bowl. Add the lime zest to the dressing for an extra flavor.

Drizzle the lime-mint dressing over the fruit salad and gently toss to coat the fruit with the dressing. Be careful not to overmix, as some fruits are delicate.

To let the flavors merge, serve the salad immediately or sit in the fridge for 10-15 minutes. Garnish with extra mint leaves or your preferred toppings, such as chia seeds or coconut flakes.

For a heartier meal, serve the fruit salad alongside a whole grain, such as quinoa, or enjoy it with whole-grain toast for added fiber.

Zucchini and Feta Breakfast Casserole

Yield: 6 servings	**Preparation Time:** 15 minutes	**Cooking Time:** 35 minutes

Calories: 160 kcal | Carbohydrates: 15g | Total Fat: 7g | Saturated Fat: 2g | Cholesterol: 15mg | Protein: 9g | Sodium: 250mg
(per serving)

Ingredients:
- 2 medium zucchinis, grated (about 2 cups/ 400g)
- 1 cup (100g) whole wheat bread crumbs or rolled oats
- 1 small onion, finely chopped
- 2 cloves garlic, minced
- 4 large egg whites (or 2 whole eggs and 2 egg whites)
- ½ cup (75g) low-fat feta cheese, crumbled
- ½ cup (75g) red bell pepper, diced
- ¼ cup (5g) fresh parsley, chopped
- 2 tbsp (2.2g) fresh dill, chopped (or 1 tsp (1g) dried dill)
- 1 tsp (1g) dried oregano
- ½ tsp (1.1g) black pepper
- ¼ tsp (1g) salt (optional, low-sodium)
- 1 tbsp (15 ml) olive oil

Customizable Ingredients/Garnishes:
- Sliced cherry tomatoes for topping
- Fresh basil or cilantro for garnish
- Red pepper flakes for a spicy kick
- Sautéed mushrooms or spinach for added vegetables

Instructions:

Turn the oven on to 375°F (190°C). Lightly coat an 8-8-inch baking dish with olive oil.

Place the shredded zucchini in a fresh kitchen towel or cheesecloth to squeeze extra moisture. This is a critical step in avoiding a soggy dish.

Squeezed zucchini, rolled oats or whole wheat bread crumbs, sliced red bell pepper, chopped onion, minced garlic, crumbled feta cheese, dried oregano, black pepper, and salt (if used) should all be combined in a big mixing dish. Mix well to combine.

In a separate bowl, gently beat the egg whites (or whole eggs and egg whites). Pour the eggs into the zucchini mixture and stir until all ingredients are evenly incorporated.

Evenly distribute the ingredients into the baking dish. If using, arrange sliced cherry tomatoes on top for added color and flavor.

Bake for 30-35 minutes or until the casserole is set and the top is browned. Bake in a preheated oven. A toothpick inserted in the center should emerge clean.

Remove it from the oven and allow it to cool for 5-10 minutes before slicing. Garnish with fresh cilantro or basil if preferred. Serve warm.

Serve alongside whole-grain toast or a small side of avocado for extra fiber and healthy fats.

Lunch Recipes

Quinoa Salad with Roasted Vegetables and Feta

Yield: 4 servings   **Preparation Time:** 15 minutes   **Cooking Time:** 30 minutes

Calories: 260 kcal | Carbohydrates: 35g | Total Fat: 10g | Saturated Fat: 2g | Cholesterol: 10mg | Protein: 7g | Sodium: 210mg
(per serving)

Ingredients:

- 1 cup (170g) quinoa, rinsed and drained
- 2 cups (480 ml) low-sodium vegetable broth (or water)
- 1 medium zucchini, diced
- 1 medium red bell pepper, diced
- 1 medium red onion, diced
- 1 medium sweet potato, peeled and diced
- 1 tbsp (15 ml) olive oil
- ½ tsp (1g) ground cumin
- ½ tsp (1g) paprika
- Salt to taste (preferably low-sodium variety)
- Freshly ground black pepper to taste
- ¼ cup (40g) crumbled feta cheese
- 2 tbsp (7g) fresh parsley, chopped
- 1 tbsp (15 ml) fresh lemon juice
- 1 tsp (2g) lemon zest (optional)

Customizable Ingredients/Garnishes:

- Chopped avocado for extra healthy fats
- Sliced almonds or pumpkin seeds
- Fresh spinach or arugula for added greens

Instructions:

In a medium saucepan, combine the rinsed quinoa with the vegetable broth (or water). After bringing it to a boil over medium heat, lower the heat. After approximately 15 minutes of simmering undercover, the quinoa should absorb all the liquid. Take the quinoa from the stove and use a fork to fluff it up. Set aside to cool slightly.

Set the oven to 400°F (200°C). Arrange the diced sweet potato, red onion, bell pepper, and zucchini on a baking sheet. Drizzle with olive oil, then season with salt, pepper, paprika, and ground cumin. Toss the vegetables to coat evenly. Roast the veggies in the oven for 20- 25 minutes, stirring occasionally, until they become tender and golden brown.

Once the roasted vegetables are ready, transfer them to a large mixing bowl. Add the cooked quinoa and toss gently to combine.

Stir in the crumbled feta cheese, fresh parsley, lemon juice, and optional lemon zest. If necessary, add a little more salt and pepper to the seasoning.

The quinoa salad may be served warm or at room temperature. Garnish with additional toppings, such as avocado, sliced almonds, or extra greens.

Lentil and Spinach Soup with Herbs

Yield: 4 servings   **Preparation Time:** 10 minutes   **Cooking Time:** 35 minutes

Calories: 240 kcal | Carbohydrates: 36g | Total Fat: 5g | Saturated Fat: 0.5g | Cholesterol: 0mg | Protein: 14g | Sodium: 180mg
(per serving)

Ingredients:

- 1 cup (190g) of dried lentils
- 1 tbsp (15 ml) olive oil
- 1 medium onion, finely chopped
- 2 carrots, diced
- 2 celery stalks, diced
- 3 garlic cloves, minced
- 6 cups (1440 ml) low-sodium vegetable broth
- 1 tsp (2g) ground cumin
- 1 tsp (2g) dried thyme
- ½ tsp (0.5g) dried oregano
- 1 bay leaf
- 4 cups (120g) fresh spinach, roughly chopped
- 1 tbsp (2g) fresh parsley, chopped
- Juice of 1 lemon (optional for brightness)
- Salt to taste (preferably low-sodium)
- Freshly ground black pepper to taste

Instructions:

In a large pot set over medium heat, warm the olive oil. Add the celery, carrots, and onion in the chopped state. Sauté for 5-7 minutes until the vegetables soften. Add the minced garlic. Cook for a further minute or until fragrant after adding the garlic.

Stir in the rinsed lentils(brown or green), ground cumin, dried thyme, dried oregano, and bay leaf. Mix well to coat the lentils and vegetables with the spices.

After adding the veggie broth, heat the mixture until it boils. Once boiling, lower the heat to low, cover the pot, and allow the soup to cook until the lentils are soft but not mushy, 25-30 minutes.

Once the lentils are cooked, add the chopped spinach to the soup and let it wilt for 2-3 minutes. Season the soup with salt and pepper to taste. If desired, add 1 lemon juice to brighten the flavors.

Spoon soup into dishes and sprinkle with chopped fresh parsley. Serve warm with whole-grain bread or avocado on the side.

For added protein, stir in a serving of cooked quinoa or barley into the soup.

This soup may be frozen for up to three months or kept in the refrigerator for up to five days, making it ideal for meal prep.

Chickpea Salad with Lemon-Tahini Dressing

Yield: 4 servings　　　　**Preparation Time:** 10 minutes　　　　**Cooking Time:** None

Calories: 280 kcal | Carbohydrates: 28g | Total Fat: 14g | Saturated Fat: 2g | Cholesterol: 0mg | Protein: 9g | Sodium: 180mg
(per serving)

Ingredients:
For the Salad:
- 1 can (15 oz/425g) of rinsed and drained chickpeas
- 1 cup (150g) cucumber, diced
- 1 cup (150g) cherry tomatoes, halved
- 1 small red onion, finely chopped
- 1 bell pepper (any color), diced
- ¼ cup (5g) fresh parsley, chopped
- 2 tbsp (10g) fresh mint, chopped
- 2 cups (60g) fresh spinach or arugula

For the Lemon-Tahini Dressing:
- 3 tbsp (45 ml) tahini
- 2 tbsp (30 ml) of freshly squeezed lemon juice (about one lemon)
- 1 tbsp (15 ml) olive oil
- 1 tsp (5g) maple syrup or honey
- 1 small garlic clove, minced
- 2-3 tbsp (30 ml) water
- Salt to taste (low-sodium variety recommended)
- Freshly ground black pepper to taste

Customizable Ingredients/Garnishes:
- Chopped avocado for extra healthy fats
- Sliced almonds or pumpkin seeds
- Crumbled feta
- Red pepper flakes for heat

Instructions:

Combine the drained chickpeas, diced cucumber, cherry tomatoes, red onion, and bell pepper in a large mixing bowl. Toss in the chopped parsley and mint (if using), as well as spinach or arugula.

Whisk together the tahini, fresh lemon juice, olive oil, minced garlic, and maple syrup (if using). Gradually add one spoonful of water at a time until the dressing becomes creamy yet pourable. Season with salt and pepper to taste.

Assemble the salad:

Add the lemon-tahini dressing to the chickpea salad. Gently spin to coat all ingredients. If preferred, add more lemon juice, salt, and pepper to adjust the seasoning.

Divide the salad among four bowls and garnish with additional toppings, such as avocado slices, sliced almonds, or a sprinkle of red pepper flakes.

Pair it with whole grain pita or crackers for added fiber, or serve alongside grilled vegetables for a complete meal.

For added protein, consider topping the salad with grilled tofu, a hard-boiled egg (using only the whites for lower cholesterol), or some quinoa.

Whole Wheat Wraps with Hummus and Fresh Veggies

Yield: 4 servings　　　　**Preparation Time:** 10 minutes　　　　**Cooking Time:** None

Calories: 300 kcal | Carbohydrates: 45g | Total Fat: 10g | Saturated Fat: 1g | Cholesterol: 0mg | Protein: 10g | Sodium: 340mg
(per serving)

Ingredients:
- 4 large whole wheat tortillas (8-10 inches in diameter)
- 1 cup (240g) hummus
- 1 medium cucumber, sliced
- 1 medium carrot, peeled and shredded
- 1 red bell pepper, thinly sliced
- 1 small red onion, thinly sliced
- 2 cups (50g) fresh spinach or arugula
- ¼ cup (15g) fresh parsley, chopped
- Juice of 1 lemon (for extra flavor)
- Salt and pepper to taste (optional)

Customizable Ingredients/Garnishes:
- Avocado slices for healthy fats
- Sliced olives for added flavor
- Sliced cherry tomatoes
- Alfalfa sprouts for crunch.
- Red pepper flakes to add a little spiciness

Instructions:

Wash and slice all the vegetables as directed—thinly slice the cucumber, bell pepper, and onion; shred the carrot; and roughly chop the fresh spinach or arugula.

Lay a whole wheat tortilla flat on a clean surface. Leaving a thin border all the way around, evenly distributes 2-3 tablespoons of hummus over the tortilla.

Arrange a few slices of cucumber, shredded carrot, bell pepper, onion, and a handful of spinach or arugula on the hummus. Add some fresh parsley and squeeze some lemon juice on top. Add salt and pepper to taste, if desired.

Like a burrito, fold in the edges of the tortilla and firmly roll it from one end to the other. If preferred, slice it in half.

Continue this procedure with the remaining tortillas. Serve the wraps immediately or store them in the refrigerator in an airtight container for a nutritious and easy-to-make meal that can be consumed for up to a day.

Black Bean and Corn Salad with Avocado

Yield: 4 servings   **Preparation Time:** 15 minutes   **Cooking Time:** None

Calories: 290 kcal | Carbohydrates: 36g | Total Fat: 14g | Saturated Fat: 2g | Cholesterol: 0mg | Protein: 9g | Sodium: 200mg
(per serving)

Ingredients:

- 1 can (15 oz/425g) of rinsed and drained black beans
- 1 cup (200g) of corn kernels, either fresh, frozen, or canned (if using frozen kernels, defrost them first).
- 1 large avocado, diced
- 1 cup (150g) cherry tomatoes, halved
- 1 small red onion, finely diced
- 1 small red bell pepper, diced
- ¼ cup fresh cilantro, chopped
- 1 clove garlic, minced
- 2 tbsp (30g) freshly squeezed lime juice (about one lime)
- 1 tbsp (15 ml) olive oil
- 1 tsp (2.5g) ground cumin
- Salt to taste (preferably low-sodium)
- Freshly ground black pepper to taste

Customizable Ingredients/Garnishes:

- Sliced jalapeño for heat
- Chopped green onions for extra flavor
- Crumbled feta (optional)
- Red pepper flakes for added spice

Instructions:

Drain and rinse the black beans. Thaw frozen corn entirely before using it. Dice the avocado, cherry tomatoes, red bell pepper, and red onion.

In a big bowl, mix the black beans, corn, avocado, cherry tomatoes, red onion, bell pepper, and cilantro. Toss gently to mix the ingredients.

In a small bowl, mix the fresh lime juice, olive oil, pepper, minced garlic, and salt until well blended.

Dress the salad. After adding the lime and olive oil dressing, toss the salad lightly to ensure all items are uniformly coated. Adjust the seasoning as required by adding more lime juice, salt, or pepper.

Serve the salad fresh, or chill in the refrigerator for 10-15 minutes to allow the flavors to meld.

For extra crunch, sprinkle some pumpkin or sunflower seeds on top.

Grilled Veggie Sandwich on Whole Grain Bread

Yield: 2 servings   **Preparation Time:** 10 minutes   **Cooking Time:** 15 minutes

Calories: 380 kcal | Carbohydrates: 50g | Total Fat: 15g | Saturated Fat: 2g | Cholesterol: 0mg | Protein: 10g | Sodium: 320mg
(per serving)

Ingredients:

- 4 slices whole grain bread (preferably 100% whole grain)
- 1 small zucchini, thinly sliced
- 1 small red bell pepper, cut into strips
- 1 small eggplant, thinly sliced
- 1 small red onion, thinly sliced
- 1 tbsp (15 ml) olive oil
- 1 tsp (5 ml) balsamic vinegar (optional)
- 1 clove garlic, minced
- ½ tsp (0.5) dried oregano
- Salt and pepper to taste (low-sodium preferred)
- ¼ cup (60g) hummus
- ¼ cup (8g) fresh spinach or arugula
- 1 small avocado, sliced

Customizable Ingredients/Garnishes:

- Sliced tomatoes
- Fresh basil or cilantro
- Crumbled feta (optional for a bit of creaminess)
- Red pepper flakes for spice

Instructions:

Heat your grill or grill pan to medium-high heat.

In a small bowl, toss the zucchini, red bell pepper, eggplant, and red onion with olive oil, oregano, chopped garlic, and a dash of salt and pepper. Drizzle with balsamic vinegar, if using, for extra flavor.

Place the seasoned vegetables on the preheated grill or grill pan. Grill 3-4 minutes per side until the vegetables are tender and have excellent grill marks. Remove from the grill and set aside.

Take each piece of whole-grain bread and spread a thin hummus coating on one side. Layer the grilled vegetables evenly on two slices of bread. If using, top the veggies with a handful of fresh spinach or arugula and sliced avocado. Sandwich the remaining bread pieces, hummus side down, on top of the sandwiches.

Place the assembled sandwiches back on the grill or in a grill pan for a warm, pressed sandwich. After cooking for two to three minutes on each side, gently push down with a spatula; the bread should be crispy and golden.

Immediately serve the sandwiches by slicing them in half. Optionally, garnish with extra fresh herbs, such as basil or cilantro.

For extra vegetables and fiber, pair this sandwich with a small bowl of vegetable soup or a cup of gazpacho.

Zucchini Noodles with Pesto and Cherry Tomatoes

Yield: 2 servings   **Preparation Time:** 10 minutes   **Cooking Time:** 5 minutes

Calories: 210 kcal | Carbohydrates: 12g | Total Fat: 17g | Saturated Fat: 2g | Cholesterol: 0mg | Protein: 6g | Sodium: 140mg
(per serving)

Ingredients:

- ¼ cup (6g) fresh basil leaves
- 2 tbsp (15g) pine nuts or walnuts (for a budget-friendly option)
- 1 tbsp (15 ml) olive oil
- 1 small clove garlic, minced
- 2 tbsp (15g) nutritional yeast (or, for a non-vegan alternative, 2 tbsp (10g) grated Parmesan)
- 1 tbsp (15 ml) fresh lemon juice
- Salt and pepper to taste (low-sodium preferred)

Customizable Ingredients/Garnishes:

- Sliced avocado for extra healthy fats
- Crushed red pepper flakes (optional)
- Chopped fresh parsley for garnish
- Toasted seeds (like sunflower seeds) for crunch

Instructions:

Using a spiralizer or julienne peeler, spiralize the zucchini into noodles. Set aside.

In a food processor, pulse the fresh basil, lemon juice, pine nuts, nutritional yeast, garlic, olive oil, salt, and pepper. Blend until smooth. If the pesto is too thick, add a little water (one or two teaspoons) to thin it.

Heat 1 tablespoon of olive oil in a large skillet over medium heat. Add the zucchini noodles and cook, stirring periodically, for 2-3 minutes. Be careful not to overcook, as zucchini releases water quickly and can become mushy.

When the zucchini noodles are done, add the cherry tomatoes in halves to the pan and heat them for a further minute.

Remove the skillet from the heat. Add the prepared pesto to the zucchini noodles and cherry tomatoes, tossing gently to coat the noodles evenly with the pesto.

Divide the zucchini noodle mixture between two plates. Garnish with additional toppings like avocado slices, crushed red pepper flakes, or toasted seeds for added texture and flavor.

Add lean protein like grilled tofu, chickpeas, or lentils to fill the meal without adding cholesterol.

Stuffed Bell Peppers with Brown Rice and Herbs

Yield: 4 servings   **Preparation Time:** 15 minutes   **Cooking Time:** 15 minutes

Calories: 260 kcal | Carbohydrates: 45g | Total Fat: 7g | Saturated Fat: 1g | Cholesterol: 0mg | Protein: 6g | Sodium: 180mg
(per serving)

Ingredients:

- 4 large bell peppers (any color)
- 1 cup (185g) uncooked brown rice
- 2 cups (480g) low-sodium vegetable broth or water
- 1 medium onion, finely chopped
- 2 cloves garlic, minced
- 1 small zucchini, diced
- 1 cup (150g) cherry tomatoes, halved
- ¼ cup (15g) fresh parsley, chopped
- 2 tbsp (5g) chopped fresh basil or 1 tbsp (1.5g) dried
- 1 tsp (1.5g) dried oregano
- 1 tbsp (15 ml) olive oil
- Juice of 1 lemon (about 2 tbsp/30 ml)
- Salt and pepper to taste (low-sodium recommended)

Customizable Ingredients/Garnishes:

- Crumbled feta cheese (optional for added creaminess)
- Chopped pine nuts or walnuts for texture
- Red pepper flakes for heat
- Fresh spinach (can be sautéed and mixed into the filling)

Instructions:

Put the vegetable broth and brown rice in a saucepan. Over medium heat, bring to a boil, then lower the heat to a simmer, cover, and cook for approximately 35-40 minutes, or until the rice is soft and has soaked up all the liquid. Fluff with a fork and set aside.

Preheat your oven to 375°F (190°C). Slice off the bell peppers' tops, then remove the seeds and membranes. Place the bell peppers vertically in a baking dish. Cut a thin slice off the bottom of each pepper to make it stand upright.

Place the olive oil in a big pan and heat it to medium. Add the chopped onion, garlic, and sauté until softened for 3-4 minutes. Add the diced zucchini and cook for 3-4 minutes, stirring occasionally. Add the cherry tomatoes and cook for a further 2 minutes.

After turning off the heat, add the cooked rice, lemon juice, fresh parsley, basil, and oregano to the pan. Season with salt and pepper to taste. Mix until all ingredients are evenly combined.

Gently stir the filling into the hollowed-out bell peppers by spooning the rice and veggie mixture. If desired, sprinkle a small amount of crumbled feta on top of each stuffed pepper for added flavor.

Bake the filled bell peppers, covered with foil, in the oven for 25-30 minutes or until the peppers are soft. Remove the foil for the last ten minutes of baking to let the tops softly brown.

Remove the stuffed bell peppers from the oven and allow them to cool for a few minutes before serving.

Garnish with additional fresh herbs or red pepper flakes if desired.

Edamame and Quinoa Salad with Sesame Dressing

Yield: 4 servings | **Preparation Time:** 15 minutes | **Cooking Time:** 15 minutes

Calories: 300 kcal | Carbohydrates: 33g | Total Fat: 14g | Saturated Fat: 2g | Cholesterol: 0mg | Protein: 12g | Sodium: 210mg
(per serving)

Ingredients:
For the Salad:
- 1 cup (185g) quinoa, rinsed and drained
- 2 cups (480 ml) water or low-sodium vegetable broth
- 1 cup (155g) shelled edamame (frozen or fresh)
- 1 small cucumber, diced
- 1 small red bell pepper, diced
- 1 small carrot, shredded
- 2 green onions, chopped
- ¼ cup (5g) fresh cilantro or parsley, chopped
- 1 tbsp (9g) sesame seeds (optional)

For the Sesame Dressing:
- 2 tbsp (30 ml) sesame oil
- 1 tbsp (15ml) rice vinegar
- 1 tbsp (15 ml) of gluten-free tamari or low-sodium soy sauce.
- 1 tbsp (15 ml) fresh lemon juice
- 1 tbsp (15 ml) maple syrup or honey
- 1 clove garlic, minced
- 1 tsp (5g) grated fresh ginger
- Salt and pepper to taste

Customizable Ingredients/Garnishes:
- Sliced avocado for extra healthy fats
- Sliced almonds or pumpkin seeds
- Chili flakes for a bit of heat
- Microgreens for extra freshness

Instructions:

Rinse the quinoa and add water (or veggie broth) to a medium pot. Bring to a boil over medium heat, then lower the heat to a simmer, cover, and cook for 12-15 minutes, or until the quinoa has absorbed all the liquid. Allow it to cool down a little

While the quinoa is cooking, bring a small pot of water to a boil. Add the shelled edamame and cook for 3-4 minutes, until tender. Drain and set aside.

Combine the diced cucumber, red bell pepper, shredded carrot, green onions, and chopped cilantro (or parsley) in a large mixing bowl. Add the cooked quinoa and edamame to the bowl and toss gently to combine.

Whisk together the sesame oil, soy sauce, lemon juice, rice vinegar, honey (if using), chopped garlic, and grated ginger. Season with salt and pepper to taste.

Drizzle the sesame dressing over the quinoa and veggie combination. Toss to coat all parts evenly. Lemon juice, salt, or pepper may adjust the seasoning.

Split the salad into four dishes and top with sliced almonds, avocado slices, or sesame seeds, if desired.

Caprese Salad with Fresh Mozzarella and Basil

Yield: 4 servings | **Preparation Time:** 15 minutes | **Cooking Time:** None

Calories: 220 kcal | Carbohydrates: 50g | Total Fat: 18g | Saturated Fat: 6g | Cholesterol: 20mg | Protein: 9g | Sodium: 150mg
(per serving)

Ingredients:
- 4 medium ripe tomatoes, sliced (about 2 cups/490g)
- 8 oz (230g) fresh mozzarella cheese, sliced (preferably part-skim)
- 1 cup (25g) fresh basil leaves
- 2 tbsp (30 ml) extra virgin olive oil
- 1 tbsp (15 ml) balsamic vinegar (optional)
- Salt and pepper to taste
- 1 tsp (1.5g) dried oregano (optional)

Customizable Ingredients/Garnishes:
- Sliced avocado for extra healthy fats
- Toasted pine nuts or sliced almonds for added texture
- Whole grain croutons for extra crunch
- Microgreens for garnish

Instructions:

Slice the tomatoes and fresh mozzarella into even slices, about ¼ inch thick. Arrange them alternately on a serving platter, overlapping slightly (tomato slice, then mozzarella slice, then a basil leaf, and repeat).

Tuck whole basil leaves between the tomato and mozzarella slices to distribute the flavors evenly.

Evenly drizzle the salad with extra virgin olive oil. If desired, add a drizzle of balsamic vinegar for a slightly tangy touch.

Add a little salt, pepper, and dried oregano (if using) to the salad. Adjust the seasoning to taste.

Serve immediately as a light meal or as a side dish with a main course.

Sweet Potato and Black Bean Tacos

Yield: 4 servings (8 tacos)   **Preparation Time:** 10 minutes   **Cooking Time:** 25 minutes

Calories: 300 kcal | Carbohydrates: 48g | Total Fat: 8g | Saturated Fat: 1g | Cholesterol: 0mg | Protein: 9g | Sodium: 250mg
(per serving)

Ingredients:
- 2 medium sweet potatoes (260g), chopped and skinned.
- 1 tbsp (15 ml) olive oil
- 1 tsp (2g) ground cumin
- ½ tsp (1g) smoked paprika
- ¼ tsp (0.5g) ground cayenne pepper
- Salt and pepper to taste (low-sodium recommended)
- 1 can (15 oz/425g) of rinsed and drained black beans
- 8 small corn tortillas (preferably whole grain or low-sodium)
- 1 small red onion, finely diced
- 1 small avocado, diced
- 1 cup (150g) cherry tomatoes, halved
- 1 cup (20g) fresh cilantro, chopped
- 1 lime, cut into wedges
- 1 tbsp (15 ml) fresh lime juice
- 1 small garlic clove, minced (optional)

Customizable Ingredients/Garnishes:
- Sliced jalapeño for extra heat
- Chopped red cabbage for crunch
- Low-fat Greek yogurt (or plant-based yogurt) as a sour cream alternative
- Hot sauce for added spice

Instructions:

Spread the diced sweet potatoes on a baking sheet and toss them with a small pinch of salt, pepper, olive oil, ground cumin, smoked paprika, and cayenne (if using). Spread the sweet potatoes in a single layer and roast for 20-25 minutes, turning once throughout the cooking process or until tender and lightly browned.

Put the black beans in a small saucepan and cook over medium heat while the sweet potatoes bake. Add the fresh lime juice and minced garlic, and stir periodically for 5-7 minutes or until cooked thoroughly. Season with salt and pepper to taste.

In a dry skillet, cook the corn tortillas for 30 seconds on each side over medium heat or until they are soft and warm. Alternatively, encase them in foil and bake them for five minutes.

Spoon a heaping tablespoon of black beans and roasted sweet potatoes into each heated tortilla. Top with diced red onion, cherry tomatoes, avocado, and fresh cilantro. For a tangy touch, squeeze some fresh lime juice over the tacos.

Serve the tacos immediately, garnished with additional toppings or garnishes like sliced jalapeños, red cabbage, or a dollop of yogurt.

Serve these tacos with fresh salsa or guacamole for extra flavor and texture.

Cauliflower Rice Stir-Fry with Vegetables

Yield: 4 servings   **Preparation Time:** 10 minutes   **Cooking Time:** 15 minutes

Calories: 140 kcal | Carbohydrates: 17g | Total Fat: 7g | Saturated Fat: 1g | Cholesterol: 0mg | Protein: 5g | Sodium: 280mg
(per serving)

Ingredients:
- 1 medium head cauliflower, riced (or 4 cups (400g) store-bought cauliflower rice)
- 1 tbsp (15 ml) olive oil
- 1 small onion, diced
- 2 cloves garlic, minced
- 1 cup (90g) broccoli florets
- 1 red bell pepper, thinly sliced
- 1 medium carrot, thinly sliced
- 1 cup (150g) snap peas (optional)
- 2 tbsp (30 ml) of tamari or low-sodium soy sauce
- 1 tbsp (15 ml) rice vinegar
- 1 tbsp (6g) fresh ginger, grated
- 1 tsp (15 ml) sesame oil (optional)
- Salt and pepper to taste (low-sodium recommended)
- 1 tbsp (9g) sesame seeds (optional)
- 2 green onions, sliced (for garnish)
- Lime wedges (for serving, optional)

Instructions:

If using a whole head of cauliflower, remove the leaves and cut it into florets. Pulse the florets in a food processor until they resemble rice, being careful not to ground them too finely. Set aside.

In a large skillet or wok, warm one tablespoon of olive oil over medium heat. Add the chopped onion and cook for 3–4 minutes or until tender. Stir in the grated ginger and minced garlic and simmer for an additional minute or until fragrant.

Add the broccoli florets, red bell pepper, carrot, and snap peas (if using) to the skillet. Stir-fry the veggies for 5-7 minutes or until they are crisp-tender but retain their color.

Add the cauliflower rice and simmer, stirring regularly, for 3–4 minutes or until cooked through and slightly soft. The cauliflower might go mushy if it is overcooked, so take caution while cooking it.

Add the low-sodium soy sauce (or tamari), rice vinegar, and sesame oil (if using) to the stir-fry. Stir well to coat the veggies uniformly. Season with salt and pepper to taste.

Divide the stir-fry into bowls and garnish with sesame seeds, sliced green onions, and a lime wedge for freshness. Optionally, add chili flakes or sliced avocado for extra flavor.

Roasted Beet and Goat Cheese Salad

Yield: 4 servings   **Preparation Time:** 10 minutes   **Cooking Time:** 45 minutes

Calories: 220 kcal | Carbohydrates: 17g | Total Fat: 15g | Saturated Fat: 3g | Cholesterol: 5mg | Protein: 6g | Sodium: 150mg
(per serving)

Ingredients:

For the Salad:
- 4 medium beets, scrubbed and trimmed
- 2 tbsp (30 ml) olive oil, divided
- 1 tbsp (15 ml) balsamic vinegar
- 4 cups (120g) mixed greens (arugula, spinach, or mixed salad greens)
- ¼ cup (30g) crumbled goat cheese
- ¼ cup (30g) walnuts, toasted and chopped
- 2 tbsp (8g) fresh parsley, chopped

For the Dressing:
- 2 tbsp (30 ml) olive oil
- 1 tbsp (15 ml) balsamic vinegar
- 1 tsp (5 ml) Dijon mustard
- 1 tbsp (15ml) maple syrup or honey
- Salt and pepper to taste (low-sodium preferred)

Customizable Ingredients/Garnishes:
- Chopped fresh mint or basil
- Sliced oranges or pomegranate
- Pumpkin seeds for crunch

Instructions:

Preheat the oven to 400°F (200°C). Spread out a piece of aluminum foil, pour in a tablespoon of olive oil, then enclose the beets in the foil to form a sealed package. Fork-pierced beets should be soft after 40-45 minutes of roasting. Allow them to cool, then peel and cut them into wedges.

As the beets roast, toast the walnuts for 3-4 minutes over medium heat in a dry pan or until aromatic and lightly toasted. Set aside to cool.

In a small bowl, mix two tablespoons of olive oil, one tablespoon of balsamic vinegar, Dijon mustard, honey (if using), salt, and pepper. Taste and adjust seasoning as needed.

Mix the mixed greens with 1 tablespoon each of olive oil and balsamic vinegar in a bowl. Arrange the roasted beet wedges on top of the greens. Sprinkle with crumbled goat cheese, toasted walnuts, and chopped parsley.

After making the dressing, pour it over the salad and toss carefully to mix everything.

Divide the salad into four servings and garnish with optional toppings like avocado, mint, or orange for added flavor and texture.

Spinach and Feta Quiche with Whole Wheat Crust

Yield: 6 servings   **Preparation Time:** 15 minutes   **Cooking Time:** 45 minutes

Calories: 220 kcal | Carbohydrates: 19g | Total Fat: 12g | Saturated Fat: 3g | Cholesterol: 30mg | Protein: 9g | Sodium: 280mg
(per serving)

Ingredients:
- 1 cup (120g) whole wheat flour
- ¼ tsp (1.5g) salt
- ¼ cup (60 ml) olive oil or avocado oil
- 3-4 tbsp (45-60 ml) cold water

For the Quiche Filling:
- 1 tbsp (15 ml) olive oil
- 1 small onion, finely chopped
- 3 cups (90g) fresh spinach, roughly chopped (or one 10-oz package (280g) of frozen spinach, thawed and squeezed dry)
- 4 large egg whites (or 2 whole eggs and 2 egg whites)
- ¾ cup (180 ml) of unsweetened almond milk or milk from any plant
- ½ cup (75g) crumbled feta cheese
- ¼ tsp (0.5g) ground nutmeg (optional)
- Salt and pepper to taste

Customizable Ingredients/Garnishes:
- Sliced cherry tomatoes for garnish
- Chopped fresh herbs for taste, such as parsley or basil
- Red pepper flakes for heat
- Chopped mushrooms or bell peppers

Instructions:

Preheat the oven to 375°F (190°C). Combine the salt and whole wheat flour in a medium-sized bowl. After adding the olive oil, toss the mixture until it crumbles. Gradually add 3-4 tablespoons of cold water until the dough comes together. Form the dough into a ball.

On a surface that has been lightly floured, roll the dough into a circle that is approximately 12 inches in diameter. Press the dough evenly onto the bottom and edges of a 9-inch pie dish after transferring it there.

Pour the crust lightly with a fork and bake for 10 minutes to prevent it from becoming soggy when filling is added.

In a big skillet over medium heat, warm one tablespoon of olive oil. Add the onion and sauté it for 3-4 minutes. Add the frozen or fresh spinach and simmer for an additional 2-3 minutes, or until the spinach has wilted. Remove from heat and set aside.

Whisk the egg whites (or eggs and egg whites), unsweetened almond milk, salt, pepper, and grated nutmeg (if using) in a medium-sized bowl.

Spread the sautéed spinach and onion mixture evenly over the pre-baked crust. Top with a scattering of the crumbled feta cheese.

Cover the spinach and feta in the crust with the egg mixture.

Place the quiche in the oven and bake for 30-35 minutes or until the filling is set and slightly golden.

Let the quiche cool for a half hour to an hour and a half before cutting and serving.

Pair this quiche with a simple side salad of mixed greens, cucumbers, and cherry tomatoes for a well-rounded, heart-healthy meal.

Asian-Inspired Cabbage Salad with Peanut Dressing

Yield: 4 servings   **Preparation Time:** 15 minutes   **Cooking Time:** None

Calories: 200 kcal | Carbohydrates: 22g | Total Fat: 11g | Saturated Fat: 1.5g | Cholesterol: 0mg | Protein: 6g | Sodium: 400mg
(per serving)

Ingredients:

For the Salad:
- 4 cups (280g) green cabbage, thinly sliced
- 2 cups (140g) red cabbage, thinly sliced
- 1 medium carrot, shredded
- 1 red bell pepper, thinly sliced
- 2 green onions, chopped
- ¼ cup (4g) fresh cilantro, chopped
- ¼ cup (10g) fresh mint, chopped

For the Peanut Dressing:
- ¼ cup (64g) natural peanut butter
- 2 tbsp (30 ml) of tamari or soy sauce
- 1 tbsp (15 ml) rice vinegar
- 1 tbsp (15 ml) lime juice (about ½ lime)
- 1 tbsp (15 ml) maple syrup or honey
- 1 clove garlic, minced
- 1 tsp (2g) grated fresh ginger
- 2-3 tbsp (45-60 ml) water
- A pinch of red pepper

Instructions:

In a large mixing bowl, combine the thinly sliced green and red cabbage, shredded carrot, sliced red bell pepper, green onions, fresh cilantro, and fresh mint (if using). Toss to mix well.

In a small bowl, whisk together the peanut butter (unsweetened), low-sodium soy sauce, rice vinegar, lime juice, honey (or maple syrup), minced garlic, grated ginger, and red pepper flakes (if using). One spoonful at a time, gradually add water to the dressing until it achieves the right consistency—it should be creamy yet pourable.

Add the peanut dressing to the cabbage mixture and gently toss to cover the veggies evenly.

Divide the salad into four servings and garnish with chopped peanuts, sesame seeds, or any other desired toppings.

Vegetable Sushi Rolls with Brown Rice

Yield: 4 servings   **Preparation Time:** 25 minutes   **Cooking Time:** 30 minutes

Calories: 250 kcal | Carbohydrates: 40g | Total Fat: 7g | Saturated Fat: 1g | Cholesterol: 0mg | Protein: 6g | Sodium: 200mg
(per serving)

Ingredients:

For the Sushi Rice:
- 1 cup (190g) brown sushi rice
- 2 cups (480 ml) water
- 2 tbsp (30 ml) rice vinegar
- 1 tbsp (12g) sugar (optional, use a small amount for flavor balance)
- ¼ tsp (1.5g) salt (low-sodium preferred)

For the Sushi Rolls:
- 4 nori sheets (seaweed sheets)
- ½ medium cucumber, julienned
- 1 small carrot, julienned
- 1 small avocado, thinly sliced
- ½ medium red bell pepper, thinly sliced
- 4-6 slices firm tofu, grilled or pan-fried (optional for added protein)
- 1 tbsp (9g) sesame seeds (optional)
- Soy sauce (low-sodium, for dipping)

Optional Fillings/Garnishes:
- Fresh spinach leaves
- Mango slices for sweetness
- Pickled ginger for serving
- Wasabi for heat

Instructions:

Rinse the brown rice under cold water. Add two cups of water to the rice in a medium saucepan. Bring it to a boil, lower the heat, cover, and cook for 30-35 minutes, or until the rice is soft and the water has been absorbed. Remove the heat and leave it covered for 10 minutes.

In a small bowl, mix the rice vinegar, sugar (if using), and salt. Gently fold the mixture into the cooked rice, taking care not to smash it. Let the rice come to room temperature before putting the rolls together.

While the rice cools, julienne the cucumber, carrot, bell pepper, and slice the avocado and any other optional fillings, such as mango or tofu.

Place a bamboo sushi rolling mat (or a clean kitchen towel) on a flat surface. Place a sheet of plastic wrap on top of the mat, then lay one nori sheet, shiny side down, on the plastic wrap.

To avoid stickiness, softly moisten your hands. Leaving a 1-inch space at the upper edge, cover the nori with a thin, equal coating of brown rice.

Arrange a few strips of cucumber, carrot, bell pepper, and avocado (and optional spinach or tofu) horizontally across the center of the rice.

Using the bamboo mat, begin to roll the sushi from the bottom, keeping the fillings in place. Roll tightly, but be careful not to press too hard. When you reach the top, lightly dampen the exposed edge of the nori to seal the roll. Using a sharp knife, cut the sushi roll into 8 equal pieces. Continue with the remaining fillings and nori sheets.

Place the sushi rolls on a plate. Sprinkle with sesame seeds if desired. Serve with low-sodium soy sauce, pickled ginger, and wasabi on the side.

Add extra vegetables such as asparagus or radishes to the rolls for variety. For an extra kick, serve with sriracha or homemade spicy mayo made from Greek yogurt and hot sauce.

Dinner Recipes

Baked Lemon Herb Salmon with Asparagus

Yield: 4 servings | **Preparation Time:** 10 minutes | **Cooking Time:** 20 minutes

Calories: 360 kcal | Carbohydrates: 6g | Total Fat: 22g | Saturated Fat: 3g | Cholesterol: 70mg | Protein: 34g | Sodium: 170mg
(per serving)

Ingredients:
- 4 (6 oz/680g) salmon fillets, skinless
- 1 bunch of asparagus, trimmed (about 1 lb /450g)
- 2 tbsp (30 ml) olive oil, divided
- 2 tbsp (30 ml) of freshly squeezed lemon juice (approximately one lemon)
- 1 tsp (2g) lemon zest
- 2 cloves garlic, minced
- 1 tsp (1g) dried rosemary or 2 tsp (2g) chopped fresh rosemary
- 2 tsp (2g) chopped fresh thyme or 1 tsp (1g) dried
- Salt and pepper to taste (low-sodium preferred)
- Lemon slices for garnish

Customizable Ingredients/Garnishes:
- Fresh parsley or dill for extra flavor
- Sliced avocado
- Toasted almonds for added crunch

Instructions:

Preheat your oven to 400°F (200°C).

Grease a large baking sheet lightly with olive oil or line it with parchment paper.

Place the salmon fillets on the prepared baking sheet. Combine 1 tablespoon olive oil, lemon zest, juice, garlic, thyme, rosemary, and thyme. Evenly drizzle the mixture over the salmon fillets. Season with salt and pepper.

Arrange the asparagus spears around the salmon fillets on the same baking sheet. Sprinkle the asparagus with a bit of salt and pepper and drizzle the remaining 1 tablespoon of olive oil over it. Toss the asparagus to coat evenly.

After preheating the oven, place the baking sheet inside and bake for 15-18 minutes, or until the asparagus is crisp but still soft and the salmon is cooked through. The internal temperature of the salmon should reach 145°F (63°C).

Remove the baking sheet from the oven. If preferred, garnish the salmon with fresh herbs like parsley or dill in addition to lemon slices. Serve immediately.

Grilled Chicken with Quinoa and Spinach Salad

Yield: 4 servings | **Preparation Time:** 15 minutes | **Cooking Time:** 20 minutes

Calories: 430 kcal | Carbohydrates: 28g | Total Fat: 19g | Saturated Fat: 3g | Cholesterol: 70mg | Protein: 32g | Sodium: 240mg
(per serving)

Ingredients:
- 4 skinless, boneless (about 4-5 ounces/500g) chicken breasts
- 1 tbsp (15 ml) olive oil
- 2 tbsp (30 ml) fresh lemon juice
- 2 garlic cloves, minced
- 1 tsp (1g) dried oregano
- Salt and pepper to taste

For the Quinoa Salad:
- 1 cup (170g) quinoa, rinsed
- 2 cups (480 ml) low-sodium vegetable broth or water
- 4 cups (120g) fresh spinach, roughly chopped
- 1 cup (150g) cherry tomatoes, halved
- ½ cucumber, diced
- ¼ cup (8g) fresh parsley, chopped
- ¼ cup (40g) red onion, thinly sliced

For the Dressing:
- 2 tbsp (30 ml) olive oil
- 1 tbsp (15 ml) balsamic vinegar
- 1 tsp (5 ml) Dijon mustard

Instructions:

Mix the lemon juice, minced garlic, dried oregano, olive oil, salt, and pepper in a small bowl. Transfer the marinade to the chicken breasts by placing them in a shallow dish or a plastic bag that can be sealed. Marinate in the refrigerator for at least 15 minutes or up to 1 hour for more flavor.

Set the grill or stovetop grill pan over medium-high heat. After removing the chicken from the marinade, grill it for 6-8 minutes on each side or until it is cooked through and reaches an internal temperature of 165°F (74°C). Allow it to rest for 5 minutes before slicing.

In a medium saucepan, combine the rinsed quinoa and vegetable broth (or water). Bring to a boil over medium-high heat, then lower the temperature, cover, and let the quinoa absorb the liquid for about 15 minutes. Using a fork, fluff, and set aside to cool somewhat.

Cooked quinoa, chopped spinach, cherry tomatoes, cucumber, parsley, and red onion should all be combined in a big mixing basin.

Combine olive oil, Dijon mustard, lemon juice, a dash of salt, and pepper in a small bowl. Pour the dressing over the quinoa and vegetables, then gently toss to blend.

Divide the quinoa salad evenly among four plates. Place some grilled chicken pieces on top of each platter.

Garnish the salad with optional ingredients like sliced avocado, feta cheese, or toasted nuts. Serve immediately.

Vegetable Stir-Fry with Tofu and Brown Rice

Yield: 4 servings **Preparation Time:** 15 minutes **Cooking Time:** 20 minutes

Calories: 360 kcal | Carbohydrates: 52g | Total Fat: 11g | Saturated Fat: 2g | Cholesterol: 0mg | Protein: 15g | Sodium: 380mg
(per serving)

Ingredients:
- 1 block (14 oz/400g) firm tofu
- 1 tbsp (15 ml) soy sauce or tamari
- 1 tbsp (15 ml) olive oil
- 1 tbsp (8g) cornstarch
- 1 small onion, sliced
- 1 red bell pepper, sliced
- 1 medium zucchini, sliced
- 1 cup (90g) broccoli florets
- 1 medium carrot, thinly sliced
- 1 cup (150g) snap peas
- 2 cloves garlic, minced
- 1 tbsp (6g) fresh ginger, grated
- 3 tbsp (45 ml) soy sauce or tamari
- 1 tbsp (15 ml) rice vinegar
- 1 tbsp (15 ml) sesame oil (optional)
- 1 tbsp (15 ml) maple syrup or honey
- 1 tbsp (15 ml) fresh lime juice
- 1 tbsp (15 ml) water
- 1 tsp (3g) cornstarch (for thickening)
- 1 cup (190g) brown rice, rinsed
- 2 cups (480g) water or low-sodium vegetable broth

Customizable Ingredients/Garnishes:
- Toasted sesame seeds for garnish
- Chopped green onions for garnish
- Red pepper flakes for heat

Instructions:

In a medium saucepan, combine the rinsed brown rice and water (or vegetable broth). Once it reaches a boil, lower the heat to a simmer, cover, and let the rice cook for 40-45 minutes until it is soft and the liquid has been completely absorbed. Fluff with a fork and set aside.

After draining, press the tofu between paper towels to eliminate any remaining moisture. Once dry, cut the tofu into 1-inch cubes.

Toss the cubed tofu in 1 tablespoon of soy sauce and 1 tablespoon of cornstarch for a crispier texture. In a nonstick pan, heat one tablespoon of olive oil over medium heat. Add the tofu and cook, stirring periodically, for 6-8 minutes or until it is crispy and brown on both sides. Remove and set aside the tofu from the pan.

Add the sliced onion, red bell pepper, zucchini, broccoli, carrot, and snap peas to the same skillet. Stir-fry the vegetables for 5-6 minutes until they are tender but crisp. For 1-2 minutes, stir-fry the grated ginger and minced garlic.

In a small bowl, whisk together cornstarch, honey, soy sauce, lime juice, rice vinegar, water, and sesame oil (if using). Add sesame oil if using. Stir well to combine.

Add the sauce to the stir-fried veggies, and put the tofu back in the pan. Toss to coat everything evenly and cook for 2-3 minutes until the sauce thickens and the tofu is heated.

Divide the cooked brown rice among four plates. Top with the vegetable stir-fry and tofu. Garnish with optional toppings like toasted sesame seeds, chopped green onions, or red pepper flakes.

Stuffed Portobello Mushrooms with Spinach and Cheese

Yield: 4 servings **Preparation Time:** 10 minutes **Cooking Time:** 20 minutes

Calories: 180 kcal | Carbohydrates: 10g | Total Fat: 10g | Saturated Fat: 3g | Cholesterol: 15mg | Protein: 10g | Sodium: 260mg
(per serving)

Ingredients:
- 4 large portobello mushroom caps, stems removed
- 1 tbsp (15 ml) olive oil
- 1 small onion, finely diced
- 2 garlic cloves, minced
- 4 cups (120g) fresh spinach
- ½ cup (120g) part-skim ricotta cheese or cottage cheese
- ¼ cup (25g) grated Parmesan cheese
- ¼ tsp (0.5g) ground black pepper
- ¼ tsp (1.5g) salt (low-sodium preferred)
- ¼ tsp (0.5g) red pepper flakes
- 1 tbsp (4g) fresh parsley, chopped
- 1 tbsp (6g) whole wheat breadcrumbs

Customizable Ingredients/Garnishes:
- Chopped sun-dried tomatoes for added flavor
- Fresh basil or cilantro for garnish

Instructions:

Turn the oven up to 375°F (190°C). Lightly oil or line a baking sheet with parchment paper.

Drizzle the portobello mushroom caps with olive oil, then arrange them, gill side up, on the preheated baking sheet. Bake for 8-10 minutes to soften the mushrooms slightly. Remove from the oven and set aside.

In a pan, warm the leftover olive oil over medium heat. Add the diced onion and garlic, sautéing for 3-4 minutes until softened and fragrant. Cook the chopped spinach for 2-3 minutes or until it wilts. Add salt, pepper, and red pepper flakes (if using) for seasoning.

Take the pan off the burner and add the grated Parmesan and part-skim ricotta cheese. Mix well until combined.

The spinach and cheese should be equally distributed inside the four portobello mushroom caps. If using breadcrumbs, sprinkle them on top for a crunchy finish.

Bake the filled mushrooms for 10-12 minutes or until the filling is cooked through and the tops begin to turn brown. When removing them from the oven, sprinkle with freshly cut parsley. Serve immediately.

Roasted Cauliflower and Chickpeas with Tahini Sauce

Yield: 4 servings   **Preparation Time:** 10 minutes   **Cooking Time:** 30 minutes

Calories: 280 kcal | Carbohydrates: 24g | Total Fat: 16g | Saturated Fat: 2g | Cholesterol: 0mg | Protein: 8g | Sodium: 180mg
(per serving)

Ingredients:
For the Roasted Cauliflower and Chickpeas:
- 1 large head cauliflower, cut into florets
- 1 can (15 oz/400g) of rinsed and drained chickpeas
- 2 tbsp (15 ml) olive oil
- 1 tsp (2g) ground cumin
- 1 tsp (2g) smoked paprika
- ½ tsp (1g) ground turmeric (optional)
- ½ tsp (1g) ground coriander
- Salt and pepper to taste

For the Tahini Sauce:
- ¼ cup (60g) tahini
- 2 tbsp (30 ml) fresh lemon juice
- 1 clove garlic, minced
- 2 tbsp (30 ml) water (to thin the sauce)
- 1 tsp (15 ml) olive oil (optional)
- Salt and pepper to taste

Customizable Ingredients/Garnishes:
- Chopped fresh parsley or cilantro
- Toasted sesame seeds for extra crunch
- Red pepper flakes for heat
- Lemon wedges for serving

Instructions:

Preheat the oven to 400°F (200°C). Line a large baking sheet with parchment paper.

In a large mixing basin, toss cauliflower florets and chickpeas with olive oil, cumin, smoked paprika, turmeric, coriander, salt, and pepper. Mix until the spices are evenly coated.

Arrange the chickpeas and cauliflower in a single layer on the preheated baking sheet. Roast, flipping halfway through to ensure equal roasting, in a preheated oven for 25-30 minutes or until the cauliflower is soft and golden brown and the chickpeas are crispy.

Mix the tahini, water, lemon juice, minced garlic, and optional olive oil in a small bowl. Add an additional tablespoon of water to thin the mixture for a creamy, pourable sauce. Season with salt and pepper to taste.

After roasting, move the chickpeas and cauliflower to a serving plate. Drizzle with the tahini sauce and top with toasted sesame seeds, chopped cilantro or parsley, and red pepper flakes, if preferred.

For added freshness, serve right now with lemon slices on the side

Whole Wheat Pasta Primavera with Seasonal Vegetables

Yield: 4 servings   **Preparation Time:** 10 minutes   **Cooking Time:** 20 minutes

Calories: 320 kcal | Carbohydrates: 55g | Total Fat: 7g | Saturated Fat: 1g | Cholesterol: 0mg | Protein: 12g | Sodium: 160mg
(per serving)

Ingredients:
- 8 oz (225g) whole wheat pasta (spaghetti, penne, or your choice)
- 1 tbsp (15 ml) olive oil
- 1 small onion, thinly sliced
- 2 cloves garlic, minced
- 1 cup (90g) broccoli florets
- 1 small zucchini, sliced
- 1 small yellow squash, sliced
- 1 red bell pepper, thinly sliced
- 1 cup (150g) cherry tomatoes, halved
- 1 cup (30g) baby spinach (optional)
- ¼ cup (10g) fresh basil, chopped
- ¼ cup (8g) fresh parsley, chopped
- Juice of 1 lemon
- Salt and pepper to taste (low-sodium recommended)

Optional Garnishes:
- Grated Parmesan cheese
- Crushed red pepper flakes for heat
- Toasted pine nuts for extra texture
- Lemon zest for added flavor

Instructions:

Bring a large pot of water to a boil. Add pasta. When cooking whole wheat pasta, the goal is al dente (typically approximately 8–10 minutes). Add a touch of salt and follow the package's directions. Drain the pasta, reserving ¼ cup of pasta water, and set aside.

While the pasta cooks, place a large pan over medium heat with 1 tablespoon of olive oil. Add the onion slices and simmer for 3–4 minutes or until tender. Add the minced garlic and cook for another 1 minute until fragrant.

Add the broccoli florets, zucchini, yellow squash, and red bell pepper to the skillet. Stir-fry for 5-7 minutes until the vegetables are tender but crisp. If using, add the baby spinach during the last 2 minutes to wilt it slightly.

Add the cherry tomatoes halves and simmer for another 1-2 minutes or until the tomatoes soften. After turning off the heat, add the lemon juice, fresh parsley, and basil to the pan. Toss to combine.

Combine the cooked pasta and veggies in a skillet. Pour the pasta water aside to loosen the mixture and toss everything together.

Season with salt and pepper to taste. Divide the pasta into four dishes. Optional garnishes include toasted pine nuts, crushed red pepper flakes, or grated Parmesan.

Zucchini Noodles with Marinara and Turkey Meatballs

Yield: 4 servings	**Preparation Time:** 15 minutes	**Cooking Time:** 25 minutes

Calories: 350 kcal | Carbohydrates: 15g | Total Fat: 18g | Saturated Fat: 3g | Cholesterol: 65mg | Protein: 30g | Sodium: 350mg
(per serving)

Ingredients:

For the Turkey Meatballs:
- 1 lb (450g) ground lean turkey (93% lean or higher)
- 1 small onion, finely chopped
- 1 clove garlic, minced
- ¼ cup (15g) whole wheat breadcrumbs
- 1 large egg white
- 2 tbsp (6g) chopped fresh parsley or 1 tbsp (1g) dry
- 1 tsp (1g) dried oregano
- ¼ tsp (1.5g) salt (low-sodium preferred)
- ¼ tsp (0.5g) black pepper
- 2 tbsp (15 ml) olive oil

For the Marinara Sauce:
- 2 cups (480 ml) marinara sauce
- 1 tsp (15 ml) olive oil
- 2 cloves garlic, minced
- ½ tsp (0.5g) dried basil
- ½ tsp (0.5g) dried oregano
- Pinch of red pepper flakes (optional)

For the Zucchini Noodles:
- 4 medium zucchinis, spiralized into noodles (zoodles)
- 1 tbsp (15 ml) olive oil

Customizable Ingredients/Garnishes:
- Grated Parmesan cheese
- Fresh basil for garnish
- Crushed red pepper flakes for heat

Instructions:

Combine the ground turkey, finely chopped onion, minced garlic, whole wheat breadcrumbs, egg white, parsley, oregano, salt, and pepper in a large bowl. Mix until all the ingredients are well incorporated.

Using your fingertips, form 12–16 little meatballs (approximately 1 inch in diameter) out of the turkey mixture.

Heat 1 tablespoon of olive oil in a large skillet over medium heat. Add the meatballs and cook, flipping regularly, for 8-10 minutes or until browned on both sides and cooked through. Remove from the skillet and set aside.

Heat 1 teaspoon of olive oil over medium heat in the same skillet.

Minced garlic should be added and cooked for 1-2 minutes or until aromatic.

Add the low-sodium marinara sauce, dried basil, oregano, and red pepper flakes (if using). Let the sauce cook for 5-7 minutes, stirring occasionally. Return the cooked turkey meatballs to the skillet and coat them in the sauce. Avoid overcooking the zucchini as it might leak water and go mushy.

In another skillet, warm 1 tablespoon of olive oil over medium heat. Add the spiralized zucchini noodles and sauté for 2-3 minutes until tender but firm (al dente). Be careful not to overcook, as the zucchini can release water and become mushy.

Divide the zucchini noodles among four plates. Top each serving with the turkey meatballs and marinara sauce. Garnish with fresh basil and a light sprinkle of Parmesan cheese if desired.

Ratatouille with Fresh Herbs and Olive Oil

Yield: 4 servings	**Preparation Time:** 15 minutes	**Cooking Time:** 40 minutes

Calories: 180 kcal | Carbohydrates: 24g | Total Fat: 9g | Saturated Fat: 1g | Cholesterol: 0mg | Protein: 4g | Sodium: 220mg
(per serving)

Ingredients:
- 2 tbsp (30 ml) olive oil
- 1 medium onion, finely chopped
- 3 cloves garlic, minced
- 1 medium eggplant, diced
- 1 medium zucchini, sliced
- 1 medium yellow squash, slice
- 1 red bell pepper, diced
- 1 yellow bell pepper, diced
- 1 can (14.5 oz/410g) of diced tomatoes
- 1 tbsp (17g) tomato paste
- 1 tsp (1g) dried oregano
- 1 tsp (1g) dried thyme
- 1 bay leaf
- ¼ cup (10g) fresh basil, chopped
- ¼ cup (8g) fresh parsley, chopped
- Salt and pepper to taste (low-sodium)

Instructions:

Heat 2 tablespoons of olive oil in a large pot or Dutch oven over medium heat. Add the chopped onion and sauté for 4-5 minutes until softened. Add the minced garlic and cook until aromatic, about 1 more minute.

Add the diced eggplant, zucchini, yellow squash, and bell peppers to the pot. Stir well to coat the vegetables in the olive oil. Simmer the veggies for 8 to 10 minutes, stirring now and again, until they become somewhat tender.

Add the bay leaf, dried thyme, dried oregano, and chopped tomatoes with their juice. Bring the mixture to a simmer. After turning the heat low, cover and simmer the veggies for 25-30 minutes, stirring now and again, until they are soft and the flavors are well combined.

After removing the bay leaf, add the parsley and fresh basil and stir. Season with salt and pepper to taste. Cook for 2-3 minutes to allow the herbs to infuse their flavor.

Remove from heat and serve the Ratatouille hot, garnished with fresh thyme or additional basil leaves if desired.

Grilled Lemon Garlic Chicken with Quinoa

Yield: 4 servings	**Preparation Time:** 30 minutes	**Cooking Time:** 25 minutes

Calories: 380 kcal | Carbohydrates: 30g | Total Fat: 13g | Saturated Fat: 2g | Cholesterol: 75mg | Protein: 32g | Sodium: 300mg
(per serving)

Ingredients:

- 4 skinless, boneless chicken breasts (about 4-5 ounces/ 800-900g)
- 3 tbsp (45 ml) olive oil
- 1 big lemon's juice (about 3 tbsp / 45 ml)
- 2 cloves garlic, minced
- 1 tsp (1g) dried oregano
- 1 tsp (1g) dried thyme
- ½ tsp (1g) black pepper
- ½ tsp (3g) salt
- 1 tbsp (3g) fresh parsley, chopped
- 1 cup (170g) quinoa, rinsed
- 2 cups (480 ml) low-sodium vegetable broth or water

Optional Garnishes and Customizable Ingredients:
- Sautéed spinach or grilled vegetables for a vegetable boost
- Chopped fresh parsley or basil for garnish
- Lemon wedges for serving

Instructions:

Marinate the chicken (optional but recommended). In a small bowl, mix the olive oil, oregano, lemon juice, thyme, minced garlic, salt, and pepper. Pour the marinade over the chicken breasts in a shallow dish or resealable plastic bag. For maximum taste, marinate in the fridge for up to 2 hours or for at least 30 minutes.

Set a stovetop grill pan or grill to medium-high heat. After removing the chicken from the marinade, grill it for 6-8 minutes on each side or until it is cooked through. Remove from the grill and let rest for 5 minutes before slicing.

In a medium saucepan, combine the rinsed quinoa and vegetable broth (or water). Bring to a boil, then reduce the heat to low, cover, and simmer for 15 minutes or until the quinoa has absorbed all the liquid. Take the quinoa from the stove and use a fork to fluff it up.

Toss the cooked quinoa with olive oil, lemon juice, and a little salt and pepper. Toss to combine.

Divide the quinoa among four plates. Place a grilled chicken breast on top of each plate. Garnish with fresh parsley and optional lemon wedges for extra flavor. Add sautéed spinach or grilled vegetables on the side if desired.

Herb-Crusted Baked Cod with Steamed Broccoli

Yield: 4 servings	**Preparation Time:** 10 minutes	**Cooking Time:** 20 minutes

Calories: 330 kcal | Carbohydrates: 20g | Total Fat: 13g | Saturated Fat: 2g | Cholesterol: 55mg | Protein: 32g | Sodium: 300mg
(per serving)

Ingredients:

- 4 cod fillets (4-6 oz each/400-600g)
- 3 tbsp (45 ml) olive oil
- 1 cup (120g) whole wheat breadcrumbs or panko for extra crunch
- 2 tbsp (6g) fresh parsley, chopped
- 1 tbsp (3g) chopped fresh thyme or 1 tsp (1g) dry
- 1 tsp (1g) dried or 1 tbsp (1.5g) chopped fresh dill
- 1 clove garlic, minced
- 1 tsp (2g) lemon zest
- 1 tbsp (15 ml) Dijon mustard
- Salt and pepper to taste (low-sodium recommended)
- Lemon wedges (for serving)
- 1 large broccoli head divided into florets
- 1 tbsp (15 ml) olive oil (optional)
- Lemon zest (optional for garnish)

Customizable Ingredients/Garnishes:
- Red pepper flakes for extra heat
- Sliced almonds for garnish on the broccoli
- Fresh basil or chives for extra flavor

Instructions:

Preheat the oven to 400°F (200°C). Lightly oil or line a baking sheet with parchment paper.

In a bowl, mix together whole wheat breadcrumbs, lemon zest, minced garlic, thyme, dill, fresh parsley, salt, and pepper. Lightly wet the breadcrumbs by drizzling with one tablespoon of olive oil and stirring.

Gently pat the cod fillets dry using paper towels. Apply a thin layer of Dijon mustard to each fish, and then equally top the fillets with the herb breadcrumb mixture to form a crust.

Cod fillets should be placed on the ready baking sheet. Bake the fish for 12-15 minutes or until it is opaque and flakes readily when tested with a fork (it should be cooked inside to 145°F/63°C). Remove from the oven and set aside.

While the cod is baking, steam the broccoli. In a large pot, bring about 1 inch of water to a simmer and place a steamer basket inside. Add the broccoli florets to the basket, cover, and steam for four to five minutes or until they are soft but still vibrant green.

After removing the steamed broccoli from the saucepan, sprinkle it with one tablespoon (if using) of olive oil. For extra flavor, sprinkle some lemon zest on top and season with salt and pepper to suit.

Divide the herb-crusted baked cod fillets and steamed broccoli among four plates. Garnish the cod with lemon wedges and serve immediately.

Lentil Loaf with Tomato Glaze

Yield: 6 servings   **Preparation Time:** 15 minutes   **Cooking Time:** 1 hour

Calories: 260 kcal | Carbohydrates: 37g | Total Fat: 7g | Saturated Fat: 1g | Cholesterol: 0mg | Protein: 12g | Sodium: 200mg
(per serving)

Ingredients:

- 1 cup (200g) dry green or brown lentils
- 2 ½ cups (600 ml) water or low-sodium vegetable broth
- 1 tbsp (15 ml) olive oil
- 1 small onion, finely chopped
- 2 cloves garlic, minced
- 1 medium carrot, grated
- 1 small celery stalk, finely chopped
- 1 cup (90g) rolled oats (quick oats or old-fashioned)
- ¼ cup (30g) ground flaxseed
- 3 tbsp (45 ml) of water and 1 tbsp (7g) of ground flaxseed (flax "egg")
- ¼ cup (8g) chopped fresh parsley
- 1 tbsp (15 ml) soy sauce
- 1½ tbsp (25 ml) Dijon mustard
- 1 tsp (1g) dried thyme
- 1 tsp (2g) smoked paprika
- ½ tsp (1g) ground cumin
- Salt and pepper to taste (low-sodium recommended)
- ¼ cup (60g) tomato paste
- 1 tbsp (15 ml) balsamic vinegar
- 1 tbsp (15 ml) maple syrup

Instructions:

Rinse the lentils under cold water. Heat 2 ½ cups of water (or veggie broth) and the lentils in a medium pot until they boil. Simmer them for 20 to 25 minutes over low heat with a cover to achieve tender but not mushy lentils. Drain any excess liquid and set aside.

Preheat your oven to 350°F (175°C). Grease the loaf pan very lightly or line it with parchment paper.

Place the olive oil in a pan and heat it to medium. Add the chopped onion, garlic, grated carrot, and celery. Cook for 5-7 minutes until softened. Remove from heat.

Cooked lentils, sautéed veggies, oats, ground flaxseed, flax "egg," parsley, soy sauce, Dijon mustard, thyme, cumin, smoked paprika, and salt and pepper should all be combined in a big bowl. Mix well until fully combined. Mash the ingredients using a potato masher, being careful to preserve some texture.

Pour the lentil mixture into the loaf pan, smoothing the top and pushing down firmly.

Mix the tomato paste, ½ tbsp Dijon mustard, maple syrup, and balsamic vinegar.

Spread the tomato glaze evenly over the top of the lentil loaf.

Place the bread in the preheated oven for 45 minutes or until it is firm and has a gently golden top. Let the loaf cool for 10-15 minutes before slicing and serving. For added texture and flavor, sprinkle with toasted nuts or pumpkin seeds before serving.

Serve this lentil loaf with a side of roasted vegetables or a green salad for added fiber and nutrients.

Grilled Shrimp Tacos with Cabbage Slaw

Yield: 4 servings   **Preparation Time:** 15 minutes   **Cooking Time:** 10 minutes

Calories: 320 kcal | Carbohydrates: 28g | Total Fat: 12g | Saturated Fat: 2g | Cholesterol: 150mg | Protein: 25g | Sodium: 300mg
(per serving)

Ingredients:

- 1 lb (450g) large shrimp, peeled and deveined
- 2 tbsp (30 ml) olive oil
- 1 tsp (2g) chili powder
- 1 tsp (2g) cumin
- 1 tsp (2g) smoked paprika
- ½ tsp (1g) garlic powder
- Salt and pepper to taste (low-sodium)
- Juice of 1½ lime
- 2 cups (180g) green cabbage, shredded
- 1 cup (90g) red cabbage, shredded
- 1 medium carrot, shredded
- ¼ cup (4g) fresh cilantro, chopped
- 1 tbsp (20 ml) maple syrup or honey
- 8 small corn tortillas (preferably whole grain or low-sodium)
- Fresh avocado slices (optional)
- Lime wedges (for garnish)
- Sliced jalapeño (optional, for heat)
- Fresh cilantro for garnish

Instructions:

Toss the shrimp in a bowl with olive oil, chili powder, cumin, smoked paprika, garlic powder, salt, pepper, and lime juice. Let it marinate for at least 10 minutes while preparing the other ingredients.

Set a stovetop grill pan or grill to medium-high heat. Grill the shrimp for 2-3 minutes per side or until they are pink and opaque. Remove from heat and set aside.

Combine the shredded green and red cabbage, carrot, and cilantro in a large bowl.

Mix the lime juice, olive oil, honey or maple syrup, salt, and pepper in a small bowl. After adding the dressing, stir the cabbage mixture to ensure uniform coating.

In a dry skillet, cook the corn tortillas for 30 seconds on each side or until they are soft and warm.

Divide the grilled shrimp among the tortillas. Add the cabbage slaw on top and optional toppings such as sliced jalapeños, avocado slices, and additional cilantro. Serve with lime wedges on the side.

Spicy Thai Green Curry with Vegetables

Yield: 4 servings	**Preparation Time:** 10 minutes	**Cooking Time:** 20 minutes

Calories: 320 kcal | Carbohydrates: 44g | Total Fat: 12g | Saturated Fat: 5g | Cholesterol: 0mg | Protein: 6g | Sodium: 450mg
(per serving)

Ingredients:

- 1 tbsp (15 ml) olive oil or avocado oil
- 1 small onion, finely chopped
- 2 cloves garlic, minced
- 1 tbsp (6g) fresh ginger, grated
- 3 tbsp (45g) Thai green curry paste
- 1 can (14 oz/400 ml) light coconut milk
- ½ cup (120 ml) low-sodium vegetable broth
- 1 small zucchini, sliced
- 1 small eggplant, diced
- 1 red bell pepper, thinly sliced
- 1 cup (90g) broccoli florets
- 1 medium carrot, thinly sliced
- 1 cup (30g) baby spinach
- 1 tbsp (15 ml) low-sodium soy sauce or tamari
- 1 tbsp (15 ml) fresh lime juice
- 1 tsp (4g) brown sugar (optional)
- Salt and pepper to taste

For Serving:

- 2 cups (340g) cooked brown rice or quinoa
- Fresh cilantro, chopped (for garnish)
- Fresh basil leaves (optional)
- Lime wedges (for garnish)

Instructions:

Heat the olive oil in a large skillet or saucepan over medium heat. Chop the onion and sauté it for 3-4 minutes or until tender. Add the ginger and garlic and simmer for an additional minute or until fragrant.

Stir in the Thai green curry paste and simmer for one to two minutes to allow the flavors to meld.

Add veggie broth and light coconut milk. Bring the mixture to a gentle simmer.

Add the zucchini, eggplant, red bell pepper, broccoli, and carrot to the skillet. Simmer the veggies for 10-12 minutes, stirring now and again until soft but not mushy. Add the baby spinach during the last 2 minutes to wilt it slightly.

Stir in the soy sauce (or tamari), lime juice, and optional brown sugar. Season with salt and pepper to taste. If desired, add more chili peppers or curry paste to increase the degree of spiciness.

Prepare the rice/quinoa.

For extra fiber and whole grains, serve the curry over cooked brown rice or quinoa.

Garnish with fresh cilantro, basil leaves, and lime wedges. Add crushed peanuts or toasted cashews for extra crunch and sliced chili peppers for extra heat.

Herb-Roasted Turkey Breast with Seasonal Vegetables

Yield: 4 servings	**Preparation Time:** 15 minutes	**Cooking Time:** 60-75 minutes

Calories: 350 kcal | Carbohydrates: 28g | Total Fat: 13g | Saturated Fat: 2g | Cholesterol: 70mg | Protein: 36g | Sodium: 300mg
(per serving)

Ingredients:

- 1.5-2 lb (900g) boneless, skinless turkey breast
- 2 tbsp (30 ml) olive oil
- 2 tbsp (6g) fresh rosemary, chopped
- 1 tbsp (3g) fresh thyme, chopped
- 1 tbsp (3g) fresh parsley, chopped
- 3 cloves garlic, minced
- 1 tsp (2g) lemon zest
- 1½ tsp (3g) black pepper
- 1 tsp (6g) salt (low-sodium preferred)
- Juice of 1 lemon
- 1 lb (450g) baby carrots
- 1 lb (450g) Brussels sprouts, halved
- 1 medium sweet potato, cubed
- 1 red onion, quartered
- 1 tbsp (15 ml) olive oil
- 1 tsp (1g) dried thyme
- 1 tsp (2g) smoked paprika

Instructions:

Preheat your oven to 375°F (190°C).

Mix olive oil, rosemary, thyme, parsley, minced garlic, lemon zest, black pepper, and salt together. Rub this mixture evenly over the turkey breast.

Take a roasting pan and put the turkey breast in. Drizzle the turkey with one lemon juice. Roast the turkey for 60-75 minutes, or until the internal temperature reaches 165°F (74°C) when checked with a meat thermometer. Let the turkey rest for 10 minutes before slicing.

While the turkey is roasting, place the carrots, Brussels sprouts, sweet potato, and red onion on a baking sheet. Drizzle with olive oil and sprinkle with dried thyme, smoked paprika, black pepper, and salt. Toss to coat the vegetables evenly.

Spread the vegetables in a single layer and roast in the oven alongside the turkey for 25-30 minutes or until the vegetables are tender and lightly browned.

After slicing, present the turkey breast with veggies. Add some fresh parsley as a garnish and serve with lemon wedges for more taste.

Drizzle the turkey and vegetables with a little balsamic reduction for extra flavor if desired.

Snacks and Appetizers

Roasted Chickpeas with Paprika and Cumin

Yield: 4 servings   **Preparation Time:** 5 minutes   **Cooking Time:** 30 minutes

Calories: 150 kcal | Carbohydrates: 20g | Total Fat: 6g | Saturated Fat: 1g | Cholesterol: 0mg | Protein: 6g | Sodium: 200mg
(per serving)

Ingredients:
- 1 can (15 oz/400g) of washed, drained, and patted dry chickpeas
- 1 tbsp (15 ml) olive oil
- 1 tsp (2g) ground cumin
- 1 tsp (2g) smoked paprika (or regular paprika)
- ¼ tsp (0.5g) ground cayenne pepper (optional for heat)
- ½ tsp (1g) garlic powder
- ¼ tsp (1.5g) salt (low-sodium recommended)
- ¼ tsp (0.5g) black pepper

Optional Garnishes:
- Fresh lemon zest for brightness
- Chopped parsley for garnish
- Red pepper flakes for extra heat

Instructions:

Set a silicone baking mat or parchment paper on a baking sheet and preheat the oven to 400°F (200°C).

After draining, give the chickpeas a good rinse. Using paper towels or a fresh towel, pat them dry. It's essential that the chickpeas are as dry as possible to ensure they roast up crispy.

The dry chickpeas should be combined with olive oil, smoked paprika, ground cumin, garlic powder, cayenne pepper (if used), salt, and black pepper in a bowl. Thoroughly mix to uniformly coat the chickpeas with the spices.

Arrange the seasoned chickpeas in a single layer on the preheated baking sheet. Roast the chickpeas in the preheated oven for 25-30 minutes, stirring the pan halfway through or until they are crispy and golden brown.

Once taken out of the oven, let the chickpeas cool for a little while. If desired, garnish with lemon zest or fresh parsley before serving.

Serve these Roasted Chickpeas as a crunchy snack, or toss them on top of a green salad for added texture and protein.

Use as a topping for soups, grain bowls, or wraps to add flavor and a satisfying crunch.

Cucumber Slices with Avocado Hummus

Yield: 4 servings   **Preparation Time:** 10 minutes   **Cooking Time:** None

Calories: 200 kcal | Carbohydrates: 16g | Total Fat: 13g | Saturated Fat: 2g | Cholesterol: 0mg | Protein: 4g | Sodium: 180mg
(per serving)

Ingredients:
- 1 ripe avocado
- 1 can (15 oz/400g) of rinsed and drained chickpeas
- 2 tbsp (30 ml) olive oil
- 2 tbsp (30g) tahini
- 2 tbsp (30g) fresh lemon juice
- 1 clove garlic, minced
- ¼ tsp (0.5g) ground cumin
- ¼ tsp smoked paprika (optional for flavor)
- ¼ tsp (1.5g) salt (low-sodium recommended)
- 2-3 tbsp (30-45 ml) water (if needed)
- Fresh cilantro or parsley, chopped
- 2 large cucumbers sliced into rounds or sticks
- Fresh dill or mint (optional for garnish)

Optional Garnishes:
- Flakes of red pepper for some spiciness
- Sesame seeds for extra crunch

Instructions:

In a food processor, combine the ripe avocado, chickpeas, olive oil, tahini, lemon juice, minced garlic, cumin, smoked paprika (if using), and salt. Blend, scraping down the sides as necessary until smooth.

If the hummus is too thick, add two to three tablespoons of water (or more, if necessary) and mix until it reaches the right consistency.

After giving the hummus a taste test, add more salt, lemon juice, or spices as needed.

Transfer the hummus to a serving dish, top with a little olive oil drizzle, chopped parsley or cilantro, and, if you like, sesame seeds or red pepper flakes.

Wash the cucumbers thoroughly and slice them into rounds or sticks. Place the cucumber slices on a plate for serving.

Serve the avocado hummus alongside the cucumber slices. If desired, garnish the cucumber slices with fresh dill or mint for added freshness.

This hummus can also be spread on whole-grain toast or rolled up with fresh veggies for a heart-healthy meal.

Pair the hummus with fresh veggies like carrot sticks, bell pepper slices, or celery for a nutrient-packed, colorful platter.

Baked Sweet Potato Chips with Sea Salt

Yield: 4 servings   **Preparation Time:** 10 minutes   **Cooking Time:** 30 minutes

Calories: 320 kcal | Carbohydrates: 44g | Total Fat: 12g | Saturated Fat: 5g | Cholesterol: 0mg | Protein: 6g | Sodium: 450mg
(per serving)

Ingredients:
- 2 large sweet potatoes, scrubbed clean
- 1 tbsp (15 ml) olive oil
- ½ tsp (3g) sea salt (low-sodium preferred)
- ¼ tsp (0.5g) black pepper (optional)

Optional Garnishes:
- Fresh rosemary, finely chopped (for extra flavor)
- Smoked paprika (for a kick of spice)
- Lemon zest (for brightness)

Instructions:

Preheat your oven to 375°F (190°C). Line two large baking sheets with parchment paper or a silicone baking mat.

Thinly slice the sweet potatoes to about 1/8-inch thick. Uniform slices ensure even baking.

Place the sweet potato slices in a large bowl. Drizzle with 1 tablespoon of olive oil and sprinkle with sea salt (and pepper if using). Toss to coat the slices evenly.

Arrange the sweet potato slices on the ready baking sheets in a single layer. Make sure they are not overlapping to allow for even crisping.

Bake in the preheated oven for 12-15 minutes. Then, flip the slices and bake for an additional 10-15 minutes or until the chips are crispy and golden. Keep an eye on them to avoid burning; the chips can cook quickly in the final minutes.

Remove the baking sheets from the oven and let the chips cool for a few minutes.

For added flavor, sprinkle with fresh rosemary, smoked paprika, cayenne pepper, or lemon zest. Serve immediately.

Serve these Baked Sweet Potato Chips as a snack or appetizer with a heart-healthy dip like hummus or guacamole.

Pair them with a side of grilled chicken or a vegetable-based sandwich for a light lunch.

You can bake chips using other root vegetables, such as carrots, parsnips, or beets.

Almond-Crusted Cauliflower Bites

Yield: 4 servings   **Preparation Time:** 15 minutes   **Cooking Time:** 30 minutes

Calories: 180 kcal | Carbohydrates: 12g | Total Fat: 12g | Saturated Fat: 1g | Cholesterol: 0mg | Protein: 7g | Sodium: 160mg
(per serving)

Ingredients:
- 1 large head of cauliflower
- 1 cup (100g) almonds, finely ground or almond meal
- ¼ cup (30g) whole wheat flour
- 2 large egg whites
- 1 tsp (3g) garlic powder
- 1 tsp (2g) smoked paprika
- ½ tsp (1g) ground cumin
- ¼ tsp (0.5g) black pepper
- ¼ tsp (1.5g) salt (low-sodium preferred)
- 1 tbsp (15 ml) olive

Optional Garnishes:
- Fresh parsley or cilantro, chopped
- Lemon wedges for serving
- Red pepper flakes

Instructions:

Preheat your oven to 400°F (200°C). Line a baking sheet with parchment paper or lightly grease it with olive oil.

Combine the ground almonds, whole wheat flour, garlic powder, smoked paprika, cumin, salt, and black pepper. Mix well and set aside.

Chop the cauliflower into bite-sized pieces, making sure each piece is around the same size so that baking turns out evenly.

In another bowl, whisk the egg whites until slightly frothy. Dip each cauliflower floret into the egg whites, allowing the excess to drip off, then coat it in the almond mixture. Press the almond coating onto the cauliflower to ensure it sticks well. Place the coated florets on the prepared baking sheet in a single layer.

Bake in the preheated oven for 25-30 minutes, flipping the florets halfway through, until golden brown and crispy.

Once done, remove the cauliflower bites from the oven. Add some fresh cilantro or parsley as a garnish, and serve with lemon wedges for a zesty, refreshing finish.

Pair with a light mixed greens salad for a balanced meal.

These bites also work well as a side dish to complement grilled chicken or baked fish for a heart-healthy meal.

Fresh Fruit Skewers with Yogurt Dip

Yield: 4 servings   **Preparation Time:** 15 minutes   **Cooking Time:** None

Calories: 120 kcal | Carbohydrates: 24g | Total Fat: 1g | Saturated Fat: 0.5g | Cholesterol: 5mg | Protein: 5g | Sodium: 30mg
(per serving)

Ingredients:

- 1 cup (150g) strawberries, hulled and halved
- 1 cup (150g) pineapple chunks
- 1 cup (150g) grapes (red or green)
- 1 kiwi, peeled and cut into chunks
- 1 small apple, cut into chunks
- 1 small banana, sliced (optional)
- 8 wooden or bamboo skewers
- 1 cup (240g) plain, low-fat Greek yogurt
- 1 tbsp (15 ml) maple syrup or honey (if desired for sweetness)
- 1 tsp (5 ml) vanilla extract
- 1 tsp (5 ml) fresh lemon juice
- 1 pinch (0.25g) cinnamon (optional)

Optional Garnishes:

- Chopped fresh mint or basil for garnish
- Lemon zest for extra flavor
- Chia seeds or toasted nuts for a bit of crunch

Instructions:

Wash and cut the strawberries, pineapple, grapes, kiwi, apple, and any other fruits you're using into bite-sized chunks. Make sure the pieces are around the same size to ensure equal skewering.

Thread the fruit pieces onto the wooden skewers in alternating patterns to create colorful skewers. Leave a bit of space at the ends of each skewer for easy handling.

Combine the Greek yogurt, lemon juice, honey or maple syrup (if using), vanilla essence, and a dash of cinnamon (if preferred) in a small bowl. Mix until smooth and well combined.

Refrigerate the yogurt dip for 10-15 minutes before serving to let the flavors meld.

Arrange the fruit skewers on a serving platter alongside the yogurt dip. Garnish with fresh mint or basil leaves, lemon zest, or chia seeds for added texture and flavor.

Spicy Guacamole with Whole Grain Tortilla Chips

Yield: 4 servings   **Preparation Time:** 15 minutes   **Cooking Time:** 10 minutes

Calories: 230 kcal | Carbohydrates: 22g | Total Fat: 16g | Saturated Fat: 2g | Cholesterol: 0mg | Protein: 4g | Sodium: 180mg
(per serving)

Ingredients:

For the Spicy Guacamole:

- 2 ripe avocados, peeled, pitted, and mashed
- 1 small jalapeño, finely chopped (adjust based on spice preference)
- 1 small tomato, diced
- ¼ cup (40g) red onion, finely chopped
- 1 clove garlic, minced
- ¼ cup (4g) fresh cilantro, chopped
- Juice of 1 lime
- ½ tsp (1g) ground cumin
- ¼ tsp (1.5g) salt (low-sodium recommended)
- ¼ tsp (0.5g) black pepper
- ½ tsp (1g) crushed red pepper flakes

For the Whole Grain Tortilla Chips:

- 4 large whole grain tortillas (or whole wheat tortillas)
- 1 tbsp (15 ml) olive oil
- ½ tsp (1g) garlic powder
- ½ tsp (1g) chili powder
- ¼ tsp (1.5g) salt (low-sodium recommended)

Instructions:

Preheat your oven to 350°F (175°C). Line a baking sheet with parchment paper.

Cut the whole-grain tortillas into triangular chip-sized pieces using a sharp knife or pizza cutter.

Combine the olive oil, garlic powder, chili powder, and salt. Lightly brush the tortilla pieces with the seasoned oil mixture on both sides.

Arrange the tortilla triangles in a single layer on the prepared baking sheet. Bake for 10-12 minutes or until golden and crispy. Keep an eye on them to prevent burning. Remove from the oven and let cool.

Prepare the Spicy Guacamole. Using a fork, mash the ripe avocados in a medium-sized basin until they are smooth but still have some chunks.

Stir in the finely chopped jalapeño, diced tomato, red onion, minced garlic, cilantro, lime juice, cumin, salt, and pepper. Mix well to combine.

Adjust the seasoning if needed. If you like extra heat, add crushed red pepper flakes or more jalapeño.

Serve the spicy guacamole in a bowl alongside the baked whole-grain tortilla chips. If desired, garnish with additional cilantro and lime wedges.

Zucchini Fritters with Greek Yogurt Dip

Yield: 4 servings   **Preparation Time:** 15 minutes   **Cooking Time:** 15 minutes

Calories: 200 kcal | Carbohydrates: 18g | Total Fat: 13g | Saturated Fat: 1.5g | Cholesterol: 0mg | Protein: 5g | Sodium: 120mg
(per serving)

Ingredients:

For the Zucchini Fritters:
- 2 medium zucchinis, grated
- ¼ cup (30g) whole wheat flour (or almond flour for gluten-free)
- 2 large egg whites
- 2 tbsp (6g) fresh parsley, chopped
- 1 clove garlic, minced
- ¼ tsp (0.5g) black pepper
- ½ tsp (3g) salt (low-sodium preferred)
- ½ tsp (1g) ground cumin (optional)
- 2 tbsp (30 ml) olive oil (for frying)

For the Greek Yogurt Dip:
- 1 cup (240 ml) plain, low-fat Greek yogurt
- 1 tbsp (15 ml) fresh lemon juice
- 1 tbsp (2g) fresh dill, chopped (or parsley)
- 1 clove garlic, minced
- Pinch of salt (low-sodium preferred)
- Pinch of black pepper

Optional Garnishes:
- Lemon wedges for serving
- Chopped fresh herbs like mint or basil for garnish
- Red pepper flakes for extra heat

Instructions:

Grate the zucchini and place it in a clean kitchen towel. Squeeze out as much excess water as possible to ensure the fritters stay crisp.

In a large bowl, combine the grated zucchini, whole wheat flour, egg whites, parsley, minced garlic, black pepper, salt, and cumin (if using). Mix until everything is well incorporated.

Form small patties (about 2-3 tablespoons each) from the zucchini mixture. Flatten them slightly with your hands.

Heat 2 tablespoons of olive oil in a large skillet over medium heat. Add the fritters in batches, making sure not to overcrowd the pan. Cook each fritter for 3-4 minutes on each side until golden brown and crisp. Remove from the skillet and place on paper towels to absorb excess oil.

Combine the Greek yogurt, fresh lemon juice, chopped dill, minced garlic, salt, and black pepper. Stir well until smooth and creamy.

Refrigerate the dip for 10-15 minutes to allow the flavors to blend.

Serve the zucchini fritters warm with the Greek yogurt dip on the side. Garnish with fresh herbs, lemon wedges, or a sprinkle of red pepper flakes if desired.

Spiced Apple Chips with Cinnamon

Yield: 4 servings   **Preparation Time:** 10 minutes   **Cooking Time:** 2 hours

Calories: 60 kcal | Carbohydrates: 17g | Total Fat: 0g | Saturated Fat: 0g | Cholesterol: 0mg | Protein: 0g | Sodium: 0mg
(per serving)

Ingredients:
- 2 large apples (any variety, such as Fuji or Gala)
- 1 tsp (2.5g) ground cinnamon
- ¼ tsp (0.5g) ground nutmeg (optional)
- Pinch of ground ginger (optional)

Optional Garnishes:
- Lemon zest for brightness
- Drizzle of honey for extra sweetness (optional)

Instructions:

Preheat your oven to 225°F (110°C). Line two large baking sheets with parchment paper.

Wash and core the apples. Slice the apples very thinly (about ⅛ inch thick) to ensure even cooking. You can leave the skin on for added fiber.

In a small bowl, mix together the ground cinnamon, ground nutmeg, and ground ginger. Lay the apple slices in a single layer on the prepared baking sheets. Lightly sprinkle the spice mixture over the apple slices.

Bake in the preheated oven for 1 hour. After 1 hour, flip the apple slices and bake for another 1 hour, or until the apples are crisp and lightly browned. Keep an eye on them in the final minutes to prevent burning.

After baking, remove the apple chips from the oven and allow them to cool fully. As they cool, they will continue to become crispier.

Serve the apple chips as a snack, or store them in an airtight container for up to a week.

After baking, drizzle the apple chips with honey or maple syrup for a touch of extra sweetness.

Use them as a topping for oatmeal, salads, or granola for added texture and flavor.

Edamame with Sea Salt and Lemon

Yield: 4 servings | **Preparation Time:** 20 minutes | **Cooking Time:** 25 minutes

Calories: 180 kcal | Carbohydrates: 30g | Total Fat: 4g | Saturated Fat: 0.5g | Cholesterol: 30mg | Protein: 6g | Sodium: 340mg
(per serving)

Ingredients:

- 2 cups (240g) frozen edamame (in the pod)
- 1 tbsp (18g) sea salt (low-sodium recommended)
- Juice of 1 lemon
- Lemon zest from ½ lemon (optional, for extra flavor)

Optional Garnishes:

- Red pepper flakes
- Sesame seeds for added texture
- Fresh parsley or cilantro, chopped

Instructions:

About 4 cups of water should be brought to a boil in a medium saucepan. Cook the frozen edamame for 5-7 minutes or until the pods are soft and cooked all the way through.

Drain the edamame and transfer them to a serving bowl. While still warm, sprinkle with sea salt, squeeze the juice of one lemon over the edamame, and toss to coat evenly. Optionally, zest half a lemon over the top for extra flavor.

Add optional garnishes such as red pepper flakes, sesame seeds, or fresh herbs for extra flavor and presentation. Serve immediately.

Serve this Edamame with Sea Salt and Lemon as a snack or appetizer. It pairs well with dishes like sushi, grilled chicken, or brown rice bowls.

You can also enjoy it as a protein-packed side dish with quinoa, whole-grain pasta, or a vegetable stir-fry.

Baked Veggie Spring Rolls with Dipping Sauce

Yield: 4 servings (12 rolls) | **Preparation Time:** 15 minutes | **Cooking Time:** 10 minutes

Calories: 230 kcal | Carbohydrates: 22g | Total Fat: 16g | Saturated Fat: 2g | Cholesterol: 0mg | Protein: 4g | Sodium: 180mg
(per serving)

Ingredients:

For the Spring Rolls:

- 12 spring roll wrappers (rice paper or whole wheat wrappers)
- 1 cup (120g) shredded carrots
- 1 cup (90g) shredded cabbage
- 1 small zucchini, julienned
- 1 red bell pepper, julienned
- 1 cup (100g) bean sprouts
- 2 green onions, finely chopped
- 2 cloves garlic, minced
- 1 tbsp (15 ml) soy sauce (low-sodium)
- 1 tbsp (15 ml) sesame oil (or olive oil)
- 1 tsp (2g) fresh ginger, grated
- 1 tbsp (1g) fresh cilantro, chopped

For the Dipping Sauce:

- ¼ cup (60 ml) low-sodium soy sauce
- 1 tbsp (15 ml) rice vinegar
- 1 tsp (5 ml) sesame oil
- 1 tsp (5 ml) honey (optional for sweetness)
- ½ tsp (1g) red pepper flakes (optional for heat)
- 1 tsp (5 ml) fresh lime juice

Optional Garnishes:

- Sesame seeds
- Chopped fresh cilantro or mint
- Lime wedges

Instructions:

In a large skillet or wok, heat 1 tablespoon of sesame oil over medium heat. Add the minced garlic and grated ginger, sautéing for about 30 seconds until fragrant.

Add the shredded carrots, cabbage, zucchini, and red bell. Stir-fry the vegetables for 4-5 minutes until they are slightly softened but still crisp. Stir in the bean sprouts, green onions, soy sauce, and fresh cilantro (if using). Cook for another 2 minutes, then remove from heat.

If using rice paper wrappers, dip each wrapper in warm water for about 10 seconds to soften. If using whole wheat spring roll wrappers, follow the package instructions.

Place about 2 tablespoons of the veggie filling in the center of each wrapper. Fold the bottom edge over the filling, then fold in the sides and roll tightly, like a burrito. Repeat until all the filling is used.

Preheat your oven to 400°F (200°C). Line a baking sheet with parchment paper.

Place the spring rolls on the baking sheet. To help them crisp up, lightly brush each one with olive oil or cooking spray. Bake the rolls for 20-25 minutes, rotating them midway through, until they are crispy and golden.

In a small bowl, whisk together the soy sauce, rice vinegar, sesame oil, honey (if using), red pepper flakes, and fresh lime juice. Adjust seasoning to taste.

Serve the baked veggie spring rolls hot with the dipping sauce on the side. Garnish with sesame seeds, fresh cilantro, or lime wedges as desired.

Serve these Baked Veggie Spring Rolls with a side of brown rice or quinoa for a more substantial meal.

Pair with a light miso soup or green salad for a balanced and nutritious meal.

Roasted Red Pepper and Walnut Dip

Yield: 6 servings   **Preparation Time:** 10 minutes   **Cooking Time:** 10 minutes

Calories: 160 kcal | Carbohydrates: 7g | Total Fat: 14g | Saturated Fat: 1.5g | Cholesterol: 0mg | Protein: 4g | Sodium: 150mg
(per serving)

Ingredients:

- 2 large roasted red bell peppers (jarred or homemade)
- 1 cup (120g) walnuts, toasted
- 1 clove garlic, minced
- 2 tbsp (30 ml) olive oil
- 1 tbsp (15 ml) lemon juice
- 1 tsp (2g) ground cumin
- 1 tsp (2g) smoked paprika or regular paprika
- ¼ tsp (0.5g) cayenne pepper (optional for heat)
- 1 tbsp (15 ml) pomegranate molasses (optional for sweetness)
- ¼ tsp (1.5g) salt (low-sodium recommended)
- ¼ tsp (0.5g) black pepper

Optional Garnishes:

- Fresh parsley, chopped
- Pomegranate seeds for a burst of sweetness
- Drizzle of extra olive oil

Instructions:

Toast the walnuts in a dry skillet over medium heat for 5-7 minutes, stirring frequently, until fragrant and lightly browned. Set aside to cool.

If using fresh red bell peppers, preheat the oven to 450°F (230°C). After placing the peppers on a baking sheet, roast them for 20-25 minutes, rotating them halfway through until the skins are blistered and browned. Remove the peppers from the oven, cover with foil, and let steam for 10 minutes. Peel the skins off and remove the seeds.

In a food processor or blender, combine the roasted red peppers, toasted walnuts, minced garlic, olive oil, lemon juice, cumin, smoked paprika, cayenne pepper (if using), salt, and black pepper. Blend until smooth. For a chunkier texture, pulse the mixture until it reaches your desired consistency.

Taste and adjust the seasoning as needed. If you like a sweeter dip, add 1 tablespoon of pomegranate molasses (optional).

Transfer the dip to a serving bowl. If desired, garnish with fresh parsley, pomegranate seeds, or a drizzle of olive oil.

Serve this Roasted Red Pepper and Walnut Dip with whole-grain pita chips, fresh vegetable sticks (carrots, cucumbers, bell peppers), or whole-grain crackers.

Mini Stuffed Peppers with Cream Cheese

Yield: 4 servings   **Preparation Time:** 10 minutes   **Cooking Time:** 15 minutes

Calories: 90 kcal | Carbohydrates: 17g | Total Fat: 0g | Saturated Fat: 0g | Cholesterol: 0mg | Protein: 0g | Sodium: 0mg
(per serving)

Ingredients:

- 12 mini sweet peppers (assorted colors)
- 4 oz (100g) light cream cheese (reduced-fat)
- ¼ cup (60g) plain Greek yogurt (low-fat or fat-free)
- 1 clove garlic, minced
- 2 tbsp (6g) fresh parsley, chopped
- 2 tbsp (6g) fresh chives, chopped
- ½ tsp (1g) black pepper
- ¼ tsp (1.5g) salt (low-sodium recommended)
- 1 tbsp (15 ml) lemon juice
- 2 tbsp (10g) grated Parmesan cheese

Optional Garnishes:

- Fresh basil or cilantro, chopped
- Red pepper flakes for a bit of heat
- Lemon zest for added flavor

Instructions:

Preheat your oven to 375°F (190°C). Line a baking sheet with parchment paper.

Slice the mini peppers in half lengthwise, removing the seeds and membranes. Place them on the prepared baking sheet and cut side up.

In a medium bowl, mix together the light cream cheese, Greek yogurt, minced garlic, parsley, chives, black pepper, salt, and lemon juice. Stir until smooth and well combined.

Using a small spoon or piping bag, fill each pepper half with the cream cheese mixture. If using, sprinkle with grated Parmesan cheese.

Bake in the preheated oven for 12-15 minutes or until the peppers are tender and the filling is lightly golden on top.

Remove the peppers from the oven and garnish with fresh herbs, lemon zest, or red pepper flakes if desired. Serve warm.

Serve these Mini Stuffed Peppers with Cream Cheese as an appetizer or snack for parties, or enjoy them as a side dish with a green salad or whole grain crackers.

These peppers also make a great accompaniment to grilled or roasted dishes like chicken, fish, or tofu.

Savory Oatmeal Energy Bites

Yield: 4 servings   **Preparation Time:** 10 minutes   **Cooking Time:** 30 minutes

Calories: 190 kcal | Carbohydrates: 16g | Total Fat: 12g | Saturated Fat: 1.5g | Cholesterol: 16mg | Protein: 6g | Sodium: 120mg
(per serving)

Ingredients:
- 1 cup (90g) rolled oats (whole grain)
- ¼ cup (35g) flaxseed meal
- ¼ cup (35g) sunflower seeds
- ¼ cup (30g) nutritional yeast (optional, for a cheesy flavor)
- 2 tbsp (9g) chia seeds
- ¼ cup (60g) almond butter (or any nut butter)
- 2 tbsp (30 ml) olive oil
- 2 tbsp (30 ml) water (or as needed)
- 1 clove garlic, minced
- 1 tbsp (3.5g) fresh parsley, chopped
- 1 tsp (2.5g) ground cumin
- ½ tsp (1.5g) smoked paprika
- ½ tsp (3g) salt (low-sodium recommended)
- ¼ tsp (0.5g) black pepper

Optional Garnishes:
- Sesame seeds for rolling
- Fresh herbs like cilantro or dill

Instructions:

In a large bowl, combine the rolled oats, flaxseed meal, sunflower seeds, nutritional yeast (if using), and chia seeds. Mix well.

In a small bowl, combine the almond butter, olive oil, water, minced garlic, fresh parsley, cumin, smoked paprika, salt, and black pepper. Stir until smooth.

Pour the wet mixture into the dry ingredients and mix until well combined. If the mixture is too dry, add water (1 teaspoon at a time) until it holds together.

Roll the mixture into 1-inch balls. If desired, roll the bites in sesame seeds for added crunch and flavor.

Place the energy bites on a plate and refrigerate for at least 30 minutes to firm up before serving.

For added variety, you can customize the flavor by mixing in roasted red pepper flakes, grated carrots, or finely chopped spinach.

Serve these bites with a light salad or soup for a quick and nutritious meal.

Herb and Garlic Popcorn

Yield: 4 servings   **Preparation Time:** 5 minutes   **Cooking Time:** 10 minutes

Calories: 120 kcal | Carbohydrates: 15g | Total Fat: 7g | Saturated Fat: 1g | Cholesterol: 0mg | Protein: 2g | Sodium: 150mg
(per serving)

Ingredients:
- ½ cup (60g) popcorn kernels (yields about 8 cups popped)
- 2 tbsp (15 ml) olive oil or avocado oil
- 2 cloves garlic, minced
- 1 tsp (1.5g) dried oregano
- 1 tsp (1g) dried thyme
- 1 tsp (1g) dried rosemary, crushed
- ½ tsp (1.5g) garlic powder (optional for extra garlic flavor)
- ½ tsp (3g) salt (low-sodium recommended)
- ¼ tsp (0.5g) black pepper
- 1 tbsp (5g) nutritional yeast (optional for a cheesy flavor)

Optional Garnishes:
- Fresh parsley, chopped for garnish
- Lemon zest for added brightness
- Red pepper flakes for heat

Instructions:

In a large pot with a lid, heat 1 tablespoon of olive oil over medium-high heat. Add the popcorn kernels and cover with the lid. Shake the pot occasionally as the kernels pop. Once the popping slows to about 2 seconds between pops, remove from heat. This should take about 3-5 minutes. Transfer the popcorn to a large bowl.

In a small skillet, heat the remaining 1 tablespoon of olive oil over medium heat. Add the minced garlic and cook for 1-2 minutes until fragrant and lightly golden. Be careful not to burn the garlic. Remove from heat.

Pour the garlic-infused olive oil over the popped popcorn. Add the dried oregano, thyme, rosemary, garlic powder (if using), salt, and pepper. Toss well to coat the popcorn evenly with the herbs and seasoning.

For added flavor, sprinkle nutritional yeast over the popcorn and toss again. If desired, garnish with fresh parsley, lemon zest, or red pepper flakes.

For a different flavor profile, experiment with other herbs and spices such as paprika, cumin, or dill.

Salads

Mediterranean Quinoa Salad with Chickpeas

Yield: 4 servings	**Preparation Time:** 15 minutes	**Cooking Time:** 15 minutes

Calories: 320 kcal | Carbohydrates: 39g | Total Fat: 14g | Saturated Fat: 2g | Cholesterol: 0mg | Protein: 10g | Sodium: 250mg
(per serving)

Ingredients:

- 1 cup (170g) quinoa, rinsed
- 2 cups (480 ml) water
- 1 can (15 oz/240g) chickpeas, drained and rinsed
- 1 cup (150g) cucumber, diced
- 1 cup (150g) cherry tomatoes, halved
- ¼ cup (40g) red onion, finely chopped
- ¼ cup (30g) Kalamata olives, pitted and sliced
- ¼ cup (15g) fresh parsley, chopped
- ¼ cup (10g) fresh mint, chopped
- ¼ cup (35g) crumbled feta cheese

For the Dressing:

- 3 tbsp (45 ml) olive oil
- 2 tbsp (30 ml) fresh lemon juice
- 1 clove garlic, minced
- 1 tsp (1g) dried oregano
- ¼ tsp (1.5g) salt
- ¼ tsp (0.5g) black pepper

Optional Garnishes:

- Lemon wedges for serving
- Fresh basil or cilantro for extra herbs

Instructions:

To remove the quinoa's naturally occurring coating, which may give it an unpleasant flavor, thoroughly rinse it under cold water through a fine-mesh sieve.

Combine the quinoa and water in a medium saucepan. Bring to a boil over medium heat, then reduce to a simmer, cover, and cook for 12-15 minutes until all the water is absorbed and the quinoa is tender. Remove from the heat, use a fork to fluff, and let it cool.

Whisk together the olive oil, lemon juice, minced garlic, oregano, salt, and black pepper until well combined.

Combine the cooled quinoa, chickpeas, cucumber, cherry tomatoes, red onion, Kalamata olives, parsley, and mint (if using).

After adding the dressing to the salad, stir to mix. Taste and adjust seasoning if needed.

You can add more fresh herbs or lemon wedges as decoration and crumbled feta cheese on top if you like. Serve immediately or refrigerate for later.

For added protein, top with grilled tofu or salmon.

For a fast and healthy meal, keep leftovers in the fridge for up to three days.

Spinach and Strawberry Salad with Balsamic Vinaigrette and Chickpeas

Yield: 4 servings	**Preparation Time:** 10 minutes	**Cooking Time:** None

Calories: 260 kcal | Carbohydrates: 26g | Total Fat: 13g | Saturated Fat: 2g | Cholesterol: 0mg | Protein: 8g | Sodium: 200mg
(per serving)

Ingredients:

- 6 cups (180g) fresh baby spinach
- 1 cup (150g) strawberries, hulled and sliced
- 1 can (15 oz/240g) chickpeas, drained and rinsed
- ¼ cup (40g) red onion, thinly sliced
- ¼ cup (30g) slivered almonds, toasted
- ¼ cup (35g) feta cheese
- 1 small avocado, sliced (optional)

For the Balsamic Vinaigrette:

- ¼ cup (60 ml) balsamic vinegar
- 2 tbsp (30 ml) olive oil
- 1 tsp (5g) Dijon mustard
- 1 tsp (7 ml) honey or maple syrup
- 1 clove garlic, minced
- ¼ tsp (1.5g) salt
- ¼ tsp black pepper

Instructions:

Whisk together minced garlic, balsamic vinegar, olive oil, Dijon mustard, honey (if using), salt, and black pepper until smooth and emulsified.

Combine the baby spinach, sliced strawberries, chickpeas, and red onion in a large salad bowl.

Over medium heat, toast the slivered almonds for 2-3 minutes until lightly golden and fragrant. Remove from heat and set aside.

Pour the balsamic vinaigrette over the salad and toss gently to combine. Add the toasted almonds and, if desired, top with crumbled feta cheese and sliced avocado for extra flavor and texture.

Garnish with fresh herbs like basil or mint and a little lemon zest if desired. Serve immediately.

Serve this Spinach and Strawberry Salad with Balsamic Vinaigrette and Chickpeas as a light lunch or dinner, or pair it with grilled chicken, salmon, or tofu for added protein.

Cabbage and Carrot Slaw with Apple Cider Dressing

Yield: 4 servings | **Preparation Time:** 15 minutes | **Cooking Time:** None

Calories: 120 kcal | Carbohydrates: 15g | Total Fat: 6g | Saturated Fat: 1g | Cholesterol: 0mg | Protein: 2g | Sodium: 120mg
(per serving)

Ingredients:
- 2 cups (140g) green cabbage, finely shredded
- 1 cup (70g) red cabbage, finely shredded
- 1 cup (110g) carrots, grated or julienned
- 1 small red bell pepper, julienned
- 2 green onions, chopped
- ¼ cup (15g) fresh parsley, chopped

For the Apple Cider Dressing:
- ¼ cup (60 ml) apple cider vinegar
- 1 tbsp (15g) Dijon mustard
- 1 tbsp (15 ml) honey or maple syrup
- 2 tbsp (30 ml) olive oil
- 1 clove garlic, minced
- ¼ tsp (1.5g) salt
- ¼ tsp (0.5g) black pepper
- 1 tsp (3g) poppy seeds (optional)

Optional Garnishes:
- Toasted sunflower seeds or pumpkin seeds
- Fresh herbs like cilantro or dill
- Lemon zest for extra brightness

Instructions:

Combine the green and red cabbage, carrots, red bell pepper, and green onions. Toss to mix.

If using, add the chopped parsley for a burst of fresh flavor and color.

Whisk together the apple cider vinegar, Dijon mustard, honey, olive oil, minced garlic, salt, black pepper, and poppy seeds (if using). Whisk until the dressing is well combined and emulsified.

Pour the apple cider dressing over the cabbage and carrot mixture. Toss everything together until the vegetables are well coated with the dressing.

For best results, refrigerate the slaw for at least 20-30 minutes.

Before serving, garnish with optional toasted sunflower seeds or pumpkin seeds for added crunch, or sprinkle with fresh herbs or lemon zest.

Serve this Cabbage and Carrot Slaw as a side dish with grilled chicken, fish, or tofu for a complete, heart-healthy meal.

This slaw can also be used as a topping for tacos or burgers, adding freshness and flavor to any dish.

Kale Salad with Avocado and Lemon Dressing

Yield: 4 servings | **Preparation Time:** 15 minutes | **Cooking Time:** None

Calories: 180 kcal | Carbohydrates: 14g | Total Fat: 13g | Saturated Fat: 2g | Cholesterol: 0mg | Protein: 4g | Sodium: 120mg
(per serving)

Ingredients:
- 6 cups (200g) fresh kale, stems removed and chopped
- 1 large avocado, diced
- 1 cup (150g) cherry tomatoes, halved
- ½ cup (75g) red bell pepper, diced
- ¼ cup (40g) red onion, thinly sliced
- 2 tbsp (18g) sunflower seeds or pumpkin seeds

For the Lemon Dressing:
- ¼ cup (60 ml) fresh lemon juice
- 2 tbsp (30 ml) olive oil
- 1 tsp (5g) Dijon mustard
- 1 tsp (7 ml) honey or maple syrup
- 1 clove garlic, minced
- ¼ tsp (1.5g) salt (low-sodium recommended)
- ¼ tsp (0.5g) black pepper

Optional Garnishes:
- Fresh herbs like parsley, cilantro, or basil
- Crumbled feta (optional for added creaminess)
- Lemon zest for extra brightness

Instructions:

Place the chopped kale in a large salad bowl. Drizzle 1 tablespoon of olive oil or lemon juice over the kale and massage it with your hands for 2-3 minutes. This makes the kale softer and more delicate.

Once the kale is softened, add the diced avocado, cherry tomatoes, red bell pepper, and red onion to the bowl and toss to combine.

Whisk together the fresh lemon juice, olive oil, Dijon mustard, honey, minced garlic, salt, and black pepper until well combined.

Pour the lemon dressing over the kale and vegetables. Gently toss the salad to properly distribute the dressing among the components.

If desired, garnish the salad with sunflower seeds or pumpkin seeds, fresh herbs, and a sprinkle of lemon zest. Serve immediately.

Cranberry Walnut Salad with Citrus Vinaigrette

Yield: 6 servings   **Preparation Time:** 10 minutes   **Cooking Time:** 0 minutes

Calories: 180 kcal | Carbohydrates: 22g | Total Fat: 10g | Saturated Fat: 1g | Cholesterol: 0mg | Protein: 3g | Sodium: 70mg
(per serving)

Ingredients:

- 6 cups (180g) mixed greens (e.g., spinach, arugula, romaine)
- ½ cup (60g) dried cranberries
- ¼ cup (30g) lightly toasted and chopped walnuts
- 1 medium apple, thinly sliced
- ¼ cup (35g) crumbled feta cheese

For the Citrus Vinaigrette:

- 3 tbsp (45 ml) fresh orange juice
- 1 tbsp (15 ml) fresh lemon juice
- 1 tsp (2g) orange zest
- 1 tsp (5g) Dijon mustard
- 1 tsp (7 ml) honey or maple syrup
- 1 tbsp (15 ml) extra-virgin olive oil
- Salt and pepper to taste

Instructions:

Whisk together the orange juice, orange zest, lemon juice, Dijon mustard, and honey until well combined.

While whisking to emulsify the dressing, gradually pour in the olive oil.

Add a pinch of salt and pepper for seasoning. Set aside.

Put the mixed greens in a big salad bowl.

Scatter the cranberries, walnuts, apple slices, and optional feta cheese over the greens.

Before serving, pour the citrus vinaigrette over the salad.

Gently toss to ensure that the dressing coats every ingredient equally.

Serve the salad immediately, or if making it ahead of time, chill it for up to an hour before serving.

Mixed Greens with Grapes and Pecans

Yield: 4 servings   **Preparation Time:** 10 minutes   **Cooking Time:** None

Calories: 190 kcal | Carbohydrates: 13g | Total Fat: 15g | Saturated Fat: 2g | Cholesterol: 0mg | Protein: 3g | Sodium: 120mg
(per serving)

Ingredients:

- 6 cups (180g) mixed greens (baby spinach, arugula, or spring mix)
- 1 cup (150g) seedless red or green grapes, halved
- ¼ cup (30g) pecans, toasted and chopped
- ¼ cup (35g) crumbled feta cheese (optional for added creaminess)
- ¼ small red onion, thinly sliced

For the Vinaigrette:

- 2 tbsp (30 ml) olive oil
- 1 tbsp (15 ml) balsamic vinegar (or apple cider vinegar)
- 1 tsp (5g) Dijon mustard
- 1 tsp (7 ml) honey (optional for sweetness)
- 1 clove garlic, minced
- ¼ tsp (1.5g) salt (low-sodium recommended)
- ¼ tsp (0.5g) black pepper

Optional Garnishes:

- Fresh herbs such as parsley or mint
- Lemon zest for added brightness

Instructions:

In a large salad bowl, place the mixed greens as the base. Add the halved grapes, toasted pecans, red onion slices, and crumbled feta cheese (if using).

Over medium heat, toast the pecans for 2-3 minutes until lightly golden and fragrant. Stir occasionally to avoid burning. Allow to cool slightly before incorporating into the salad.

Whisk together Dijon mustard, olive oil, balsamic vinegar, honey (if using), minced garlic, salt, and black pepper until smooth and emulsified.

Over the salad, drizzle with the vinaigrette and gently toss to coat the greens evenly.

If desired, garnish with a sprinkling of lemon zest or fresh herbs for an extra taste. Serve immediately.

Other fruits, such as sliced pears or apples, may be added for more taste and texture.

Chickpea and Avocado Salad with Lime Dressing

Yield: 4 servings   **Preparation Time:** 15 minutes   **Cooking Time:** None

Calories: 220 kcal | Carbohydrates: 21g | Total Fat: 14g | Saturated Fat: 2g | Cholesterol: 0mg | Protein: 5g | Sodium: 170mg
(per serving)

Ingredients:
- 1 can (15 oz/240g) chickpeas, drained and rinsed
- 1 cup (150g) cucumber, diced
- 1 large avocado, diced
- 1 cup (150g) cherry tomatoes, halved
- ¼ cup (40g) red onion, finely diced
- ¼ cup (15g) fresh cilantro, chopped
- ¼ cup (15g) fresh parsley, chopped (optional)

For the Lime Dressing:
- 3 tbsp (45 ml) of freshly squeezed lime juice (about 1 big lime)
- 2 tbsp (30 ml) olive oil
- 1 tsp (5g) Dijon mustard
- 1 tsp (7 ml) honey or maple syrup
- 1 clove garlic, minced
- ¼ tsp (1.5g) salt (low-sodium recommended)
- ¼ tsp (0.5g) black pepper

Optional Garnishes:
- Chili flakes for a bit of heat
- Lemon zest for extra brightness
- Toasted sunflower seeds for added crunch

Instructions:

Combine the chickpeas, diced avocado, cucumber, cherry tomatoes, red onion, cilantro, and parsley (if using). Toss gently.

Whisk together the fresh lime juice, olive oil, Dijon mustard, honey (if using), minced garlic, salt, and black pepper until well combined.

Pour the lime dressing over the chickpea and avocado mixture. Gently toss the salad to ensure all components are equally coated with the dressing.

Garnish the salad with chili flakes, lemon zest, or toasted sunflower seeds if desired. Serve immediately.

For a Mediterranean twist, add feta cheese (optional) or olives to enhance the flavor profile.

Citrus Salad with Pomegranate Seeds and Mint

Yield: 4 servings   **Preparation Time:** 15 minutes   **Cooking Time:** None

Calories: 140 kcal | Carbohydrates: 20g | Total Fat: 6g | Saturated Fat: 1g | Cholesterol: 0mg | Protein: 1g | Sodium: 90mg
(per serving)

Ingredients:
- 2 oranges, peeled and sliced into rounds
- 1 grapefruit, peeled and sliced into rounds
- 1 blood orange (optional), peeled and sliced into rounds
- ½ cup (90g) pomegranate seeds
- ¼ cup (10g) fresh mint leaves, chopped or torn
- 2 tbsp (30 ml) fresh lime juice
- 1 tbsp (15 ml) olive oil
- 1 tsp (7 ml) honey or maple syrup
- 1 tsp (2g) lemon zest (optional)
- ¼ tsp (1.5g) salt (low-sodium recommended)
- ¼ tsp (0.5g) black pepper

Optional Garnishes:
- Crushed pistachios or almonds for added crunch
- Feta cheese (optional for a savory twist)
- Additional mint leaves for garnish

Instructions:

Peel the oranges, grapefruit, and blood orange (if using). Slice the fruits into rounds and arrange them on a large serving plate.

Sprinkle the pomegranate seeds evenly over the citrus slices.

Whisk together the lime juice, olive oil, honey (if using), salt, black pepper, and lemon zest (if using) until well combined.

Drizzle the lime dressing over the citrus and pomegranate seeds.

Top the salad with fresh chopped mint leaves. For extra texture, sprinkle crushed pistachios or almonds and add a few whole mint leaves as garnish. Serve immediately.

Roasted Vegetable Salad with Tahini Dressing

Yield: 4 servings   **Preparation Time:** 15 minutes   **Cooking Time:** 25 minutes

Calories: 250 kcal | Carbohydrates: 12g | Total Fat: 16g | Saturated Fat: 2g | Cholesterol: 0mg | Protein: 5g | Sodium: 180mg
(per serving)

Ingredients:

- 1 medium sweet potato, peeled and diced
- 1 red bell pepper, diced
- 1 zucchini, sliced into rounds
- 1 red onion, cut into wedges
- 1 cup broccoli florets
- 1 tbsp (15 ml) olive oil
- 1 tsp (2g) ground cumin
- 1 tsp (2g) paprika
- ¼ tsp (1.5g) salt
- ¼ tsp (0.5g) black pepper
- 4 cups (120g) mixed greens (spinach, arugula, or spring mix)

For the Tahini Dressing:

- ¼ cup (60g) tahini
- 2 tbsp (30 ml) fresh lemon juice
- 1 clove garlic, minced
- 2 tbsp (30 ml) warm water (more as needed for consistency)
- 1 tsp (5 ml) olive oil
- 1 tsp (7 ml) honey or maple syrup
- ¼ tsp (1.5g) salt
- ¼ tsp (0.5g) black pepper

Optional Garnishes:

- Toasted sesame seeds for extra crunch
- Fresh parsley or cilantro, chopped
- Lemon zest for added brightness

Instructions:

Preheat your oven to 400°F (200°C). Line a baking sheet with parchment paper.

Toss the diced sweet potato, red bell pepper, zucchini, red onion, and broccoli florets with 1 tablespoon of olive oil, ground cumin, paprika, salt, and black pepper. Ensure the vegetables are evenly coated.

Spread the vegetables in an even layer on the prepared baking sheet. Roast for 20-25 minutes, stirring halfway through, until they are tender and lightly browned.

Whisk together the tahini, lemon juice, minced garlic, olive oil, honey (if using), salt, black pepper, and warm water. Adjust the consistency by adding more water as needed until the dressing is smooth and creamy.

Divide the mixed greens between four plates or bowls.

Once the vegetables are roasted, arrange them on top of the mixed greens. Drizzle the tahini dressing over the salad and toss gently to combine.

If desired, garnish with toasted sesame seeds, fresh herbs, or lemon zest. Serve immediately.

Lentil Salad with Cherry Tomatoes and Feta

Yield: 4 servings   **Preparation Time:** 10 minutes   **Cooking Time:** 20 minutes

Calories: 280 kcal | Carbohydrates: 32g | Total Fat: 12g | Saturated Fat: 3g | Cholesterol: 5mg | Protein: 12g | Sodium: 220mg
(per serving)

Ingredients:

- 1 cup (190g) dry green or brown lentils
- 3 cups (720 ml) water or low-sodium vegetable broth
- 1 cup (150g) cherry tomatoes, halved
- ½ cup (75g) cucumber, diced
- ¼ cup (40g) red onion, finely chopped
- ¼ cup (15g) fresh parsley, chopped
- ¼ cup (35g) crumbled feta cheese
- 2 tbsp (30 ml) fresh lemon juice
- 2 tbsp (30 ml) olive oil
- 1 tsp (5g) Dijon mustard
- 1 clove garlic, minced
- ¼ tsp (1.5g) salt
- ¼ tsp (0.5g) black pepper
- 1 tsp (1g) dried oregano

Optional Garnishes:

- Fresh mint or basil for extra flavor
- Toasted pine nuts or sunflower seeds

Instructions:

Rinse the lentils thoroughly under cold water. Place them in a medium saucepan with 3 cups of water or low-sodium vegetable broth.

After bringing the lentils to a boil, lower the heat so they simmer. Cook for 15-20 minutes until tender. Drain and let them cool slightly.

Combine the cherry tomatoes, diced cucumber, red onion, and parsley in a large bowl.

Whisk together the lemon juice, minced garlic, black pepper, olive oil, Dijon mustard, salt, and oregano (if using) until smooth and emulsified.

Add the cooked lentils to the bowl with the vegetables. Pour the dressing over the salad and toss gently to combine.

Gently fold in the crumbled feta cheese (if using). Taste and adjust seasoning as needed.

If desired, garnish with fresh herbs or toasted nuts/seeds. Serve right away or store in the refrigerator for up to three days.

Broccoli Salad with Almonds and Cranberries

Yield: 4 servings   **Preparation Time:** 15 minutes   **Cooking Time:** None

Calories: 180 kcal | Carbohydrates: 15g | Total Fat: 11g | Saturated Fat: 1.5g | Cholesterol: 0mg | Protein: 5g | Sodium: 150mg
(per serving)

Ingredients:

- 4 cups (280g) fresh broccoli florets, chopped into bite-sized pieces
- ¼ cup (30g) dried cranberries (unsweetened if possible)
- ¼ cup (30g) sliced almonds, toasted
- ¼ red onion, finely chopped
- ¼ cup (30g) shredded carrots (optional for added color and nutrition)

For the Dressing:

- ¼ cup (60g) plain Greek yogurt (low-fat or fat-free)
- 2 tbsp (30 ml) olive oil
- 1 tbsp (15 ml) apple cider vinegar
- 1 tsp (7 ml) honey or maple syrup
- 1 tsp (5g) Dijon mustard
- 1 clove garlic, minced
- ¼ tsp (1.5g) salt (low-sodium recommended)
- ¼ tsp (0.5g) black pepper

Optional Garnishes:

- Fresh parsley or chives, chopped
- Lemon zest for added brightness

Instructions:

Combine the broccoli florets, dried cranberries, toasted almonds, and finely chopped red onion. If using, add shredded carrots for extra color and crunch.

To toast the almonds, heat a small skillet over medium heat and cook the sliced almonds for 2-3 minutes, frequently stirring until gently golden. Remove from heat and let them cool.

Whisk together the Greek yogurt, minced garlic, apple cider vinegar, olive oil, honey (if using), Dijon mustard, salt, and black pepper.

Pour the yogurt dressing over the broccoli mixture and toss gently.

Garnish the salad with lemon zest and fresh parsley or chives if desired. Serve immediately or refrigerate for 30 minutes to let the flavors meld.

Arugula Salad with Pears and Gorgonzola

Yield: 4 servings   **Preparation Time:** 10 minutes   **Cooking Time:** None

Calories: 210 kcal | Carbohydrates: 15g | Total Fat: 16g | Saturated Fat: 3g | Cholesterol: 5mg | Protein: 4g | Sodium: 180mg
(per serving)

Ingredients:

- 4 cups (120g) fresh arugula
- 2 ripe pears, thinly sliced
- ¼ cup (30g) Gorgonzola cheese, crumbled (use reduced-fat for a lower-fat option)
- ¼ cup (30g) walnuts, toasted and chopped
- ¼ red onion, thinly sliced
- 2 tbsp (15g) dried cranberries

For the Vinaigrette:

- 3 tbsp (45 ml) olive oil
- 1 tbsp (15 ml) balsamic vinegar
- 1 tbsp (15 ml) fresh lemon juice
- 1 tsp (5g) Dijon mustard
- 1 tsp (7 ml) honey or maple syrup
- ¼ tsp (1.5g) salt (low-sodium recommended)
- ¼ tsp (0.5g) black pepper

Optional Garnishes:

- Lemon zest for added brightness
- Fresh herbs like parsley or mint

Instructions:

In a large salad bowl, place the fresh arugula as the base. Add the thinly sliced pears, crumbled Gorgonzola cheese, toasted walnuts, and sliced red onion. Optionally, sprinkle in dried cranberries for extra sweetness.

Whisk together the olive oil, balsamic vinegar, lemon juice, Dijon mustard, honey (if using), salt, and black pepper until well combined.

Drizzle the vinaigrette over the arugula and pears, then gently toss the salad to evenly coat all ingredients with the dressing.

If desired, garnish with fresh herbs or lemon zest. Serve immediately.

For an added crunch, consider topping with toasted seeds or pumpkin seeds.

Carrot and Raisin Salad with Greek Yogurt Dressing

Yield: 4 servings   **Preparation Time:** 15 minutes   **Cooking Time:** 15 minutes

Calories: 165 kcal | Carbohydrates: 28g | Total Fat: 3g | Saturated Fat: 0.5g | Cholesterol: 0mg | Protein: 5g | Sodium: 80mg
(per serving)

Ingredients:

- 4 medium carrots, peeled and shredded (about 2 cups/240g)
- ½ cup (75g) raisins
- ¼ cup (15g) chopped fresh parsley
- ¼ cup (30g) toasted sunflower seeds

For the Greek Yogurt Dressing:

- ½ cup (120g) plain Greek yogurt (low-fat or fat-free)
- 1 tbsp (15 ml) honey or maple syrup
- 1 tbsp (15 ml) apple cider vinegar
- 1 tbsp (15 ml) lemon juice
- ½ tsp (3g) Dijon mustard
- ¼ tsp (1.5g) salt (low-sodium recommended)
- ¼ tsp (0.5g) black pepper
- 2 tbsp (30 ml) water

Optional Garnishes:

- Fresh mint or cilantro for extra flavor
- Lemon zest for a citrusy touch

Instructions:

Utilizing a food processor or box grater, peel and shred the carrots. Place the shredded carrots in a large salad bowl.

Toss the carrots with the raisins and, if desired, fresh parsley for extra flavor. For some crunch, add toasted sunflower seeds.

Prepare the Greek Yogurt Dressing. Whisk together the Greek yogurt, honey (if using), apple cider vinegar, lemon juice, Dijon mustard, salt, and black pepper. Add water one tablespoon at a time to get the desired consistency.

Pour the Greek yogurt dressing over the carrot and raisin mixture. Toss until the dressing coats the salad evenly.

Optionally, garnish with fresh mint, cilantro, or lemon zest. Serve immediately or refrigerate for 15 minutes to allow the flavors to meld.

Tropical Mango Salad with Black Beans and Lime Dressing

Yield: 4 servings   **Preparation Time:** 15 minutes   **Cooking Time:** None

Calories: 250 kcal | Carbohydrates: 34g | Total Fat: 11g | Saturated Fat: 1.5g | Cholesterol: 0mg | Protein: 6g | Sodium: 200mg
(per serving)

Ingredients:

- 1 large ripe mango, peeled and diced
- 1 can (15 oz/240g) black beans, drained and rinsed
- 1 red bell pepper, diced
- 1 cup (150g) cherry tomatoes, halved
- 1 small red onion, finely chopped
- 1 avocado, diced
- ¼ cup (15g) fresh cilantro, chopped
- 2 cups (60g) fresh spinach or mixed greens (optional for a more substantial salad)

For the Lime Dressing:

- ¼ cup (60 ml) fresh lime juice
- 2 tbsp (30 ml) olive oil
- 1 tsp (7 ml) honey or maple
- 1 clove garlic, minced
- ½ tsp ground cumin
- ¼ tsp (1.5g) salt (low-sodium recommended)
- ¼ tsp (0.5g) black pepper

Optional Garnishes:

- Toasted pumpkin seeds or sunflower seeds for crunch
- Sliced jalapeño for heat
- Lime zest for extra brightness

Instructions:

Combine the diced mango, black beans, red bell pepper, cherry tomatoes, red onion, avocado, and fresh cilantro. If using, toss in the spinach or mixed greens to create a more substantial salad.

Whisk together the fresh lime juice, olive oil, honey (if using), minced garlic, ground cumin, salt, and black pepper until well combined.

Pour the lime dressing over the salad. Toss until the dressing coats the salad evenly.

Optionally, garnish with toasted pumpkin or sunflower seeds for added crunch and sliced jalapeños for a kick of spice. Sprinkle with lime zest for extra flavor. Serve immediately.

Desserts

Dark Chocolate Avocado Mousse

Yield: 4 servings   **Preparation Time:** 10 minutes   **Cooking Time:** 30 minutes

Calories: 240 kcal | Carbohydrates: 25g | Total Fat: 18g | Saturated Fat: 4g | Cholesterol: 0mg | Protein: 3g | Sodium: 60mg
(per serving)

Ingredients:

- 2 ripe avocados, peeled and pitted
- ¼ cup (25g) unsweetened cocoa powder
- ¼ cup (50g) dark chocolate chips (70% or higher cacao), melted
- 3-4 tbsp (60 ml) maple syrup or honey
- 1 tsp (5 ml) vanilla extract
- ¼ cup (60 ml) almond milk or oat milk (unsweetened)
- Pinch of salt

Optional Garnishes:

- Fresh berries (strawberries, raspberries, or blueberries)
- Cacao nibs or dark chocolate shavings
- Chopped nuts (such as almonds or walnuts)
- Mint leaves for freshness

Instructions:

Melt the dark chocolate chips in a double boiler or microwave until smooth. Set aside to cool slightly.

In a food processor or blender, combine the ripe avocados, cocoa powder, melted dark chocolate, maple syrup (or honey), vanilla extract, almond milk, and a pinch of salt. Blend the ingredients until it becomes creamy and smooth. If preferred, increase the amount of honey or maple syrup to adjust the sweetness.

Put the mousse into separate glasses or bowls for serving. Cover and chill for at least half an hour to let the flavors mingle and the mousse thicken.

Before serving, garnish with fresh berries, cacao nibs, dark chocolate shavings, chopped nuts, or mint leaves for added texture and flavor.

Coconut Chia Seed Pudding with Pineapple

Yield: 4 servings   **Preparation Time:** 10 minutes   **Cooking Time:** 4 hours or overnight

Calories: 180 kcal | Carbohydrates: 20g | Total Fat: 10g | Saturated Fat: 6g | Cholesterol: 0mg | Protein: 3g | Sodium: 20mg
(per serving)

Ingredients:

- 1 cup (240 ml) unsweetened coconut milk (light coconut milk for lower fat content)
- ¼ cup (40g) chia seeds
- 2 tbsp (30 ml) maple syrup or honey
- 1 tsp (5 ml) vanilla extract
- 1 cup (160g) fresh pineapple, diced (or canned pineapple, drained)
- ¼ cup (20g) unsweetened shredded coconut (optional for topping)

Optional Garnishes:

- Fresh mint leaves
- Toasted coconut flakes
- Chopped nuts (like almonds or walnuts)

Instructions:

Whisk together the coconut milk, vanilla extract, maple syrup (or honey), and chia seeds. Stir well to ensure the chia seeds are evenly distributed.

Cover the bowl and refrigerate for at least 4 hours or overnight for best results. The chia seeds will absorb the liquid and form a thick, pudding-like consistency.

While the chia pudding sets, prepare the pineapple by dicing it into small pieces. If using canned pineapple, make sure to drain it well.

Once the chia pudding has thickened, stir it. Divide the pudding evenly between four serving bowls. Place a heaping portion of chopped pineapple on top of each bowl.

Sprinkle unsweetened shredded coconut, toasted coconut flakes, or chopped nuts over the pudding for added texture and flavor. Garnish with fresh mint leaves if desired.

This Coconut Chia Seed Pudding with Pineapple can be stored in the fridge for up to three days.

Top the pudding with toasted almonds, pumpkin seeds, or granola for added crunch.

Baked Apples with Oats and Cinnamon

Yield: 4 servings   **Preparation Time:** 10 minutes   **Cooking Time:** 30 minutes

Calories: 180 kcal | Carbohydrates: 33g | Total Fat: 5g | Saturated Fat: 2g | Cholesterol: 0mg | Protein: 2g | Sodium: 5mg
(per serving)

Ingredients:
- 4 medium apples (such as Honeycrisp, Gala, or Granny Smith)
- ¼ cup (20g) old-fashioned rolled oats
- 2 tbsp (15g) chopped walnuts or almonds (optional)
- 2 tbsp (15g) raisins or dried cranberries (optional)
- 1 tbsp (15 ml) maple syrup or honey
- 1 tsp (2.5g) ground cinnamon
- ½ tsp (2.5 ml) vanilla extract
- 1 tbsp (15 ml) coconut oil or olive oil (optional for richness)
- ½ cup (120 ml) water

Optional Garnishes:
- Plain Greek yogurt or coconut yogurt (for serving)
- Fresh berries or mint leaves
- A sprinkle of additional cinnamon

Instructions:

Preheat the oven to 350°F (175°C) and lightly grease a small baking dish with oil or cooking spray.

Using an apple corer or a small paring knife, carefully core each apple, leaving the bottom intact to create a well for the filling. Place the apples in the prepared baking dish.

Combine the rolled oats, chopped nuts (if using), raisins (if using), maple syrup or honey, cinnamon, and vanilla extract. Stir well to combine. If desired, mix in 1 tablespoon of melted coconut oil or olive oil for a richer filling.

Spoon the oat mixture evenly into the cored apples, packing it down gently. Pour ½ cup of water into the bottom of the baking dish to prevent the apples from drying out while baking.

Cover the dish with aluminum foil and bake in the preheated oven for 20 minutes. Then remove the foil and bake for an additional 5-10 minutes, or until the apples are tender but not mushy and the filling is golden brown.

Serve the baked apples warm, optionally topped with a dollop of plain Greek yogurt or coconut yogurt for creaminess. Garnish with fresh berries or mint leaves, and sprinkle with extra cinnamon if desired.

Healthy Banana Bread with Walnuts

Yield: 10 servings   **Preparation Time:** 10 minutes   **Cooking Time:** 55 minutes

Calories: 190 kcal | Carbohydrates: 30g | Total Fat: 7g | Saturated Fat: 1g | Cholesterol: 0mg | Protein: 4g | Sodium: 140mg
(per serving)

Ingredients:
- 3 ripe bananas, mashed
- 2 large eggs (or flax eggs for a vegan option: 2 tbsp (15g) flaxseed meal + 5 tbsp (75 ml) water)
- ¼ cup (60 ml) honey or maple syrup
- ¼ cup (60 ml) unsweetened applesauce (or plain Greek yogurt)
- 1 tsp (5 ml) vanilla extract
- 1 ½ cups (180g) whole wheat flour (or spelt flour)
- 1 tsp (5g) baking soda
- ½ tsp (2g) baking powder
- ½ tsp (2g) ground cinnamon
- ¼ tsp (1.5g) salt (low-sodium recommended)
- ½ cup (60g) chopped walnuts (optional for crunch)

Optional Add-ins and Garnishes:
- 1 tsp (3g) ground flaxseeds or chia seeds for added fiber
- ¼ cup (45g) dark chocolate chips for a hint of sweetness
- Extra walnuts or sliced banana on top for garnish

Instructions:

Preheat your oven to 350°F (175°C). Use a little amount of olive oil to lightly grease or line a 9 × 5-inch loaf pan with parchment paper for easy removal.

Mash the bananas in a large mixing bowl with a fork until smooth.

To the mashed bananas, add the eggs (or flax eggs), honey (or maple syrup), applesauce, and vanilla extract. Whisk until well combined.

Whisk together the whole wheat flour, cinnamon, baking powder, baking soda, and salt.

Gradually add the dry components to the wet ones. Stir gently until just incorporated (avoid over-mixing). Fold in the chopped walnuts and any other optional add-ins, such as flaxseeds, chia seeds, or dark chocolate chips.

After the loaf pan is ready, pour the batter into it and distribute it evenly. If desired, sprinkle extra walnuts or sliced banana on top for garnish.

Bake for 50–55 minutes, or until a toothpick inserted into the middle of the loaf comes out clean. If the top of the loaf is browning too quickly, tent it with aluminum foil for the last 10 minutes of baking.

Before slicing, let the banana bread sit in the pan for ten minutes.

Serve as a snack with a cup of green or herbal tea for a light and nutritious treat.

Spread some nut butter on top or cover it with dark chocolate for a decadent choice.

Oatmeal Raisin Cookies with Almond Flour

Yield: 12 cookies   **Preparation Time:** 10 minutes   **Cooking Time:** 15 minutes

Calories: 160 kcal | Carbohydrates: 20g | Total Fat: 8g | Saturated Fat: 2g | Cholesterol: 0mg | Protein: 3g | Sodium: 50mg
(per serving)

Ingredients:

- 1 ¼ cups (100g) old-fashioned rolled oats
- ¾ cup (75g) almond flour
- 1 tsp (4g) baking powder
- 1 tsp (2.5g) ground cinnamon
- ¼ tsp (1.5g) salt (low-sodium recommended)
- ¼ cup (60 ml) coconut oil (melted) or olive oil
- ¼ cup (60 ml) maple syrup or honey
- 1 large egg (or flax egg: 1 tbsp (7g) flaxseed meal + 2 ½ tbsp (37 ml) water for a vegan option)
- 1 tsp (5 ml) vanilla extract
- ½ cup (75g) raisins
- ¼ cup (30g) chopped walnuts (optional for added crunch)

Optional Garnishes:

- Extra cinnamon for sprinkling on top
- Chia seeds or ground flaxseeds for extra fiber
- Dark chocolate chips for a hint of indulgence

Instructions:

Preheat your oven to 350°F (175°C) and line a baking sheet with parchment paper.

Combine the rolled oats, almond flour, baking powder, ground cinnamon, and salt. Stir well to mix the dry ingredients.

Whisk together the melted coconut or olive oil, egg or flax egg, maple syrup or honey, and vanilla extract until smooth.

Stir until well combined, and gradually add the dry ingredients to the wet components. Fold in the raisins and optional chopped walnuts to evenly distribute them throughout the dough.

Using a tablespoon or cookie scoop, drop dough balls, spaced approximately 2 inches apart, onto the baking sheet. To create a cookie shape, gently press down on each ball using the spoon's back.

Bake in the oven for 12-15 minutes or until the cookies are golden brown around the edges. If you'd like, add a bit of cinnamon to the top halfway through baking to give it even more flavor.

Let the cookies cool for 5 minutes on the baking sheet, then move them to a wire rack to finish cooling.

These cookies also make a great breakfast option, paired with Greek yogurt and fresh fruit for a balanced meal.

You can store them in an airtight container for up to 5 days or freeze them for up to 1 month.

Fruit Sorbet with Fresh Mint

Yield: 4 servings   **Preparation Time:** 10 minutes   **Cooking Time:** 3-4 hours freezing time

Calories: 90 kcal | Carbohydrates: 22g | Total Fat: 0g | Saturated Fat: 0g | Cholesterol: 0mg | Protein: 1g | Sodium: 5mg
(per serving)

Ingredients:

- 3 cups (450g) frozen mixed fruit (such as mango, pineapple, or berries)
- ¼ cup (60 ml) fresh orange juice (or water)
- 1 tbsp (15 ml) fresh lime juice
- 1 tbsp (15 ml) honey or maple syrup
- ¼ cup (10g) fresh mint leaves
- 1 tsp (5 ml) vanilla extract (optional for added flavor)

Optional Garnishes:

- Extra mint leaves
- Fresh fruit slices (like strawberries, pineapple, or kiwi)
- Lime zest for added brightness

Instructions:

If using fresh fruit, freeze it for 3-4 hours beforehand. Alternatively, use pre-frozen fruit.

In a high-speed blender or food processor, combine the frozen fruit, fresh orange juice, lime juice, honey (if using), mint leaves, and vanilla extract. Blend until smooth, scraping down the edges once in a while. If the mixture is too thick, you may adjust the consistency by adding 1 tablespoon at a time of extra orange juice or water.

Once smooth, transfer the mixture to a loaf pan or freezer-safe container. Cover and freeze for 1-2 hours to firm up the sorbet. For a softer texture, serve it immediately after blending.

Spoon the sorbet into dishes and decorate with lime zest, additional mint leaves, or fresh fruit pieces.

Pair it with whole-grain toast or granola for a more substantial breakfast or snack.

Almond Flour Brownies with Dark Chocolate

Yield: 12 servings   **Preparation Time:** 10 minutes   **Cooking Time:** 25 minutes

Calories: 150 kcal | Carbohydrates: 14g | Total Fat: 9g | Saturated Fat: 2g | Cholesterol: 30mg | Protein: 4g | Sodium: 50mg
(per serving)

Ingredients:

- 1 cup (100g) almond flour
- ¼ cup (25g) unsweetened cocoa powder
- ½ tsp (2g) baking powder
- ¼ tsp (1.5g) salt
- ¼ cup (45g) dark chocolate chips (70% or higher cacao), melted
- ¼ cup (60 ml) maple syrup or honey
- ¼ cup (60 ml) unsweetened applesauce (or mashed banana for added sweetness)
- 2 large eggs (or flax eggs for a vegan option: 2 tbsp (14g) flaxseed meal + 5 tbsp (75 ml) water)
- 1 tsp vanilla extract
- 2 tbsp (30 ml) olive oil or coconut oil, melted

Optional Add-ins and Garnishes:

- Extra dark chocolate chips for topping
- Chopped walnuts or pecans for extra crunch
- Fresh berries or mint leaves for garnish

Instructions:

Preheat the oven to 350°F (175°C). Gently oil an × 8-inch baking dish or line it with parchment paper.

Whisk the almond flour, unsweetened cocoa powder, baking powder, and salt. Set aside.

Melt the dark chocolate chips in 20-second intervals in a microwave-safe basin, stirring in between, until smooth. Let it cool slightly.

Whisk together the maple syrup (or honey), unsweetened applesauce (or mashed banana), eggs (or flax eggs), vanilla extract, and olive oil. Stir in the melted dark chocolate until well combined.

Gradually whisk the dry ingredients with the wet ones until a thick, smooth batter forms. Add extra dark chocolate chips or chopped nuts for added texture if desired.

After filling the baking dish, evenly distribute the batter. Bake in the preheated oven for 20-25 minutes or until a toothpick inserted into the center comes out mostly clean with a few moist crumbs.

Before cutting the brownies into squares, allow them to cool fully in the pan. If desired, garnish with fresh berries or mint leaves.

Pair with Greek yogurt or coconut yogurt for added protein and creaminess.

Top with fresh berries for an extra boost of antioxidants or a drizzle of dark chocolate for a more indulgent treat.

Store in an airtight container at room temperature for up to 3 days, or freeze for up to a month.

Frozen Yogurt Bark with Mixed Berries

Yield: 8 servings   **Preparation Time:** 10 minutes   **Cooking Time:** 3-4 hours

Calories: 90 kcal | Carbohydrates: 22g | Total Fat: 0g | Saturated Fat: 0g | Cholesterol: 0mg | Protein: 1g | Sodium: 5mg
(per serving)

Ingredients:

- 2 cups (480g) of low-fat or non-fat plain Greek yogurt
- 1-2 tbsp (15-30 ml) honey or maple
- 1 tsp (5 ml) vanilla extract
- ½ cup (75g) mixed berries (such as blueberries, raspberries, and strawberries, chopped if large)
- 2 tbsp (18g) chopped nuts (optional for extra crunch; try walnuts or almonds)
- 1 tbsp (10g) chia seeds (optional for extra fiber)
- 1 tbsp (6g) unsweetened shredded coconut (optional for topping)

Optional Garnishes:

- Fresh mint leaves
- Dark chocolate drizzle (70% cacao or higher)

Instructions:

Combine the plain Greek yogurt, honey (if using), and vanilla extract. Stir until smooth and well combined.

Put parchment paper on one baking sheet. Using a spatula, evenly spread the yogurt mixture over the sheet to create an approximately ¼ inch thick layer.

Sprinkle the mixed berries evenly over the yogurt layer. Then, add any optional toppings, such as chopped nuts, chia seeds, or shredded coconut.

Freeze the baking sheet for 3-4 hours or until the yogurt is solid and fully frozen.

Once frozen, remove the yogurt bark from the freezer and break it into pieces or shards. Serve immediately.

The bark may be kept in the freezer for up to a week. When you need a quick snack, simply break off a piece.

Lemon Sorbet with Fresh Herbs

Yield: 4 servings **Preparation Time:** 10 minutes **Cooking Time:** 3-4 hours

Calories: 100 kcal | Carbohydrates: 26g | Total Fat: 0g | Saturated Fat: 0g | Cholesterol: 0mg | Protein: 0g | Sodium: 5mg
(per serving)

Ingredients:
- 1 cup (240 ml) fresh lemon juice (about 4-5 lemons)
- 2 tbsp (30 ml) lemon zest
- ½ cup (120 ml) honey or maple syrup
- 1 ½ cups (360 ml) water
- ¼ cup (10g) fresh mint or basil leaves, chopped
- 1 tsp (5 ml) vanilla extract (optional for added depth of flavor)

Optional Garnishes:
- Fresh mint or basil leaves
- Lemon zest strips
- Thin lemon slices

Instructions:

In a small saucepan, simmer the water and honey (or maple syrup) over medium heat, stirring periodically to dissolve the sweetener completely. This creates a simple syrup base.

Once the sweetener has dissolved, remove the saucepan from the heat and let the syrup cool to room temperature.

Mix the lemon zest, freshly squeezed juice, and vanilla extract (if used). Stir in the chopped mint or basil leaves.

Pour the cooled simple syrup into the herb and lemon mixture. Stir well to combine all the flavors.

Pour the mixture into a shallow dish or ice cream maker. If using a shallow dish, place it in the freezer. To break up the ice crystals, stir the mixture every 30 minutes. Continue stirring for 3–4 hours or until the sorbet is completely frozen. Check the manufacturer's directions if using an ice cream machine.

Once the sorbet has frozen, scoop it into bowls and garnish with fresh mint or basil leaves, additional lemon zest, or thin lemon slices for presentation.

Healthy Carrot Cake Muffins

Yield: 12 muffins **Preparation Time:** 15 minutes **Cooking Time:** 25 minutes

Calories: 160 kcal | Carbohydrates: 21g | Total Fat: 7g | Saturated Fat: 1.5g | Cholesterol: 0mg | Protein: 4g | Sodium: 100mg
(per serving)

Ingredients:
- 1 ½ cups (180g) whole wheat flour
- 1 tsp (4g) baking powder
- 1 tsp (4g) baking soda
- 1 ½ tsp (4g) ground cinnamon
- ½ tsp (1g) ground ginger
- ¼ tsp (0.5g) ground nutmeg
- ¼ tsp (1.5g) salt (low-sodium recommended)
- 2 large eggs (or flax eggs: 2 tbsp (14g) flaxseed meal + 5 tbsp (75 ml) water for vegan option)
- ¼ cup (60 ml) olive oil or coconut oil (melted)
- ¼ cup (60 ml) unsweetened applesauce
- ⅓ cup (80 ml) honey or maple syrup
- 1 tsp (5 ml) vanilla extract
- 1 ½ cups (160g) finely grated carrots (about 2 large carrots)
- ½ cup (60g) chopped walnuts or pecans (optional for crunch)
- ¼ cup (40g) raisins (optional for sweetness)
- ¼ cup (20g) unsweetened shredded coconut (optional for texture)

Optional Garnishes:
- Extra chopped nuts for sprinkling on top
- Coconut flakes for garnish

Instructions:

Preheat your oven to 350°F (175°C) and line a 12-cup muffin tin with paper liners or lightly grease the tin.

Whisk together the whole wheat flour, baking powder, baking soda, cinnamon, ginger, nutmeg, and salt until well combined.

Whisk together the eggs (or flax eggs), olive oil (or coconut oil), unsweetened applesauce, honey (or maple syrup), and vanilla extract.

Stir in the grated carrots, chopped walnuts (if using), raisins, and shredded coconut into the wet ingredients.

Mix the wet ingredients into the dry ingredients gradually. Avoid over-mixing, as it can make the muffins dense.

Spoon ¾ of the batter into each of the prepped muffin cups. To add texture, add extra chopped nuts or coconut flakes.

Bake in the preheated oven for 20-25 minutes or until a toothpick inserted into the center of a muffin comes out clean.

Let the muffins cool in the muffin tray for 5 minutes before moving them to a wire rack to cool fully.

For a special treat, top the muffins with a light cream cheese frosting made from light cream cheese or a plant-based alternative.

These muffins keep well for up to three days at room temperature or for up to five days in the refrigerator when kept in an airtight container. They also freeze well for long-term storage.

Chocolate-Dipped Strawberries

Yield: 8 servings   **Preparation Time:** 10 minutes   **Cooking Time:** 25 minutes

Calories: 80 kcal | Carbohydrates: 1g | Total Fat: 5g | Saturated Fat: 3g | Cholesterol: 0mg | Protein: 1g | Sodium: 0mg
(per serving)

Ingredients:

- 16 fresh strawberries (medium to large, washed and dried thoroughly)
- 1 tsp (5 ml) coconut oil (optional for smoother chocolate texture)
- ½ cup (85g) dark chocolate chips (70% cacao or higher)

Optional Garnishes:

- Chopped nuts (such as almonds or pistachios)
- Unsweetened shredded coconut
- Cacao nibs
- Sea salt (a small pinch for a sweet-salty combo)

Instructions:

Wash and dry the strawberries thoroughly. They must be completely dry, as moisture can cause the chocolate to seize.

Put the coconut oil and dark chocolate chips in a microwave-safe dish. Microwave in 20-second intervals, stirring after each interval, until the chocolate is completely melted and smooth. An alternative method for melting chocolate is to use a double boiler on the stovetop.

Hold each strawberry by the stem or use a toothpick, dip it into the melted chocolate, and swirl to coat the bottom half of the strawberry. Let any excess chocolate drip off.

You can immediately top the chocolate-dipped strawberries with cacao nibs, shredded coconut, chopped almonds, or a dash of sea salt.

Transfer the dipped strawberries to a baking sheet lined with parchment paper. Move the sheet to the refrigerator and chill for 15-20 minutes or until the chocolate is firm.

Once the chocolate has set, serve the strawberries on a platter. You can store them in the refrigerator for up to a day or eat them right away.

No-Bake Chocolate Peanut Butter Bars

Yield: 12 bars   **Preparation Time:** 15 minutes   **Cooking Time:** 1-2 hours

Calories: 180 kcal | Carbohydrates: 16g | Total Fat: 11g | Saturated Fat: 2.5g | Cholesterol: 0mg | Protein: 5g | Sodium: 140mg
(per serving)

Ingredients:

- 1 ½ cups (125g) rolled oats (preferably old-fashioned oats)
- ¾ cup (190g) natural peanut butter (unsweetened, with no added oils)
- ¼ cup (60 ml) honey or maple syrup
- 1 tsp (5 ml) vanilla extract
- ¼ cup (30g) ground flaxseeds (optional for extra fiber)
- ¼ tsp (1.5g) salt (optional, low-sodium recommended)
- ½ cup dark chocolate chips (70% cacao or higher)
- 1 tbsp (15 ml) coconut oil (optional for smoother chocolate topping)

Optional Garnishes:

- Chopped peanuts for added texture
- Unsweetened shredded coconut
- Cacao nibs

Instructions:

Combine the rolled oats, peanut butter, honey (or maple syrup), vanilla extract, ground flaxseeds (if using), and salt. Mix well until a sticky dough forms.

Line an 8 × 8-inch baking dish with cooking parchment. Pour the peanut butter mixture into the dish and level it out to form a compact layer.

Put the coconut oil and dark chocolate chips in a microwave-safe dish. Microwave in 20-second intervals, stirring in between, until the chocolate is fully melted and smooth.

Pour the melted chocolate over the peanut butter and oat layer, spreading it evenly with a spatula.

Place the pan in the refrigerator for 1-2 hours or until the chocolate is set and the bars are firm.

Once chilled, remove the bars from the refrigerator and cut them into 12 squares. Serve immediately or store in the fridge for later.

Grains, Pasta, and Rice Recipes

Brown Rice Stir-Fry with Mixed Vegetables

Yield: 4 servings | **Preparation Time:** 15 minutes | **Cooking Time:** 20 minutes

Calories: 240 kcal | Carbohydrates: 25g | Total Fat: 18g | Saturated Fat: 4g | Cholesterol: 0mg | Protein: 3g | Sodium: 60mg
(per serving)

Ingredients:
- 1 cup (185g) brown rice (uncooked)
- 1 tbsp (15 ml) olive oil or sesame oil
- 1 small onion, finely chopped
- 1 red bell pepper, thinly sliced
- 1 yellow bell pepper, thinly sliced
- 1 medium zucchini, sliced
- 1 cup (70g) broccoli florets
- 1 large carrot, thinly sliced
- 2 cloves garlic, minced
- 1 tbsp (6g) fresh ginger, minced
- 2 tbsp (30 ml) low-sodium soy sauce (for a gluten-free option, use tamari)
- 1 tbsp (15 ml) rice vinegar (optional)
- 1 tsp (3g) sesame seeds (optional)
- Fresh cilantro or green onions

Optional Add-ins:
- 1 cup (155g) cooked edamame or tofu
- 1 tsp (2g) red pepper flakes
- 1 tsp (5 ml) sesame oil for a finishing drizzle

Instructions:

Rinse the brown rice under cold water, then cook it according to the package instructions. For this recipe, you'll need about 3 cups of cooked rice. Once done, set aside.

Heat the olive or sesame oil over medium heat in a large skillet or wok.

Add the chopped onion and cook for 2-3 minutes until softened. Add the minced garlic and ginger, and sauté for 1-2 minutes until fragrant.

Add the sliced bell peppers, zucchini, broccoli florets, and carrots to the skillet. Stir-fry for 5-7 minutes, stirring occasionally, until the vegetables are tender but still crisp.

Stir in the cooked brown rice, low-sodium soy sauce (or tamari), and rice vinegar. Mix everything and cook for 2-3 minutes to heat through.

Remove the stir-fry from the heat. Sprinkle sesame seeds over the top and garnish with fresh cilantro or green onions if desired.

Add a sprinkle of red pepper flakes or a drizzle of sriracha for a spicier version before serving.

This dish can also be stored in the refrigerator for up to 3 days.

Quinoa and Black Bean Pilaf with Cilantro

Yield: 4 servings | **Preparation Time:** 10 minutes | **Cooking Time:** 20 minutes

Calories: 260 kcal | Carbohydrates: 10g | Total Fat: 7g | Saturated Fat: 1g | Cholesterol: 0mg | Protein: 10g | Sodium: 300mg
(per serving)

Ingredients:
- 1 cup (170g) quinoa (rinsed)
- 1 ½ cups (360 ml) vegetable broth or water
- 1 tbsp (15 ml) olive oil
- 1 small onion, finely chopped
- 2 cloves garlic, minced
- 1 tsp (2g) ground cumin
- ½ tsp (1g) ground coriander (optional)
- 1 can (15 oz/240g) black beans, rinsed and drained
- 1 medium tomato, diced
- ¼ cup (15g) fresh cilantro, chopped
- 1 tbsp (15 ml) lime juice (optional for extra flavor)
- Salt and pepper to taste

Optional garnish:
- Extra cilantro
- Avocado slices
- Lime wedges

Instructions:

Combine the rinsed quinoa and vegetable broth (or water) in a medium saucepan. After bringing it to a boil, lower the heat to a simmer, cover, and cook the quinoa for 15 minutes or until it is tender and the liquid has been absorbed. When finished, use a fork to fluff the quinoa and put it aside.

Place the olive oil in a big pan and heat it to medium. Add the chopped onion and simmer for 3–4 minutes, stirring occasionally, until it becomes translucent and soft.

Stir in the minced garlic, cumin, and ground coriander (if using), and cook until fragrant (1 minute).

Add the drained black beans and diced tomato to the skillet. Mix and cook for 2-3 minutes to warm the beans.

Stir in the cooked quinoa and fresh cilantro. Mix everything well and cook for another 2 minutes until the ingredients are heated.

Stir in the lime juice for extra brightness. Season with salt and pepper to taste.

After taking the pan off the burner, transfer the black bean pilaf and quinoa to bowls. If desired, garnish with extra cilantro, avocado slices, or lime wedges.

For added flavor, top with avocado slices for healthy fats, or sprinkle with crushed red pepper flakes for a bit of heat.

This dish stores well in the fridge for up to 3 days.

Whole Wheat Pasta with Garlic, Olive Oil and Spinach

Yield: 4 servings   **Preparation Time:** 10 minutes   **Cooking Time:** 15 minutes

Calories: 320 kcal | Carbohydrates: 46g | Total Fat: 11g | Saturated Fat: 1.5g | Cholesterol: 0mg | Protein: 10g | Sodium: 150mg
(per serving)

Ingredients:

- 8 oz (225g) whole wheat pasta (spaghetti, linguine, or penne)
- 3 tbsp (45 ml) extra virgin olive oil
- 4 cloves garlic, thinly sliced
- 8 cups (240g) fresh spinach (about 8 oz)
- ½ tsp (1g) crushed red pepper flakes
- ½ cup (120 ml) reserved pasta water
- Juice of 1 lemon (optional for added brightness)
- Salt and pepper to taste
- 2 tbsp (10g) grated Parmesan cheese (optional or use plant-based cheese for vegan option)
- Fresh parsley or basil for garnish

Optional Add-ins or Garnishes:

- Sliced cherry tomatoes for a fresh burst of flavor
- Chopped walnuts for added crunch and heart-healthy fats
- Grilled chicken or tofu for extra protein

Instructions:

In a large pot of salted water, cook the whole wheat pasta according to the package instructions until al dente. After reserving ½ cup of pasta water, drain the pasta.

Heat the olive oil in a large skillet over medium heat. Add the thinly sliced garlic and cook for 1-2 minutes until golden and fragrant, being careful not to burn it.

Add the fresh spinach to the skillet, along with the crushed red pepper flakes (if using), salt, and pepper. Cook the spinach for 2-3 minutes, stirring regularly, until it wilts.

Add the cooked pasta to the skillet and ¼ to ½ cup of the reserved pasta water, stirring to combine and coat the pasta in the garlic oil. Cook for another 1-2 minutes until everything is heated through.

Stir in the fresh lemon juice for added brightness, then remove the skillet from heat.

Divide the pasta among bowls, sprinkle with grated Parmesan (if using), and garnish with fresh parsley or basil.

For added crunch and heart-healthy fats, sprinkle chopped walnuts or pine nuts on top.

Barley Risotto with Mushrooms and Peas

Yield: 4 servings   **Preparation Time:** 10 minutes   **Cooking Time:** 40 minutes

Calories: 300 kcal | Carbohydrates: 50g | Total Fat: 6g | Saturated Fat: 1g | Cholesterol: 0mg | Protein: 10g | Sodium: 350mg
(per serving)

Ingredients:

- 1 cup (200g) pearl barley
- 1 tbsp (15 ml) olive oil
- 1 small onion, finely chopped
- 3 cloves garlic, minced
- 2 cups (140g) mushrooms (such as cremini or button), sliced
- 4 cups (960 ml) low-sodium vegetable broth
- 1 cup (135g) frozen peas
- ½ cup (120 ml) dry white wine (optional)
- 1 tbsp (3g) fresh thyme or 1 tsp (1g) dried thyme
- ¼ cup (20g) grated Parmesan cheese (optional, or use a plant-based alternative for a vegan option)
- Fresh parsley or chives for garnish (optional)
- Salt and pepper to taste

Optional Garnishes:

- Lemon zest for added brightness
- Crushed red pepper flakes for a bit of heat

Instructions:

Heat the olive oil over medium heat in a large skillet or pot.

Add the finely chopped onion and garlic to the pan. Sauté for 2-3 minutes or until the ingredients are aromatic and tender.

After adding the sliced mushrooms to the pan, heat them for 5-7 minutes, tossing them now and again until they become soft and brown.

Add the pearl barley and simmer, stirring, for 1-2 minutes, until it toasts little and absorbs the aromas and oil.

Pour in the white wine and stir until it's absorbed chiefly about 1-2 minutes.

Gradually add ½ cup of the vegetable broth, stirring frequently. Once the liquid is absorbed, continue adding the broth in increments, allowing each addition to be absorbed before adding more. This process should take about 25-30 minutes.

When the barley is nearly cooked, stir in the frozen peas and fresh thyme. Cook for approximately 5 minutes until the barley is soft but still chewy and the peas are cooked.

To enhance the taste and creaminess, mix in the grated Parmesan cheese. Season with salt and pepper to taste.

After turning off the heat, sprinkle the risotto with lemon zest, chives, or fresh parsley. Serve immediately.

You may keep leftovers in the fridge for up to three days. Reheat in a pan with a little water or broth to restore the creamy smoothness.

Farro Salad with Roasted Vegetables and Feta

Yield: 4 servings	Preparation Time: 15 minutes	Cooking Time: 35 minutes

Calories: 290 kcal | Carbohydrates: 45g | Total Fat: 9g | Saturated Fat: 2g | Cholesterol: 0mg | Protein: 8g | Sodium: 180mg
(per serving)

Ingredients:

- 1 cup (200g) farro (uncooked)
- 2 ½ cups (600 ml) water or low-sodium vegetable broth (for cooking the farro)
- 1 medium zucchini, chopped
- 1 medium red bell pepper, chopped
- 1 small red onion, chopped
- 1 cup (150g) cherry tomatoes, halved
- 2 tbsp (30 ml) olive oil
- 1 tsp (1g) dried oregano
- Salt and pepper to taste
- ¼ cup (35g) crumbled feta cheese (optional, or use plant-based feta for a vegan option)
- 2 tbsp (8g) fresh parsley, chopped
- 1 tbsp (15 ml) fresh lemon juice
- 1 tsp (2g) lemon zest
- 1 tsp (5 ml) balsamic vinegar (optional for extra flavor)

Optional Garnishes:

- Chopped fresh basil or mint
- Toasted pine nuts or almonds for crunch

Instructions:

Rinse the farro under cold water. Combine the farro and water (or vegetable broth) in a medium saucepan. Bring to a boil, then reduce the heat to low, cover, and simmer for 25-30 minutes or until the farro is tender and chewy. Drain any excess liquid and set aside.

Preheat your oven to 400°F (200°C). Mix together 1 ½ tablespoon olive oil, dried oregano, salt, and pepper with the diced zucchini, red bell pepper, red onion, and cherry tomatoes. Spread them evenly on a baking sheet.

Bake the veggies for 20-25 minutes, tossing occasionally to maintain uniform cooking or until they are soft and beginning to caramelize.

Mix the cooked farro with the roasted vegetables.

Gently fold in the crumbled feta cheese (if using), fresh parsley, and lemon zest.

In a small bowl, whisk together the remaining ½ tbsp olive oil, fresh lemon juice, and balsamic vinegar (if using). Drizzle the dressing over the farro and vegetable mixture and toss to combine.

Divide the salad among bowls, garnish with extra parsley, basil, or toasted pine nuts if desired, and enjoy!

For extra protein, consider adding chickpeas, edamame, or grilled tofu.

The salad is a great choice for meal prep since it can be served warm or at room temperature and keeps nicely in the refrigerator for up to three days.

Wild Rice with Cranberries and Pecans

Yield: 4 servings	Preparation Time: 10 minutes	Cooking Time: 50 minutes

Calories: 250 kcal | Carbohydrates: 37g | Total Fat: 9g | Saturated Fat: 1g | Cholesterol: 0mg | Protein: 6g | Sodium: 100mg
(per serving)

Ingredients:

- 1 cup (160g) wild rice
- 2 ½ cups (600 ml) low-sodium vegetable broth or water
- ½ cup (60g) dried cranberries (unsweetened, if possible)
- ½ cup (60g) pecans, chopped and toasted
- 1 tbsp (15 ml) olive oil
- 1 small onion, finely chopped
- 2 cloves garlic, minced
- 1 tbsp (4g) fresh parsley, chopped (optional)
- 1 tsp (1g) fresh thyme
- 1 tbsp (15 ml) balsamic vinegar
- Salt and pepper to taste

Optional Garnishes:

- Fresh parsley or thyme sprigs
- Orange zest for added brightness

Instructions:

Using a fine-mesh strainer, rinse the wild rice in cold water.

Combine the wild rice and vegetable broth (or water) in a medium saucepan. Once you have brought the rice to a boil, lower the heat to a simmer, cover, and cook for 45 to 50 minutes, or until the rice is soft and most of the liquid has been absorbed. Drain any excess liquid if necessary.

While the rice cooks, toast the chopped pecans in a dry skillet over medium heat for 3-5 minutes, stirring frequently, until fragrant and slightly browned. Remove from heat and set aside.

Heat the olive oil in a big skillet over medium heat. Sauté the chopped onion for r 3-4 minutes or until it becomes softened. Add the minced garlic and thyme, and sauté for another 1-2 minutes until fragrant.

Stir in the dried cranberries and balsamic vinegar (if using) into the skillet with the onions and garlic. Cook for an additional 1-2 minutes until the cranberries soften slightly.

After the wild rice has cooked, combine it with the cranberries, sautéed onions, and garlic in a pan. Stir to combine. Fold in the toasted pecans and fresh parsley (if using). Season with salt and pepper to taste.

Transfer the wild rice mixture to a serving dish and garnish with extra parsley, thyme sprigs, or orange zest for added flavor if desired.

For extra flavor, add a sprinkle of orange zest or a drizzle of balsamic glaze before serving.

This dish can also be enjoyed cold as part of a grain salad. Leftovers can be kept in the fridge for up to three days.

Spaghetti Squash with Marinara Sauce

Yield: 4 servings   **Preparation Time:** 10 minutes   **Cooking Time:** 45 minutes

Calories: 170 kcal | Carbohydrates: 20g | Total Fat: 9g | Saturated Fat: 1g | Cholesterol: 0mg | Protein: 3g | Sodium: 180mg
(per serving)

Ingredients:

For the Spaghetti Squash:
- 1 medium spaghetti squash (about 2.5 to 3 lbs/1200-1300g)
- 1 tbsp (15 ml) olive oil
- Salt and pepper to taste

For the Marinara Sauce:
- 1 tbsp (15 ml) olive oil
- 1 small onion, finely chopped
- 3 cloves garlic, minced
- 1 can (15 oz/440 ml) crushed tomatoes (no added salt or low-sodium)
- 1 tsp (1g) dried oregano
- 1 tsp (1g) dried basil
- ¼ tsp (0.5g) red pepper flakes (optional for heat)
- Salt and pepper to taste
- 2 tbsp (8g) fresh parsley, chopped (for garnish)

Instructions:

Preheat your oven to 400°F (200°C).

Cut the spaghetti squash in half lengthwise. Remove the seeds. After adding salt and pepper, drizzle some olive oil into the squash. Transfer the squash halves, cut side down, to a parchment paper-lined baking sheet.

Squash should be roasted for 35-40 minutes or until the flesh is fork-tender. Once done, remove it from the oven and allow it to cool slightly.

After the squash cools down enough to handle, scrape off the flesh into spaghetti-like strands with a fork and put aside.

Heat 1 tablespoon of olive oil in a big pan over medium heat while the squash roasts. Add the chopped onion and sauté for 4-5 minutes until softened. Add the minced garlic and cook for another minute until fragrant.

Add the crushed tomatoes, red pepper flakes, dried oregano, dried basil, salt, and pepper to the skillet. Stir to combine and bring the sauce to a simmer. Cook, stirring periodically, until the sauce thickens, about 15 minutes.

When the spaghetti squash is done, add it to the pan with the marinara sauce and gently toss to mix.

Divide the spaghetti squash and marinara into bowls. Garnish with fresh parsley and optional toppings like grated Parmesan cheese or fresh basil leaves.

Couscous Salad with Chickpeas and Cucumbers

Yield: 4 servings   **Preparation Time:** 10 minutes   **Cooking Time:** 10 minutes

Calories: 260 kcal | Carbohydrates: 42g | Total Fat: 6g | Saturated Fat: 1g | Cholesterol: 0mg | Protein: 8g | Sodium: 180mg
(per serving)

Ingredients:
- 1 cup (180g) whole wheat couscous
- 1 ¼ cups (300 ml) low-sodium vegetable broth or water
- 1 tbsp (15 ml) olive oil
- 1 can (15 oz/425g) chickpeas, drained and rinsed
- 1 medium cucumber, diced
- 1 small red bell pepper, diced
- ¼ cup (50g) red onion, finely chopped
- ¼ cup (10g) fresh parsley, chopped
- ¼ cup (10g) fresh mint, chopped
- 2 tbsp (30 ml) fresh lemon juice (about 1 lemon)
- 1 tsp (1g) lemon zest
- 1 tsp (2g) ground cumin
- Salt and pepper to taste

Optional Garnishes:
- Crumbled feta cheese (optional for a non-vegan version)
- Chopped cherry tomatoes
- Toasted almonds or pine nuts for crunch

Instructions:

In a medium saucepan, bring the vegetable broth (or water) to a boil. Stir in the whole wheat couscous, remove from heat, cover, and let it sit for 5 minutes. Using a fork, fluff the mixture and move it to a large basin to chill somewhat.

While the couscous is cooling, dice the cucumber, red bell pepper, and red onion and set them aside.

In a small bowl, whisk together the olive oil, ground cumin, pepper, lemon zest, salt, and fresh lemon juice.

Add the drained chickpeas, diced cucumber, bell pepper, red onion, fresh parsley, and mint (if using) to the couscous. Scatter the salad with the lemon dressing and mix to incorporate it fully.

For extra flavor and texture, garnish with optional toppings such as crumbled feta cheese, chopped cherry tomatoes, or toasted nuts.

Toasted almonds or pine nuts may be added to the salad to give it more flavor and a nutty bite.

This salad keeps well in the refrigerator for up to 3 days, making it a great meal prep option.

Bulgur Wheat Salad with Tomatoes and Parsley

Yield: 4 servings   **Preparation Time:** 10 minutes   **Cooking Time:** 15 minutes

Calories: 180 kcal | Carbohydrates: 27g | Total Fat: 7g | Saturated Fat: 1g | Cholesterol: 0mg | Protein: 4g | Sodium: 60mg
(per serving)

Ingredients:
- 1 cup (180g) bulgur wheat (medium or fine)
- 1 ½ cups (360 ml) boiling water or low-sodium vegetable broth
- 1 ½ cups (300g) tomatoes, diced (about 2 medium tomatoes)
- ½ cup (80g) cucumber, diced (optional)
- 1 small red onion, finely chopped
- ½ cup (15g) fresh parsley, finely chopped
- ¼ cup (8g) fresh mint, finely chopped (optional)
- ¼ cup (60 ml) fresh lemon juice (about 1 lemon)
- 2 tbsp (30 ml) extra virgin olive oil
- 1 clove garlic, minced (optional)
- Salt and pepper to taste
- 1 tsp (2g) ground cumin (optional for added flavor)

Optional Garnishes:
- Crumbled feta cheese (optional for a non-vegan option)
- Toasted pine nuts or almonds

Instructions:

Place the bulgur wheat in a bowl and pour the boiling water (or vegetable broth) over it. Stir briefly, cover, and let it sit for 10-15 minutes until the liquid is absorbed and the bulgur is tender. Fluff the bulgur with a fork and set aside to cool.

While the bulgur is cooling, dice the tomatoes and cucumber and finely chop the red onion, parsley, and mint (if using).

In a small bowl, whisk together the lemon juice, olive oil, minced garlic (if using), ground cumin (optional), salt, and pepper.

Toss the cooled bulgur with the chopped tomatoes, cucumber, red onion, parsley, and mint. Then, add the lemon dressing and toss everything until well mixed.

Serve the bulgur salad chilled or at room temperature. Optionally, garnish with crumbled feta cheese or toasted pine nuts for added flavor and texture.

Cauliflower Rice with Herbs and Lemon Zest

Yield: 4 servings   **Preparation Time:** 10 minutes   **Cooking Time:** 10 minutes

Calories: 70 kcal | Carbohydrates: 6g | Total Fat: 4g | Saturated Fat: 0.5g | Cholesterol: 0mg | Protein: 2g | Sodium: 240mg
(per serving)

Ingredients:
- 1 large head of cauliflower, cut into florets (about 4 cups/600g riced)
- 1 tbsp (15 ml) olive oil
- 2 cloves garlic, minced
- ¼ cup (8g) fresh parsley, finely chopped
- 2 tbsp (8g) fresh dill, finely chopped (optional)
- 1 tsp (2g) lemon zest (about 1 lemon)
- 2 tbsp (30 ml) fresh lemon juice (optional for extra brightness)
- Salt and pepper to taste

Optional Garnishes:
- Chopped fresh mint or basil
- Toasted pine nuts or almonds

Instructions:

Rinse the rice in cold water to remove extra starch. This helps keep the rice light and fluffy.

Combine the rinsed rice, coconut milk, water, coconut oil, and a pinch of salt. Bring to a boil over medium heat, cover, and simmer for 20 to 25 minutes or until the rice is soft and the liquid has been absorbed.

Peel and dice the mango. Set it aside.

Zest the lime to get about 1 tsp of zest, then juice the lime to yield 1 tbsp of juice.

After the rice is cooked through, fluff it with a fork. Stir in the fresh lime juice, lime zest, and maple syrup or honey (if using) to give it a bright, sweet flavor.

Gently fold the diced mango into the rice, distributing it evenly throughout the dish.

Transfer the coconut rice to bowls, garnish with fresh mint or cilantro, and toasted shredded coconut or almonds for extra texture and flavor.

It can also be served as a light dessert, topped with additional fruit like berries or pineapple.

Brown Rice and Lentil Casserole

Yield: 4 servings   **Preparation Time:** 15 minutes   **Cooking Time:** 1 hour 10 minutes

Calories: 320 kcal | Carbohydrates: 56g | Total Fat: 6g | Saturated Fat: 1g | Cholesterol: 0mg | Protein: 12g | Sodium: 250mg
(per serving)

Ingredients:

- 1 cup (190g) brown rice
- 1 cup (190g) green or brown lentils (rinsed and drained)
- 4 cups (960 ml) low-sodium vegetable broth
- 1 small onion, chopped
- 2 cloves garlic, minced
- 1 medium carrot, chopped
- 1 celery stalk, chopped
- 1 tsp (1g) dried thyme
- 1 tsp (1g) dried oregano
- 1 tbsp (15 ml) olive oil
- Salt and pepper to taste
- ¼ cup (8g) fresh parsley chopped (for garnish)

Optional Garnishes:

- Grated Parmesan cheese (optional for a non-vegan option)
- Chopped green onions or cherry tomatoes for added flavor and texture

Instructions:

Preheat your oven to 350°F (175°C).

In a large oven-safe skillet or casserole dish, heat the olive oil over medium heat. Add the chopped onion, garlic, carrot, and celery. Sauté for 5-7 minutes until softened.

In the skillet with the vegetables, stir in the rinsed lentils and brown rice. Add the dried thyme, oregano, salt, and pepper, and stir to coat the ingredients with the seasonings.

Pour in the vegetable broth and bring the mixture to a simmer.

Once the mixture starts to simmer, cover the skillet (or transfer to a casserole dish and cover with foil). Bake in the preheated oven for 1 hour or until the lentils and rice are tender and have absorbed most of the broth.

Remove the casserole from the oven, fluff it with a fork, and adjust the seasoning if necessary. Garnish with freshly chopped parsley and optional toppings like grated Parmesan or green onions.

This dish also works well as meal prep and can be stored in the refrigerator for up to 3 days. Reheat in the microwave or oven as needed.

Coconut Rice with Mango and Lime

Yield: 4 servings   **Preparation Time:** 10 minutes   **Cooking Time:** 25 minutes

Calories: 260 kcal | Carbohydrates: 48g | Total Fat: 7g | Saturated Fat: 4g | Cholesterol: 0mg | Protein: 4g | Sodium: 50mg
(per serving)

Ingredients:

- 1 cup (190g) brown jasmine rice or regular jasmine rice (for a heart-healthier option, choose brown rice)
- 1 cup (240 ml) light coconut milk (from a can, unsweetened)
- 1 cup (240 ml) water
- 1 tbsp (15 ml) coconut oil (optional)
- 1 tbsp (15 ml) fresh lime juice (about 1 lime)
- 1 tsp (2g) lime zest
- 1 tbsp (15 ml) maple syrup or honey (optional for sweetness)
- 1 medium ripe mango, peeled and diced
- Pinch of salt

Optional Garnishes:

- Fresh mint or cilantro, chopped
- Toasted shredded coconut or toasted almonds for crunch

Instructions:

Rinse the rice under cold water to remove excess starch. This helps keep the rice light and fluffy.

In a medium saucepan, combine the rinsed rice, coconut milk, water, coconut oil (if using), and a pinch of salt. Bring the mixture to a boil over medium heat, then reduce the heat to low, cover, and simmer for 20-25 minutes, or until the rice is tender and the liquid is absorbed.

While the rice is cooking, peel and dice the mango. Set it aside.

Zest the lime to get about 1 tsp of zest, then juice the lime to yield 1 tbsp of juice.

Once the rice is fully cooked, fluff it with a fork. Stir in the fresh lime juice, lime zest, and maple syrup or honey (if using) to give it a bright, sweet flavor.

Gently fold the diced mango into the rice, distributing it evenly throughout the dish.

Transfer the coconut rice to bowls, garnish with fresh mint or cilantro, and toasted shredded coconut or almonds for extra texture and flavor.

It can also be served as a light dessert, topped with additional fruit like berries or pineapple.

Pasta Primavera with Seasonal Vegetables

Yield: 4 servings   **Preparation Time:** 15 minutes   **Cooking Time:** 20 minutes

Calories: 320 kcal | Carbohydrates: 10g | Total Fat: 10g | Saturated Fat: 1.5g | Cholesterol: 0mg | Protein: 10g | Sodium: 120mg
(per serving)

Ingredients:

- 8 oz (225g) whole wheat pasta (spaghetti, penne, or fusilli)
- 2 tbsp (30 ml) olive oil
- 1 small zucchini, sliced
- 1 small yellow squash, sliced
- 1 small red bell pepper, thinly sliced
- 1 small carrot, julienned
- 1 cup cherry tomatoes, halved
- 1 cup broccoli florets
- 3 cloves garlic, minced
- 1 tbsp (180g) fresh lemon juice
- 1 tsp (2g) lemon zest
- ½ tsp (0.5g) dried oregano
- ½ tsp (0.5g) dried basil
- Salt and pepper to taste
- ¼ cup (8g) fresh parsley chopped
- ¼ cup (30g) grated Parmesan cheese

Optional Garnishes:

- Red pepper flakes for heat
- Toasted pine nuts for added crunch

Instructions:

In a large pot of salted water, cook the whole wheat pasta according to the package instructions until al dente. Drain and set aside, reserving ½ cup of the pasta water.

While the pasta is cooking, heat 1 ½ tbsp of olive oil in a large skillet over medium heat. Add the minced garlic and sauté for 1-2 minutes until fragrant.

Add the zucchini, yellow squash, red bell pepper, carrot, and broccoli to the skillet. Sauté for 5-7 minutes until the vegetables are tender but still crisp. Add the cherry tomatoes during the last 2 minutes of cooking.

Stir in the oregano, lemon juice, lemon zest, and basil. Season with salt and pepper to taste.

Add the pasta to the skillet with the sautéed vegetables. Mix everything together, coating the spaghetti with a bit of the reserved pasta water if necessary. Cook for 1-2 minutes until everything is well combined.

Remove from heat, drizzle with the remaining ½ tbsp of olive oil. Add grated Parmesan cheese and fresh parsley as garnish. Sprinkle with toasted pine nuts or red pepper flakes.

Spinach and Ricotta Stuffed Shells with Marinara

Yield: 4 servings   **Preparation Time:** 20 minutes   **Cooking Time:** 40 minutes

Calories: 260 kcal | Carbohydrates: 48g | Total Fat: 7g | Saturated Fat: 4g | Cholesterol: 0mg | Protein: 4g | Sodium: 50mg
(per serving)

Ingredients:

For the Stuffed Shells:

- 12 large whole wheat pasta shells
- 2 cups (70g) fresh spinach (or frozen, thawed, and squeezed to remove excess water)
- 1 cup (240g) low-fat ricotta cheese
- ¼ cup (40g) grated Parmesan cheese
- 1 large egg white (or use a flax egg for a vegan option)
- 1 clove garlic, minced
- ½ tsp (0.5g) dried oregano
- ¼ tsp (0.5g) nutmeg (optional)
- Salt and pepper to taste

For the Marinara Sauce:

- 1 tbsp (15 ml) olive oil
- 1 small onion, finely chopped
- 2 cloves garlic, minced
- 1 can (15 oz/425g) crushed tomatoes
- ½ tsp (0.5g) dried basil
- ½ tsp (0.5g) dried oregano
- Salt and pepper to taste

Optional Garnishes:

- Fresh basil or parsley, chopped
- Extra grated Parmesan cheese (optional)

Instructions:

Heat up a big pot of salted water until it boils. Cook the whole wheat pasta shells according to package instructions until al dente. Drain and set aside to cool.

Prepare the Spinach and Ricotta Filling:

If using fresh spinach, place it in a pan over medium heat and cook it for 2-3 minutes or until it wilts. Remove it from the stove and let it cool a bit. Chop the spinach finely.

Combine the ricotta cheese, spinach, Parmesan (if using), egg white, minced garlic, dried oregano, nutmeg (if using), salt, and pepper. Mix until well combined.

Heat 1 tbsp of olive oil in a medium saucepan over medium heat. Add the chopped onion and sauté for 4-5 minutes until softened. Add the minced garlic once fragrant, then cook for one more minute. Stir in the crushed tomatoes, dried oregano, salt, dried basil, and pepper. Simmer the sauce for 10-15 minutes, stirring now and again.

Preheat your oven to 375°F (190°C).

Spoon the ricotta-spinach mixture into the cooked pasta shells. Put them in an ovenproof dish.

Cover the stuffed shells completely with marinara sauce.

Bake the dish for 20 minutes with the foil covering it. Remove the cover and bake for 10-15 minutes until the shells are well warm and the sauce is bubbling.

Take it out of the oven and, if wanted, top it with more Parmesan, fresh basil, or parsley.

Fish and Seafood

Grilled Mahi-Mahi with Pineapple Salsa

Yield: 4 servings   **Preparation Time:** 15 minutes   **Cooking Time:** 10 minutes

Calories: 280 kcal | Carbohydrates: 10g | Total Fat: 12g | Saturated Fat: 2g | Cholesterol: 70mg | Protein: 30g | Sodium: 180mg
(per serving)

Ingredients:
For the Mahi-Mahi:
- 4 (6 oz/170g) Mahi-Mahi fillets
- 2 tbsp (30 ml) olive oil
- 1 tbsp (15 ml) fresh lime juice
- 1 tsp (3g) garlic powder
- ½ tsp (1.5g) paprika
- Salt and pepper to taste

For the Pineapple Salsa:
- 1 cup (175g) fresh pineapple, diced
- 1 small red bell pepper, diced
- ¼ cup (50g) red onion, finely chopped
- 1 small jalapeño, seeded and minced (optional for heat)
- 2 tbsp (8g) fresh cilantro, chopped
- 2 tbsp (15 ml) fresh lime juice
- 1 tsp (2g) lime zest
- Salt and pepper to taste

Optional Garnishes:
- Extra cilantro leaves
- Lime wedges
- Avocado slices

Instructions:
Combine the diced pineapple, red bell pepper, red onion, jalapeño (if using), cilantro, lime juice, and lime zest. Season with salt and pepper to taste. Once everything is fully combined, cover and chill.

Prepare the Mahi-Mahi:

Using paper towels, gently pat dry the Mahi-Mahi fillets. Brush both sides with olive oil, season with garlic powder, paprika, salt, and pepper, and drizzle with lime juice.

Set the temperature of your grill pan or grill to medium-high. Lightly oil the grates to prevent sticking.

Grill the Mahi-Mahi:

Place the seasoned Mahi-Mahi fillets on the preheated grill. Grill for about 4-5 minutes per side or until the fish is opaque and flakes easily with a fork.

Once cooked, transfer the Mahi-Mahi fillets to a serving platter. Spoon the chilled pineapple salsa over the fillets.

Garnish with extra cilantro, lime wedges, or avocado slices if desired.

For a complete meal, pair this Grilled Mahi-Mahi with Pineapple Salsa with brown rice, quinoa, or steamed vegetables.

You can also serve it with whole wheat tortillas for a light, healthy fish taco option.

Baked Cod with Lemon, Dill, and Garlic

Yield: 4 servings   **Preparation Time:** 10 minutes   **Cooking Time:** 20 minutes

Calories: 220 kcal | Carbohydrates: 2g | Total Fat: 8g | Saturated Fat: 1.5g | Cholesterol: 60mg | Protein: 35g | Sodium: 200mg
(per serving)

Ingredients:
- 4 (6 oz/170g) cod fillets
- 2 tbsp (30 ml) olive oil
- 3 cloves garlic, minced
- 1 tbsp (4g) fresh chopped dill
- 2 tbsp (30 ml) fresh lemon juice (about 1 lemon)
- 1 tsp (2g) lemon zest
- Salt and pepper to taste
- 4 lemon slices (for garnish)

Optional Garnishes:
- Fresh parsley, chopped
- Additional lemon wedges for serving

Instructions:
Preheat the oven to 400°F (200°C). Grease a baking dish very lightly with olive oil or line it with parchment paper.

Pat the cod fillets dry using paper towels. After adding salt and pepper on both sides, put the fillets in the prepared baking dish.

Combine the olive oil, minced garlic, chopped dill, fresh lemon juice, and lemon zest. Stir until well mixed.

Drizzle the lemon, dill, and garlic mixture evenly over the cod fillets, using a brush or spoon to coat each piece. Place a lemon slice on top of each fillet.

Cod should be baked for 15-20 minutes in a preheated oven, or until it is opaque and readily flakes with a fork. The cooking time may change depending on the thickness of the fillets.

Take the cod out of the oven and, if you'd like, top it with more lemon wedges and fresh parsley. Serve hot.

For added texture, you can top the cod with toasted almonds or pine nuts.

This recipe tastes good with a simple mixed green salad with cucumber and lemon vinaigrette.

Shrimp and Veggie Skewers with Chimichurri

Yield: 4 servings	**Preparation Time:** 15 minutes	**Cooking Time:** 10 minutes

Calories: 320 kcal | Carbohydrates: 8g | Total Fat: 22g | Saturated Fat: 3g | Cholesterol: 165mg | Protein: 25g | Sodium: 280mg
(per serving)

Ingredients:

For the Shrimp and Veggie Skewers:
- 1 lb (450g) large shrimp, peeled and deveined
- 1 red bell pepper, chopped into 1-inch pieces
- 1 zucchini, sliced into ½-inch rounds
- 1 red onion, chopped into wedges
- 1 tbsp (15 ml) olive oil
- ½ tsp (1.5g) paprika
- ½ tsp (2g) garlic powder
- Salt and pepper to taste
- Wooden or metal skewers (before grilling, soak wooden skewers in water for half an hour)

For the Chimichurri Sauce:
- 1 lb (450g) large shrimp, peeled and deveined
- 1 red bell pepper, chopped into 1-inch pieces
- 1 zucchini, sliced into ½-inch rounds
- 1 red onion, chopped into wedges
- 1 tbsp (15 ml) olive oil
- ½ tsp (1.5g) paprika
- ½ tsp (2g) garlic powder
- Salt and pepper to taste

Optional Garnishes:
- Lemon wedges
- Extra fresh parsley for serving

Instructions:

Combine the chopped parsley, cilantro, garlic, olive oil, red wine vinegar, red pepper flakes (if using), lemon juice, and salt and pepper. Mix everything together, then put it aside and make the skewers.

In a large bowl, toss the shrimp, red bell pepper, zucchini, and red onion with garlic powder, salt, olive oil, paprika, and pepper until everything is evenly coated.

Alternating between shrimp, bell pepper, zucchini, and red onion, thread the veggies and shrimp onto the skewers.

Set the temperature of your grill pan or grill to medium-high. Lightly oil the grates to prevent sticking.

Grill the skewers on each side for two to three minutes until the veggies are soft and lightly charred and the shrimp are opaque and pink. Remove from the grill and set aside.

Once the skewers are grilled, drizzle the chimichurri sauce generously over the shrimp and veggies.

Serve the skewers with extra chimichurri sauce on the side, and garnish with fresh parsley and lemon wedges if desired.

Spicy Tuna Salad with Avocado and Cucumber

Yield: 2 servings	**Preparation Time:** 10 minutes	**Cooking Time:** None

Calories: 260 kcal | Carbohydrates: 48g | Total Fat: 7g | Saturated Fat: 4g | Cholesterol: 0mg | Protein: 4g | Sodium: 50mg
(per serving)

Ingredients:
- 1 can (5 oz/140g) tuna in water, drained
- 1 ripe avocado, diced
- ½ cucumber, sliced thinly
- 1 tbsp (15 ml) Greek yogurt
- 1 tsp (5 ml) Sriracha sauce (adjust to taste)
- 1 tsp (5 ml) fresh lime juice
- 1 tbsp (4g) fresh cilantro, chopped
- ¼ tsp (1g) garlic powder
- Salt and pepper to taste

Optional Garnishes:
- Sesame seeds or chopped green onions
- Extra cilantro leaves

Instructions:

Drain the tuna and place it in a medium-sized mixing bowl. Break it apart with a fork to ensure there are no large chunks.

Cut the avocado in half, remove the pit, and scoop out the flesh. Dice it into bite-sized pieces and set aside.

Add low-fat Greek yogurt, Sriracha sauce, lime juice, garlic powder, salt, and pepper in the same bowl as the tuna. Stir until the tuna is evenly coated with the dressing.

Gently fold in the diced avocado and sliced cucumber. Be careful not to mash the avocado too much so the salad maintains some texture.

Stir in the chopped cilantro to give the salad a fresh, vibrant flavor.

Transfer the spicy tuna salad to serving bowls. If desired, garnish with more cilantro and sesame seeds for crunch. You may also use chopped green onions. Serve immediately.

You may wrap it in lettuce leaves or serve it with whole-grain crackers.

Cilantro Lime Fish Tacos with Slaw

Yield: 4 servings (8 tacos) **Preparation Time:** 15 minutes **Cooking Time:** 15 minutes

Calories: 320 kcal | Carbohydrates: 8g | Total Fat: 22g | Saturated Fat: 3g | Cholesterol: 165mg | Protein: 25g | Sodium: 280mg
(per serving)

Ingredients:

For the Fish:
- 1 lb (450g) white fish (such as cod, tilapia, or mahi-mahi)
- 1 tbsp (15 ml) olive oil
- 2 tbsp (30 ml) fresh lime juice
- 1 tsp (2g) lime zest
- 2 cloves garlic, minced
- ¼ cup (8g) fresh cilantro, chopped
- 1 tsp (2g) ground cumin
- ½ tsp (1.5g) paprika
- Salt and pepper to taste

For the Slaw:
- 2 cups (170g) shredded green cabbage
- ½ cup (60g) shredded carrots
- ¼ cup (50 g) red onion, thinly sliced
- 1 tbsp (15 ml) olive oil
- 1 tbsp (15 ml) apple cider vinegar
- 1 tbsp (15 ml) fresh lime juice
- 1 tsp (5 ml) honey or maple syrup
- Salt and pepper to taste
- 1 tbsp (4g) fresh cilantro, chopped

For the Tacos:
- 8 small whole wheat or corn tortillas (preferably whole grain for a heart-healthy option)
- Lime wedges (for serving)
- Extra cilantro, chopped (for garnish)

Instructions:

Whisk together the olive oil, lime juice, zest, minced garlic, fresh cilantro, ground cumin, paprika, salt, and pepper in a small bowl. After covering the fish fillets with marinade, let them for 10-15 minutes.

Heat a grill pan, grill, or barbeque over medium heat. Add the marinated fish to the grill or pan, cooking for 4-5 minutes per side or until it is opaque and flakes easily with a fork. Remove from heat and gently break the fish into large chunks.

Combine the shredded cabbage, carrots, and red onion in a large bowl. In a small bowl, whisk together the olive oil, apple cider vinegar, honey, lime juice, salt, and pepper. Drizzle the slaw with the dressing and toss to coat. Add chopped cilantro if using, and mix well. Set aside.

In a dry skillet, cook the tortillas for 30-60 seconds on each side or until they are warm and pliable. Alternatively, you might reheat them in the oven with foil covering them.

Divide the fish evenly among the tortillas. Top each taco with a generous portion of the slaw, garnish with extra cilantro, and a squeeze of fresh lime juice.

You can also top the tacos with sliced avocado or a light Greek yogurt-based sauce for extra creaminess and flavor without adding unhealthy fats.

Baked Trout with Almond Crust

Yield: 4 servings **Preparation Time:** 10 minutes **Cooking Time:** 20 minutes

Calories: 320 kcal | Carbohydrates: 6g | Total Fat: 20g | Saturated Fat: 2.5g | Cholesterol: 75mg | Protein: 28g | Sodium: 180mg
(per serving)

Ingredients:
- 4 (6 oz/170g) trout fillets (skin-on or skinless)
- ½ cup (75g) raw almonds, finely chopped or ground
- 2 tbsp (15g) whole wheat
- 1 tbsp (4g) fresh parsley, chopped
- 1 tbsp (6g) lemon zest (about 1 lemon)
- 2 tbsp (30 ml) olive oil
- 2 cloves garlic, minced
- 1 tbsp (15 ml) fresh lemon juice
- Salt and pepper to taste
- Lemon wedges (for serving)

Optional Garnishes:
- Fresh parsley or fresh dill
- Sliced almonds for added texture

Instructions:

Preheat the oven to 400°F (200°C). Line a baking sheet with parchment paper or lightly grease it with olive oil.

Pat the trout fillets dry with paper towels. Sprinkle a little salt and pepper on each side of the fillet. Arrange the fillets skin-side down on the prepared baking sheet.

Mix the finely chopped almonds, whole wheat breadcrumbs (if using), parsley, lemon zest, minced garlic, and 1 tablespoon of olive oil until well combined.

Spread the almond mixture evenly over each trout fillet, pressing it down lightly to adhere.

After brushing the fillets with the remaining 1 tablespoon of olive oil, bake them for 15-20 minutes in a preheated oven or until they are opaque and flake easily with a fork. The crust should be golden brown and crispy.

Remove the trout from the oven and garnish with fresh parsley or dill and extra lemon wedges. Serve hot.

Serve this Baked Trout with Almond Crust and steamed vegetables like broccoli, asparagus, or green beans for added fiber and nutrients.

Sautéed Scallops with Lemon and Spinach

Yield: 4 servings   **Preparation Time:** 10 minutes   **Cooking Time:** 10 minutes

Calories: 230 kcal | Carbohydrates: 5g | Total Fat: 12g | Saturated Fat: 1.5g | Cholesterol: 35mg | Protein: 23g | Sodium: 300mg
(per serving)

Ingredients:

- 1 lb (450g) sea scallops, cleaned and patted dry
- 2 tbsp (30 ml) olive oil, divided
- 2 cloves garlic, minced
- 4 cups (140g) fresh spinach
- 2 tbsp (30 ml) fresh lemon juice
- 1 tsp (2g) lemon zest
- Salt and pepper to taste
- ½ tsp (1g) red pepper flakes (optional)
- Lemon wedges for serving
- Chopped fresh parsley (optional for garnish)

Instructions:

Use paper towels to ensure the scallops are completely dry. This helps achieve a nice sear during cooking. Season both sides with salt and pepper.

Heat 1 tablespoon of olive oil in a large nonstick skillet over medium-high heat. Once the oil is hot, add the scallops to a single layer, ensuring they are not overcrowded.

Sear the scallops on each side for 2-3 minutes until they form a golden crust and are opaque in the center. Remove the scallops from the pan and set aside on a plate.

In the same skillet, reduce the heat to medium. Add the remaining 1 tablespoon of olive oil and minced garlic. Sauté the garlic for about 30 seconds, until fragrant. Then, add the fresh spinach, lemon juice, and lemon zest. Stir occasionally and cook until the spinach wilts, about 2-3 minutes. Season with salt, pepper, and red pepper flakes (if using).

Add the cooked scallops back into the pan with the spinach for 1 minute to warm them through. Toss gently to combine.

Divide the spinach and scallops among four plates. Garnish with fresh parsley and lemon wedges for extra zest.

Ginger Garlic Salmon with Broccoli

Yield: 4 servings   **Preparation Time:** 10 minutes   **Cooking Time:** 20 minutes

Calories: 320 kcal | Carbohydrates: 6g | Total Fat: 20g | Saturated Fat: 2.5g | Cholesterol: 75mg | Protein: 28g | Sodium: 180mg
(per serving)

Ingredients:

For the Salmon:

- 4 (5-6 oz/170g) salmon fillets
- 2 tbsp (30 ml) olive oil
- 1 tbsp (6g) fresh ginger, grated
- 2 cloves garlic, minced
- 2 tbsp (30 ml) low-sodium soy sauce (or tamari for gluten-free)
- 1 tbsp (15 ml) honey or maple syrup
- 1 tbsp (15 ml) fresh lemon juice
- 1 tsp (2g) lemon zest
- Salt and pepper, to taste

For the Broccoli:

- 4 cups (300g) broccoli florets
- 1 tbsp (15 ml) olive oil
- 1 clove garlic, minced
- Salt and pepper, to taste
- Lemon wedges for serving

Optional Garnishes:

- Fresh cilantro or parsley, chopped
- Sesame seeds

Instructions:

Whisk together the olive oil, grated ginger, minced garlic, soy sauce, honey, lemon juice, and lemon zest.

Transfer the salmon fillets to a shallow dish and cover them with the marinade. Let the salmon marinate for 10 minutes, turning once to ensure all sides are coated.

While the salmon marries, toss the broccoli florets in olive oil, garlic, salt, and pepper. Arrange the broccoli evenly on a baking pan covered with foil or parchment paper.

Roast the broccoli in the preheated oven for about 15-20 minutes or until tender and slightly browned.

Heat a large skillet over medium-high heat. Remove the salmon from the marinade and pat it dry slightly to prevent excess moisture. Place the salmon fillets in the skillet, skin side down if using, and sear for about 4 minutes, until the skin is crispy.

After turning the fillets over, heat for a further 3–4 minutes or until the salmon is well cooked and readily flakes with a fork. During the last minute of cooking, drizzle the remaining marinade over the salmon.

When the salmon is done, serve it on a platter with the roasted broccoli. Garnish with fresh parsley or cilantro and sesame seeds.

Serve with extra lemon wedges for a fresh citrus burst.

Mediterranean Shrimp with Tomatoes and Olives

Yield: 4 servings   **Preparation Time:** 10 minutes   **Cooking Time:** 15 minutes

Calories: 230 kcal | Carbohydrates: 5g | Total Fat: 12g | Saturated Fat: 1.5g | Cholesterol: 35mg | Protein: 23g | Sodium: 300mg
(per serving)

Ingredients:

- 1 lb (450g) large shrimp, peeled and deveined
- 1 tbsp (15 ml) olive oil
- 1 small onion, finely chopped
- 3 cloves garlic, minced
- 1 can (14.5 oz/400g) diced tomatoes
- ¼ cup (40g) kalamata olives, pitted and halved
- 1 tsp (1g) dried oregano
- 1 tsp (1g) dried thyme
- ¼ tsp (0.5g) red pepper flakes
- 2 tbsp (8g) fresh parsley, chopped
- 2 tbsp (8g) fresh basil, chopped
- 2 tbsp (30 ml) fresh lemon juice
- Salt and pepper, to taste

Optional Garnishes:

- Extra fresh parsley or basil
- Lemon wedges
- Crumbled feta cheese

Instructions:

Pat the shrimp dry and season with salt, pepper, and a squeeze of lemon juice. Set aside while you prepare the tomato and olive sauce.

Heat olive oil in a large skillet over medium heat. Add the chopped onion and sauté for 3-4 minutes until softened and translucent. Add the minced garlic and cook for an additional 30 seconds until fragrant.

Pour in the diced tomatoes and the oregano, thyme, and red pepper flakes (if using). Mix everything together and simmer for five minutes to let the flavors blend.

Stir in the kalamata olives and lay the shrimp on top of the tomato mixture. Cover and cook for about 3-4 minutes until the shrimp are pink and opaque, flipping halfway through.

After the shrimp are done, turn off the heat and mix in the remaining lemon juice, fresh parsley, and basil. Taste-test the flavoring with salt and pepper.

Serve the Mediterranean shrimp and tomato mixture on its own or over a bed of quinoa, whole wheat couscous, or brown rice for a heart-healthy meal. Garnish with additional fresh herbs, lemon wedges, or a sprinkle of crumbled feta (optional).

Fish Cakes with Quinoa and Veggies

Yield: 4 servings (8 cakes)   **Preparation Time:** 15 minutes   **Cooking Time:** 20 minutes

Calories: 340 kcal | Carbohydrates: 28g | Total Fat: 14g | Saturated Fat: 2g | Cholesterol: 65mg | Protein: 28g | Sodium: 250mg
(per serving)

Ingredients:

For the Fish Cakes:

- 1 lb (450g) white fish fillets (such as cod, haddock, or tilapia)
- 1 cup (185g) cooked quinoa
- 1 small carrot, grated
- ½ cup (40g) finely chopped spinach
- 2 green onions, chopped
- 1 garlic clove, minced
- 1 egg, lightly beaten
- 2 tbsp (8g) fresh parsley, chopped
- 1 tbsp (15 ml) Dijon mustard
- 1 tbsp (15 ml) fresh lemon juice
- 1 tsp (2g) lemon zest
- Salt and pepper to taste
- 2 tbsp (30 ml) olive oil for cooking

For the Quinoa Veggie Side:

- 1 cup (170g) quinoa, rinsed
- 2 cups (480 ml) low-sodium vegetable broth
- 1 zucchini, diced
- ½ red bell pepper, diced
- 1 tbsp (15 ml) olive oil
- 1 clove garlic, minced
- Salt and pepper, to taste
- Fresh parsley for garnish (optional)

Instructions:

Lightly steam or bake the fish fillets until cooked (about 5-7 minutes). Fish should be flaked into tiny pieces and placed aside.

Place the quinoa and vegetable stock in a medium saucepan and bring to a boil. Reduce heat, cover, and simmer for about 15 minutes until the quinoa is fluffy and the liquid is absorbed. Set aside.

Combine the flaked fish, cooked quinoa, grated carrot, chopped spinach, green onions, garlic, egg (if using), parsley, Dijon mustard, lemon juice, and lemon zest. Season with salt and pepper. Mix until all ingredients are well incorporated.

Shape the mixture into little patties, each about 2-3 inches in diameter. You should get about 8 fish cakes.

Heat 2 tablespoons of olive oil in a large skillet over medium heat. Add the fish cakes and fry for 3–4 minutes on each side or until the outsides are crispy and golden brown. Remove from heat and set aside.

Heat 1 tablespoon of olive oil over medium heat in a large skillet. Once aromatic, add the minced garlic and sauté it for 30 seconds. Add the diced zucchini and red bell pepper, and cook for 5-7 minutes, until tender.

Stir the sautéed vegetables into the cooked quinoa. Season with salt and pepper to taste. Garnish with fresh parsley, if desired.

Arrange the vegetable combination and quinoa, then place the fish cakes next to them. For extra taste, garnish with fresh herbs or lemon slices.

Roasted Salmon with Honey Mustard Glaze

Yield: 4 servings	**Preparation Time:** 10 minutes	**Cooking Time:** 15 minutes

Calories: 330 kcal | Carbohydrates: 10g | Total Fat: 18g | Saturated Fat: 3g | Cholesterol: 80mg | Protein: 35g | Sodium: 200mg
(per serving)

Ingredients:
- 4 (6 oz/170g) salmon fillets
- 2 tbsp (30 ml) honey
- 1 tbsp (15 ml) Dijon mustard
- 1 tbsp (15 ml) whole-grain mustard
- 1 tbsp (15 ml) fresh lemon juice
- 1 tsp (2g) lemon zest
- 1 tbsp (15 ml) olive oil
- 1 garlic clove, minced
- Salt and pepper, to taste
- Fresh parsley, chopped (for garnish)
- Lemon wedges (for serving)

Optional Garnishes:
- Fresh dill or chopped green onions
- Toasted almonds for crunch

Instructions:

Preheat the oven to 400°F (200°C). Grease a baking sheet gently with olive oil or line it with parchment paper.

Whisk together the honey, lemon juice, lemon zest, Dijon mustard, whole grain mustard, olive oil, and minced garlic. Season the glaze with salt and pepper.

Use paper towels to gently pat the salmon fillets dry. Place them skin-side down on the prepared baking sheet. Sprinkle a little amount of salt and pepper on each fillet.

Generously brush the honey mustard glaze over the top of each salmon fillet.

Bake the fish for 12-15 minutes in the oven, or until the internal temperature reaches 145°F (63°C) and the fish flakes readily with a fork. The salmon should be opaque and tender.

After removing the salmon from the oven, sprinkle it with fresh parsley. Serve with lemon wedges for a fresh citrus touch.

Spaghetti with Clams and Garlic Olive Oil

Yield: 4 servings	**Preparation Time:** 10 minutes	**Cooking Time:** 20 minutes

Calories: 420 kcal | Carbohydrates: 52g | Total Fat: 14g | Saturated Fat: 2g | Cholesterol: 50mg | Protein: 24g | Sodium: 430mg
(per serving)

Ingredients:
- 12 oz (340g) whole wheat spaghetti
- 2 lbs (900g) fresh clams, scrubbed and cleaned
- 4 tbsp (60 ml) extra virgin olive oil
- 4 cloves garlic, thinly sliced
- ½ tsp (1g) red pepper flakes (optional, for heat)
- 1 cup (240 ml) dry white wine (optional for added flavor)
- ¼ cup (8g) fresh parsley, chopped
- 2 tbsp (30 ml) fresh lemon juice (about 1 lemon)
- 1 tsp (2g) lemon zest
- Salt and freshly ground black pepper to taste

Optional Garnishes:
- Extra lemon wedges
- Chopped fresh basil

Instructions:

Bring a large pot of salted water to a boil. After adding the whole wheat spaghetti, simmer it for 9-11 minutes, or until it's al dente, following the package instructions. After reserving ½ cup of pasta water, drain and put the pasta aside.

Rinse the clams under cold water and discard any with cracked shells or those that don't close when tapped.

In a big, deep-pan, warm two tablespoons of olive oil over medium heat. Add the sliced garlic and red pepper flakes (if using) and sauté for 1-2 minutes, until fragrant but not browned.

Add the clams to the skillet, followed by white wine (if used) and lemon juice. Cover the skillet and cook the clams for 5-7 minutes or until they open. Discard any that do not open.

Once the clams are cooked, add the drained pasta, the reserved pasta water, lemon zest, and the remaining 2 tablespoons of olive oil to the skillet. Toss everything together over medium heat until the pasta is well coated and warmed through. Season with salt and pepper to taste.

After adding the chopped parsley, turn off the heat and remove the skillet. If desired, garnish with extra lemon wedges and fresh basil.

Seafood Paella with Brown Rice

Yield: 4 servings	**Preparation Time:** 15 minutes	**Cooking Time:** 45 minutes

Calories: 360 kcal | Carbohydrates: 42g | Total Fat: 10g | Saturated Fat: 1.5g | Cholesterol: 120mg | Protein: 30g | Sodium: 450mg
(per serving)

Ingredients:

- 1 cup (190g) brown rice, rinsed
- 2 tbsp (30 ml) olive oil
- 1 medium onion, finely chopped
- 1 red bell pepper, diced
- 4 cloves garlic, minced
- 1 cup (160g) diced tomatoes (canned)
- 1 tsp (2g) smoked paprika
- ½ tsp (1g) turmeric or saffron (for color)
- ½ tsp (1g) ground cumin
- ½ tsp (1g) red pepper flakes
- 2½ cups (600 ml) low-sodium vegetable or seafood broth
- ½ lb (225g) shrimp, peeled and deveined
- ½ lb (225g) mussels or clams, scrubbed and cleaned
- ½ lb (225g) calamari, cleaned and cut into rings
- ½ cup (75g) frozen peas
- 1 lemon, cut into wedges
- Fresh parsley, chopped (for garnish)
- Salt and pepper, to taste

Instructions:

Heat 2 tablespoons of olive oil in a wide, deep skillet or paella pan over medium heat. Sauté the diced red bell pepper and onion for 5-6 minutes or until the vegetables are tender.

Add the red pepper flakes (if using), cumin, smoked paprika, turmeric or saffron, and chopped garlic. Stirring continually, cook for 1-2 minutes or until aromatic.

Mix the veggies and seasonings with the washed brown rice in the skillet. Allow the rice to gently roast for 2-3 minutes.

Stir in the diced tomatoes and the low-sodium broth. Bring the mixture to a simmer, reduce the heat to low, cover, and cook for about 30-35 minutes until the brown rice is tender and has absorbed most of the liquid.

Once the rice is tender, stir in the shrimp, mussels (or clams), and calamari. Cover the pan again and cook for 5-7 minutes until the shrimp is pink and the mussels (or clams) have opened. Discard any shellfish that do not open.

Add the frozen peas and heat for 2-3 minutes. Season the paella with salt and pepper to taste.

Remove the pan from the heat and let the paella rest for a few minutes. Garnish with fresh parsley and lemon wedges.

Miso-Glazed Cod with Bok Choy

Yield: 4 servings	**Preparation Time:** 10 minutes	**Cooking Time:** 20 minutes

Calories: 420 kcal | Carbohydrates: 52g | Total Fat: 14g | Saturated Fat: 2g | Cholesterol: 50mg | Protein: 24g | Sodium: 430mg
(per serving)

Ingredients:

For the Cod:
- 4 (5-6 oz/170g) cod fillets
- 2 tbsp (30g) white miso paste
- 1 tbsp (15 ml) low-sodium soy sauce
- 1 tbsp (15 ml) honey or maple syrup
- 1 tbsp (15 ml) rice vinegar
- 1 tbsp (6g) fresh ginger, grated
- 1 tbsp (15 ml) sesame oil (or olive oil)
- 1 tbsp (15 ml) water (to thin the glaze)
- 1 tbsp (9g) sesame seeds
- 2 green onions, sliced

For the Bok Choy:
- 4 heads of baby bok choy, halved lengthwise
- 1 tbsp (15 ml) olive oil or sesame oil
- 2 cloves garlic, minced
- 1 tsp (2g) fresh ginger, grated
- 1 tbsp (15 ml) low-sodium soy sauce
- 1 tbsp (15 ml) water
- Salt and pepper, to taste

Optional Garnishes:
- Lemon wedges
- Fresh cilantro or parsley, chopped

Instructions:

Preheat the oven to 400°F (200°C).

Grease a baking sheet gently with olive oil or line it with parchment paper.

In a small bowl, whisk together the miso paste, sesame oil, rice vinegar, soy sauce, honey or maple syrup, and shredded ginger. If the glaze is too thick, add a tablespoon of water.

After the baking sheet is ready, put the cod fillets on it. Brush each fillet generously with the miso glaze, coating the top and sides.

Bake in the preheated oven for 12-15 minutes or until the fish flakes easily with a fork and is cooked through. If desired, broil the cod for 2-3 minutes at the end to caramelize the glaze.

Heat up some sesame or olive oil in a big pan over medium heat while the fish bakes. Add the minced garlic and ginger, and sauté for 1-2 minutes until fragrant.

Place the halved bok choy in the skillet and cut side down. Pour in the soy sauce and water. Cover and cook for 4-5 minutes until the bok choy is tender but still crisp. Season with salt and pepper to taste.

Remove the cooked fish from the oven and top with sliced green onions and sesame seeds. Serve the cod alongside the sautéed bok choy.

Add lemon wedges on the side for a fresh citrus burst and sprinkle with fresh herbs like cilantro or parsley.

Poultry and Meat Recipes

Lemon Herb Grilled Chicken Breasts

Yield: 4 servings   **Preparation Time:** 40 minutes   **Cooking Time:** 15 minutes

Calories: 250 kcal | Carbohydrates: 1g | Total Fat: 14g | Saturated Fat: 2g | Cholesterol: 70mg | Protein: 30g | Sodium: 150mg
(per serving)

Ingredients:

- 4 boneless, skinless chicken breasts (about 6 oz/170g each)
- 3 tbsp (45 ml) olive oil
- 2 tbsp (30 ml) fresh lemon juice (about 1 lemon)
- 1 tsp (2g) lemon zest
- 2 cloves garlic, minced
- 2 tbsp (8g) fresh parsley, chopped
- 1 tbsp (2g) fresh thyme leaves
- 1 tsp (1g) dried oregano
- Salt and pepper, to taste
- Lemon wedges, for garnish (optional)
- Fresh herbs (parsley, thyme, or basil)

Optional Garnishes:

- Grilled vegetables (like zucchini, bell peppers, or asparagus)
- Brown rice or quinoa as a side

Instructions:

Whisk together olive oil, lemon zest, fresh lemon juice, minced garlic, chopped parsley, thyme, oregano, and a dash of salt and pepper.

Move the chicken breasts to a shallow dish or a large resealable bag. Cover the chicken with the marinade. Cover the dish or seal the bag, then place it in the refrigerator for at least 30 minutes or up to two hours.

Set the temperature of your grill to medium-high, about 375–400°F.

Take the chicken breasts out of the marinade and throw away any leftover marinade. Cook the chicken on the grill for 5 to 6 minutes on each side or until the juices flow clear and the internal temperature reaches 165°F (75°C). Avoid overcooking to keep the chicken juicy.

Once cooked, transfer the chicken to a plate and let it rest for a few minutes before serving. This helps the juices redistribute, ensuring tender, juicy chicken.

For a blast of freshness, garnish with more fresh herbs and lemon wedges. You can also serve the chicken with grilled vegetables or a side of whole grains like quinoa or brown rice.

Turkey and Quinoa Stuffed Peppers

Yield: 4 servings   **Preparation Time:** 15 minutes   **Cooking Time:** 40 minutes

Calories: 320 kcal | Carbohydrates: 30g | Total Fat: 10g | Saturated Fat: 2g | Cholesterol: 55mg | Protein: 27g | Sodium: 400mg
(per serving)

Ingredients:

- 4 large bell peppers (any color), tops cut off and seeds removed
- 1 lb (450g) ground turkey (lean, 93% lean or higher)
- 1 cup (185g) cooked quinoa
- 1 medium onion, finely chopped
- 2 cloves garlic, minced
- 1 medium zucchini, diced
- 1 can (14.5 oz/400g) diced tomatoes
- 1 tbsp (15 ml) olive oil
- 1 tsp (2g) cumin
- 1 tsp (2g) smoked paprika
- 1 tsp (1g) dried oregano
- ½ tsp (1g) ground black pepper
- Salt, to taste
- ½ cup (50g) shredded low-fat mozzarella cheese (optional for topping)
- Fresh parsley or cilantro, chopped
- Lemon wedges (optional for serving)

Optional Garnishes:

- Avocado slices
- Greek yogurt dollop (as a sour cream substitute)

Instructions:

Preheat the oven to 375°F (190°C). Prepare a large baking dish to hold all the bell peppers upright.

Bring a pot of water to a boil to soften the bell peppers. After blanching for 3-4 minutes, remove the bell peppers from the water and put them aside. This step is optional but will result in softer peppers.

Heat 1 tablespoon of olive oil in a large skillet over medium heat. Add the chopped onion, garlic, and sauté for 2-3 minutes until softened. Cook the chopped zucchini for 3–4 minutes or until it becomes soft.

Push the vegetables to the side of the skillet and add the ground turkey. Cook until browned, breaking it up with a spoon as it cooks (about 5-6 minutes).

Stir in the cumin, smoked paprika, oregano, black pepper, and a pinch of salt. After adding the chopped tomatoes and their liquids, simmer for 2 more minutes.

Once the turkey and vegetables are cooked, stir in the cooked quinoa and remove the mixture from heat.

Spoon the turkey-quinoa mixture into each bell pepper. After the baking dish is ready, place the filled peppers upright in it.

Bake the peppers in the baking dish covered with foil for 25 to 30 minutes or until they are soft. If you like a cheesy topping, remove the foil, sprinkle a little shredded mozzarella cheese on top of each pepper, and bake uncovered for 5 minutes to melt the cheese.

Once the stuffed peppers have roasted, remove them from the oven. Garnish with fresh cilantro or parsley, and serve with lemon wedges on the side for an added taste.

Spicy Chicken Stir-Fry with Vegetables

Yield: 4 servings	**Preparation Time:** 10 minutes	**Cooking Time:** 15 minutes

Calories: 340 kcal | Carbohydrates: 35g | Total Fat: 10g | Saturated Fat: 2g | Cholesterol: 65mg | Protein: 30g | Sodium: 350mg
(per serving)

Ingredients:

For the Stir-Fry:
- 1 lb (450g) of skinless, boneless chicken breasts sliced into small strips
- 1 tbsp (15 ml) olive oil or sesame oil
- 1 red bell pepper, sliced thin
- 1 yellow bell pepper, sliced thin
- 1 zucchini, sliced into thin rounds
- 1 cup (90g) broccoli florets
- 2 carrots, julienned
- 3 cloves garlic, minced
- 1 tbsp (7g) fresh ginger, grated
- 2 green onions, sliced (optional)
- 1 tbsp (15 ml) low-sodium soy sauce
- 2 tbsp (30 ml) low-sodium chicken broth or water
- 1 tsp (2g) red pepper flakes (adjust for spice preference)
- 1 tsp (5 ml) sriracha or hot sauce (optional for extra heat)
- 1 tbsp (15 ml) rice vinegar
- 1 tsp (3g) sesame seeds (optional garnish)

Optional Garnishes:
- Fresh cilantro, chopped
- Lime wedges

For Serving:
- 2 cups (380g) cooked brown rice or quinoa

Instructions:

Thinly slice the skinless, boneless chicken breasts into bite-sized pieces, then sprinkle with a little pinch of salt and pepper.

Slice the bell peppers, zucchini, and carrots. Cut the broccoli into bite-sized florets. Mince the garlic and grate the ginger.

Heat 1 tablespoon of olive or sesame oil in a large skillet or wok over medium-high heat.

Stir-fry the chicken strips for 4–5 minutes or until they are browned and cooked. Remove the chicken from the pan and set it aside.

Grated ginger and minced garlic should be added to the same pan. Sauté for 1 minute, then add the bell peppers, zucchini, broccoli, and carrots. Sauté the veggies for 3–4 minutes or until they are crisp-tender. Add the soy sauce, chicken broth (or water), rice vinegar, red pepper flakes, and sriracha (if using) to the pan. Cook, stirring, for a further two minutes or until thoroughly cooked and coated.

Add the cooked chicken to the pan and stir to coat in the sauce. Cook for an additional 1-2 minutes to heat through.

Serve the spicy chicken stir-fry over cooked brown rice or quinoa. Garnish with sesame seeds, fresh cilantro, and lime wedges for extra flavor.

Baked Chicken Thighs with Garlic and Rosemary

Yield: 4 servings	**Preparation Time:** 10 minutes	**Cooking Time:** 35 minutes

Calories: 230 kcal | Carbohydrates: 2g | Total Fat: 14g | Saturated Fat: 2.5g | Cholesterol: 85mg | Protein: 25g | Sodium: 300mg
(per serving)

Ingredients:
- 4 skinless, boneless chicken thighs (1 pound/450g)
- 2 tbsp (30 ml) olive oil
- 4 cloves garlic, minced
- 2 tbsp (3g) fresh rosemary, chopped
- 1 tbsp (15 ml) lemon juice
- 1 tsp (2g) lemon zest
- ½ tsp (1g) black pepper
- ½ tsp (3g) salt
- ¼ tsp (0.5g) paprika
- 1 tbsp (4g) fresh parsley, chopped (optional garnish)
- Lemon wedges for garnish

Instructions:

In a small bowl, combine chopped rosemary, olive oil, minced garlic, lemon juice, lemon zest, black pepper, and paprika (if using). Mix well to form a marinade.

The skinless, boneless chicken thighs should be placed in a resealable bag or shallow plate. When you pour the marinade over the chicken, make sure that every piece is equally covered. Let it marinate for at least 15-30 minutes (up to 2 hours) in the refrigerator for better flavor absorption.

Preheat the oven to 400°F (200°C). Grease a baking sheet gently with olive oil or line it with parchment paper.

Arrange the marinated chicken thighs on the prepared baking sheet. Bake for 25 to 30 minutes in a preheated oven or until the chicken's internal temperature reaches 165°F (75°C) and its juices flow clear. If desired, broil for 2-3 minutes to get a golden-brown finish.

When the chicken is cooked through, remove it from the oven and let it rest. Garnish with fresh parsley and serve with lemon wedges for added taste.

Mediterranean Chicken Skewers with Tzatziki

Yield: 4 servings | **Preparation Time:** 50 minutes | **Cooking Time:** 15 minutes

Calories: 290 kcal | Carbohydrates: 8g | Total Fat: 12g | Saturated Fat: 2g | Cholesterol: 80mg | Protein: 30g | Sodium: 300mg
(per serving)

Ingredients:

For the Chicken Skewers:
- 1 lb (450g) of skinless, boneless chicken breasts
- 2 tbsp (30 ml) olive oil
- 2 tbsp (30 ml) fresh lemon juice
- 1 tsp (2g) lemon zest
- 3 cloves garlic, minced
- 1 tsp (1g) dried oregano
- 1 tsp (2g) ground cumin
- ½ tsp (1.5g) paprika
- ½ tsp (1g) black pepper
- ½ tsp (3g) salt (optional)
- Wooden or metal skewers (soak wooden skewers in water for 30 minutes if using)

For the Tzatziki Sauce:
- 1 cup (240 ml) plain low-fat Greek yogurt
- ½ cucumber, grated and drained
- 1 tbsp (15 ml) fresh lemon juice
- 1 tbsp (3g) fresh dill, chopped
- 1 garlic clove, minced
- Salt and pepper, to taste

For Serving:
- Whole wheat pita bread or brown rice
- Grilled vegetables

Instructions:

Prepare the marinade. Whisk together the olive oil, paprika, lemon juice, lemon zest, minced garlic, dried oregano, cumin, paprika, black pepper, and salt (if using).

Slice chicken breasts into small cubes. Coat the chicken cubes by adding them to the marinade and tossing. Cover the bowl for at least half an hour (up to two hours) and place it in the refrigerator to allow the flavors to settle.

Grate the cucumber using a box grater. Squeeze the grated cucumber out of any extra moisture using paper towels or a clean kitchen towel, then put aside. Combine the Greek yogurt, grated cucumber, lemon juice, minced garlic, and chopped dill in a small bowl. Season with salt and pepper to taste. Mix well, then chill until serving time.

Set the heat to medium-high on your grill or grill pan.

To ensure consistent cooking, thread the marinated chicken pieces onto the skewers, allowing a little gap between each piece.

Cook the chicken until it reaches an internal temperature of 165°F (75°C), about 4–5 minutes on each side of the grill. The chicken should have excellent grill marks and be tender inside.

Serve the grilled chicken skewers with the prepared tzatziki sauce on the side. For an added taste boost, garnish with lemon wedges and fresh parsley.

To complete the meal, serve with whole wheat pita bread, brown rice, or grilled vegetables.

Slow-Cooked Beef Stew with Root Vegetables

Yield: 6 servings | **Preparation Time:** 20 minutes | **Cooking Time:** 4-8 hours

Calories: 230 kcal | Carbohydrates: 2g | Total Fat: 14g | Saturated Fat: 2.5g | Cholesterol: 85mg | Protein: 25g | Sodium: 300mg
(per serving)

Ingredients:
- 1.5 lbs (680g) lean beef stew meat, trimmed of visible fat (round or chuck cut, trimmed)
- 1 tbsp (15 ml) olive oil
- 1 large chopped onion
- 2 garlic cloves, minced
- 2 large carrots, peeled and chopped
- 2 parsnips, peeled and chopped
- 2 large sweet potatoes
- 1 large turnip, peeled and chopped
- 2 celery stalks, chopped
- 4 cups (960 ml) low-sodium beef broth
- 1 cup (240 ml) water
- 2 tbsp (30 ml) tomato paste
- 2 tsp (2g) dried thyme
- 2 tsp (1g) dried rosemary
- 1 bay leaf
- 1 tsp (2g) ground black pepper
- ½ tsp (3g) salt (optional or to taste)

Instructions:

Peel and chop all vegetables into bite-sized pieces. Set aside.

Season the lean beef stew meat with a little salt (optional) and black pepper. Add 1 tablespoon of olive oil to a large skillet over medium-high heat. Once hot, add the beef in batches (avoid overcrowding the pan) and sear on all sides until browned, about 2-3 minutes per side. Remove the beef from the pan and set aside.

In the same pan, add the chopped onion and garlic. Sauté for 2-3 minutes until softened and fragrant, scraping up any browned bits from the beef. Transfer the browned beef, onions, and garlic into the slow cooker. Add the carrots, parsnips, potatoes (or sweet potatoes), turnips, and celery. Pour in the low-sodium beef broth, water, and tomato paste. Add the dried thyme, dried rosemary, bay leaf, and black pepper. Stir everything.

Cover the slow cooker and cook on low for 6-8 hours or high for 4-5 hours. The veggies should be cooked completely, and the meat should be tender. Remove the bay leaf after cooking, and if necessary, add more salt or pepper to balance the seasoning.

To add flavor and color, ladle the beef stew into bowls and sprinkle with finely chopped parsley.

Herb-Roasted Chicken with Root Vegetables

Yield: 4 servings | **Preparation Time:** 15 minutes | **Cooking Time:** 45 minutes

Calories: 360 kcal | Carbohydrates: 28g | Total Fat: 13g | Saturated Fat: 2g | Cholesterol: 70mg | Protein: 33g | Sodium: 250mg
(per serving)

Ingredients:

For the Chicken:

- 4 boneless, skinless chicken breasts
- 2 tbsp (30 ml) olive oil
- 1 tbsp (2g) fresh chopped rosemary
- 1 tbsp (3g) fresh chopped thyme
- 1 tbsp (2g) fresh parsley, chopped
- 2 cloves garlic, minced
- 1 tsp (2g) lemon zest
- 1 tbsp (15 ml) lemon juice
- ½ tsp (1g) ground black pepper
- ½ tsp (3g) salt (optional)

For the Root Vegetables:

- 2 big carrots, peeled and chopped
- 1 large sweet potato, peeled and cubed
- 1 large parsnip, peeled and chopped
- 1 red onion, quartered
- 1 tbsp (15 ml) olive oil
- 1 tsp (2g) fresh rosemary, chopped
- 1 tsp (3g) fresh thyme, chopped
- 1 tsp (2g) ground black pepper
- ½ tsp (1.5g) paprika (optional for color)

Optional Garnishes:

- Lemon wedges

Instructions:

Prepare a roasting pan or baking sheet by gently coating it with olive oil or lining it with parchment paper.

Mix together olive oil, minced garlic, rosemary, thyme, parsley, lemon zest, lemon juice, black pepper, and salt (if using) to create an herb marinade.

Rub the herb marinade evenly over the chicken breasts. Set the chicken aside to absorb the flavors while you prepare the vegetables.

Combine the chopped carrots, sweet potato, parsnip, and red onion in a large bowl. After drizzling with olive oil, sprinkle with paprika (if using), black pepper, thyme, and rosemary. Toss the veggies to coat them uniformly with the spices by tossing them.

Place the chicken breasts in the middle of the prepped roasting pan or baking sheet. Spread the seasoned root vegetables around the chicken.

Roast for 35-40 minutes, or until the chicken reaches an internal temperature of 165°F (75°C) and the vegetables are tender and golden brown. Stir the vegetables halfway through roasting to ensure even cooking.

When the veggies and chicken are done, remove them from the oven. Let the chicken rest for five minutes before slicing. For a taste boost, serve with lemon slices and garnish with fresh parsley.

Chicken and Vegetable Curry with Coconut Milk

Yield: 4 servings | **Preparation Time:** 15 minutes | **Cooking Time:** 30 minutes

Calories: 230 kcal | Carbohydrates: 18g | Total Fat: 15g | Saturated Fat: 6g | Cholesterol: 55mg | Protein: 29g | Sodium: 400mg
(per serving)

Ingredients:

- 1 lb (450g) boneless, skinless chicken breasts
- 2 tbsp (30 ml) olive oil or coconut oil
- 1 medium onion, chopped
- 3 garlic cloves, minced
- 1 tbsp (7g) fresh ginger, minced
- 1 red bell pepper, chopped
- 1 zucchini, chopped
- 1 cup (120g) carrots, sliced
- 1 cup (90g) broccoli florets
- 1 can (14 oz/400 ml) light coconut milk
- 1 cup (240 ml) vegetable broth
- 2 tbsp (12g) curry powder
- 1 tsp (2g) ground turmeric
- 1 tsp (2g) ground cumin
- ½ tsp (1g) ground coriander
- ½ tsp (1g) red pepper flakes
- ½ tsp (1g) black pepper
- ½ tsp (3g) salt
- Juice of 1 lime

Instructions:

In a big pan, heat 1 tablespoon of olive or coconut oil over medium heat. Add the chicken pieces (bite-sized pieces), season with a pinch of salt and pepper, and cook for 5-7 minutes or until the chicken is lightly browned and cooked through. After taking the chicken out of the skillet, put it aside.

Add the remaining 1 tablespoon of oil in the same pan. Sauté the chopped onion for 2-3 minutes until softened. Add the minced garlic and ginger, and sauté for an additional 1 minute until fragrant.

Add the red bell pepper, zucchini, carrots, and broccoli florets. Cook, stirring occasionally, until the veggies are just beginning to soften, approximately 5 minutes.

Stir in the curry powder, ground turmeric, cumin, coriander, and red pepper flakes (if using). Let the spices toast for 1-2 minutes, releasing their flavor. Add the light coconut milk and vegetable broth. Stir to combine, scraping up any browned bits from the bottom of the pan.

Add the cooked chicken back into the pan. After bringing the curry to a simmer and lowering the heat to low, cook it for 10-12 minutes or until the sauce has slightly thickened.

Stir in the fresh lime juice just before serving to add brightness to the curry.

Shredded Chicken Tacos with Fresh Salsa

Yield: 4 servings (8 tacos)   **Preparation Time:** 15 minutes   **Cooking Time:** 20 minutes

Calories: 320 kcal | Carbohydrates: 30g | Total Fat: 10g | Saturated Fat: 1.5g | Cholesterol: 50mg | Protein: 28g | Sodium: 320mg
(per serving)

Ingredients:

For the Shredded Chicken:
- 1 lb (450g) boneless, skinless chicken breasts
- 3 cups (720 ml) low-sodium chicken broth or water
- 1 tsp (2g) cumin
- 1 tsp (2g) chili powder
- 1 garlic clove, minced
- ½ tsp (1g) black pepper
- ½ tsp (3g) salt (optional)

For the Fresh Salsa:
- 1 cup (150g) cherry tomatoes, chopped
- ½ red onion, finely chopped
- ¼ cup (10g) fresh cilantro, chopped
- 1 jalapeño, seeded and
- 1 lime, juiced
- ¼ tsp (1.5g) salt (optional)

For the Tacos:
- 8 small whole-grain tortillas
- ½ cup (25g) lettuce, shredded
- ¼ cup (50g) avocado, diced (about ½ medium avocado)
- ¼ cup (60g) low-fat Greek yogurt

Optional Garnishes:
- Extra lime wedges
- Extra chopped cilantro
- Hot sauce

Instructions:

In a medium saucepan, combine the chicken breasts, chicken broth, cumin, chili powder, minced garlic, black pepper, and salt (if using). Bring to a boil over medium-high heat, then lower the heat and simmer until the chicken is cooked through and measures 165°F (75°C) inside. This should take 15-20 minutes.

Remove the chicken from the broth and let it cool slightly. Using two forks, shred the chicken into bite-sized pieces. Set aside.

Combine the chopped tomatoes, red onion, cilantro, jalapeño (if using), lime juice, and salt (if using). Mix well and set aside.

Warm the whole-grain tortillas in a skillet over medium heat for 1-2 minutes on each side until pliable. Alternatively, wrap them in a moist paper towel and microwave for 20 to 30 seconds.

Place a portion of shredded chicken on each tortilla, followed by fresh salsa, shredded lettuce, and diced avocado. If desired, add a dollop of low-fat Greek yogurt.

Garnish with additional lime wedges, chopped cilantro, or hot sauce.

Lemon Garlic Chicken with Green Beans

Yield: 4 servings   **Preparation Time:** 10 minutes   **Cooking Time:** 20 minutes

Calories: 220 kcal | Carbohydrates: 9g | Total Fat: 10g | Saturated Fat: 1.5g | Cholesterol: 55mg | Protein: 25g | Sodium: 210mg
(per serving)

Ingredients:
- 1 lb (450g) boneless, skinless chicken breasts cut into thin slices
- 2 tbsp (30 ml) olive oil
- 2 garlic cloves, minced
- 1 lb (450g) fresh green beans, trimmed
- 1 lemon, juiced and zested
- ½ cup (120g) low-sodium chicken broth
- ¼ tsp (0.5g) black pepper
- ¼ tsp (1.5g) salt (optional)
- 1 tbsp (4g) fresh parsley, chopped for garnish

Instructions:

Heat 1 tablespoon of olive oil in a big skillet over medium-high heat.

Cut the chicken breasts into thin slices. Add them to the skillet and cook for 5-6 minutes, turning halfway. Transfer them to a plate and set them aside.

Add another 1 tablespoon of olive oil to the skillet.

Add the minced garlic and cook, stirring, for 30 seconds or until aromatic.

Add the green beans, stirring to coat with the garlic and oil. Simmer them for 3–4 minutes or until they start to soften.

Stir well after adding the lemon juice, zest, and chicken broth to the skillet.

Season with black pepper and salt (if using), then simmer for another 3-5 minutes, allowing the green beans to cook until tender-crisp and the flavors to meld.

Add the chicken back to the pan and toss it in with the sauce and green beans. Cook for another 2-3 minutes until everything is heated through.

Garnish with fresh parsley and serve warm.

Chicken Piccata with Capers and Lemon

Yield: 4 servings   **Preparation Time:** 10 minutes   **Cooking Time:** 20 minutes

Calories: 230 kcal | Carbohydrates: 7g | Total Fat: 9g | Saturated Fat: 1.5g | Cholesterol: 55mg | Protein: 28g | Sodium: 300mg
(per serving)

Ingredients:

- 1 lb (450g) boneless, skinless chicken breasts, sliced in half lengthwise
- ¼ cup (30g) whole wheat flour
- ¼ tsp (1.5g) salt (optional)
- ¼ tsp (0.5g) black pepper
- 2 tbsp (30 ml) olive oil
- ½ cup (120 ml) low-sodium chicken broth
- ¼ cup (120 ml) fresh lemon juice (about 2 lemons)
- 2 tbsp (10g) capers, drained and rinsed
- 1 tbsp (4g) fresh parsley, chopped, for garnish
- Lemon zest for garnish

Instructions:

Combine the whole wheat flour, salt (if using), and black pepper.

Make cutlets and dredge each chicken cutlet in the flour mixture, shaking off any excess.

In a big skillet, heat 1 tablespoon of olive oil over medium-high heat. Once hot, add half of the chicken cutlets and cook for 3-4 minutes on each side until golden brown and cooked through. To stay warm, move to a dish and cover. Repeat with the remaining chicken cutlets.

In the same skillet, add the lemon juice and low-sodium chicken broth, scraping up any browned pieces from the bottom to give more flavor.

Stir in the capers and simmer the sauce for 3-4 minutes, allowing it to reduce slightly and concentrate in flavor.

Return the chicken cutlets to the skillet, spooning the sauce over them. Simmer for 1-2 minutes until the chicken is warmed through and well-coated with the sauce.

Transfer the chicken to plates, spooning the sauce and capers over the top. If preferred, garnish with lemon zest and fresh parsley.

BBQ Chicken Quinoa Bowl

Yield: 4 servings   **Preparation Time:** 15 minutes   **Cooking Time:** 25 minutes

Calories: 370 kcal | Carbohydrates: 45g | Total Fat: 10g | Saturated Fat: 1.5g | Cholesterol: 55mg | Protein: 28g | Sodium: 420mg
(per serving)

Ingredients:

For the Bowl:

- 1 lb (450g) boneless, skinless chicken breast
- 1 cup (170g) quinoa, rinsed and drained
- 2 cups (480 ml) low-sodium chicken broth or water
- ½ cup (120 ml) low-sodium BBQ sauce (look for one without added sugars or high fructose corn syrup)
- 1 cup (150g) cherry tomatoes, halved
- 1 cup (150g) fresh corn kernels (or 1 cup (150g) thawed frozen corn)
- 1 cup (170g) black beans, drained and rinsed
- ½ cup (75g) red bell pepper, diced
- 1 avocado, sliced

For Garnish (optional):

- Fresh cilantro, chopped
- Lime wedges
- Extra BBQ sauce for drizzling

Instructions:

Combine the rinsed quinoa and low-sodium chicken broth (or water) in a medium saucepan. Bring to a boil, reduce heat to low, cover, and simmer for 15 minutes or until the liquid is absorbed. Remove from the heat and fluff with a fork. Set aside.

Warm a skillet or grill over medium-high heat. Season the chicken breast lightly with salt (optional) and black pepper.

Cook on a grill or in a pan for about 6–7 minutes on each side or until the chicken is cooked through and the internal temperature reaches 165°F (75°C). After taking it off of the fire and allowing it to rest for a few minutes, cut it into thin strips.

Toss or brush the sliced chicken with the BBQ sauce to coat evenly.

In each bowl, place a generous scoop of cooked quinoa.

Top each bowl with equal portions of BBQ chicken, cherry tomatoes, corn, black beans, red bell pepper, and avocado slices.

Sprinkle with fresh cilantro, add a lime wedge, and add a little BBQ sauce if desired.

Honey Mustard Chicken with Brussels Sprouts

Yield: 4 servings	**Preparation Time:** 10 minutes	**Cooking Time:** 25 minutes

Calories: 290 kcal | Carbohydrates: 20g | Total Fat: 10g | Saturated Fat: 1.5g | Cholesterol: 55mg | Protein: 28g | Sodium: 310mg
(per serving)

Ingredients:

- 1 lb (450g) boneless, skinless chicken breast
- 1 lb (450g) Brussels sprouts, trimmed and halved
- 1 tbsp (15 ml) olive oil
- 1 tbsp (15 ml) Dijon mustard
- 1 tbsp (15 ml) whole-grain mustard
- 1 tbsp (15 ml) honey
- ½ tsp (1.5g) garlic powder
- ¼ tsp (1.5g) salt (optional)
- ¼ tsp (0.5g) black pepper
- 1 tbsp (4g) fresh parsley, chopped (optional garnish)

Instructions:

Combine the Dijon mustard, whole-grain mustard, honey, and garlic powder in a small bowl. Stir until smooth.

Slice the chicken breast into thin cutlets. Add black pepper and salt (if using) to the cutlets. Brush each cutlet with half of the honey mustard sauce, reserving the other half for later.

In a big skillet over medium-high heat, heat 1 tablespoon of olive oil. Cook the Brussels sprouts, cut side down, for 4–5 minutes, or until they start to turn golden. Cook, stirring, until tender but still bright green, 3–4 minutes. The Brussels sprouts should be moved to a platter and left there.

In the same skillet, add the chicken cutlets and cook for 4-5 minutes on each side until golden and cooked through, with an internal temperature of 165°F (75°C).

Pour the honey mustard sauce that was set aside over the chicken in the pan and let it reheat for a minute so that the chicken is well coated.

Return the Brussels sprouts to the skillet, stirring to combine with the chicken and sauce. Garnish with fresh parsley if desired.

Asian Glazed Chicken Thighs with Sesame

Yield: 4 servings	**Preparation Time:** 10 minutes	**Cooking Time:** 25 minutes

Calories: 260 kcal | Carbohydrates: 24g | Total Fat: 12g | Saturated Fat: 2g | Cholesterol: 75mg | Protein: 24g | Sodium: 310mg
(per serving)

Ingredients:

- 1 lb (450g) boneless, skinless chicken thighs
- 1 tbsp (15 ml) sesame oil
- ¼ cup (60 ml) low-sodium soy sauce
- 2 tbsp (30 ml) honey
- 1 tbsp (15 ml) rice vinegar
- 2 garlic cloves, minced
- 1 tsp (2g) fresh ginger, grated
- ¼ tsp (0.5g) black pepper
- 1 tbsp (9g) sesame seeds, toasted
- 1 tbsp (4g) green onions, sliced (optional garnish)
- Steamed broccoli or brown rice for serving (optional)

Instructions:

Whisk together the low-sodium soy sauce, minced garlic, honey, rice vinegar, and grated ginger. Set aside.

Heat 1 tablespoon of sesame oil over medium-high heat in a big skillet.

Cook the chicken thighs in the skillet for 4–5 minutes on each side or until they are almost cooked through and golden brown.

Reduce the heat to medium, cover the chicken thighs with the sauce, and let it simmer for 8 to 10 minutes. Flip the chicken once or twice to ensure it is well covered, and then let the sauce thicken.

When the sauce has thickened and the chicken's internal temperature reaches 165°F (75°C), sprinkle toasted sesame seeds on top.

Remove the chicken from the skillet and spoon extra sauce on top. If desired, garnish with sliced green onions.

Turkey Meatloaf with Vegetables

Yield: 6 servings   **Preparation Time:** 15 minutes   **Cooking Time:** 50 minutes

Calories: 200 kcal | Carbohydrates: 15g | Total Fat: 6g | Saturated Fat: 1g | Cholesterol: 60mg | Protein: 20g | Sodium: 260mg
(per serving)

Ingredients:

- 1 lb (450g) lean ground turkey
- ½ cup (40g) whole oats, finely ground or pulsed in a food processor
- ½ cup (60g) finely diced onion
- ½ cup (75g) finely diced red bell pepper
- ½ cup (60g) carrots, shredded
- ½ cup (60g) zucchini, shredded
- ¼ cup (8g) parsley, chopped
- ½ cup (120 ml) unsweetened applesauce
- 1 large egg, beaten (or 2 tbsp (15g) ground flaxseed + 5 tbsp (75 ml) water as an egg substitute)
- 2 tbsp (30 ml) tomato paste
- 1 tsp (3g) garlic powder
- 1 tsp (1g) Italian seasoning
- ½ tsp (3g) salt
- ¼ tsp (0.5g) black pepper

Glaze:

- 2 tbsp (30 ml) low-sugar ketchup
- 1 tsp (5 ml) Dijon mustard
- 1 tsp (5 ml) honey

Instructions:

Set the oven temperature to 375°F (190°C). Line a loaf pan with parchment paper or lightly oil it.

In a large mixing bowl, add the ground turkey, ground oats, onion, red bell pepper, carrots, zucchini, parsley, applesauce, beaten egg (or flax mixture), tomato paste, garlic powder, Italian seasoning, salt, and black pepper. Mix until everything is just combined. Avoid over-mixing to keep the meatloaf tender.

Transfer the turkey mixture to the prepared loaf pan, pressing down to form an even loaf.

Mix the low-sugar ketchup, Dijon mustard, and honey in a small bowl. Spread the glaze evenly over the meatloaf.

After putting the loaf pan in the oven, bake it for 50 minutes or until the internal temperature reaches 165°F (74°C).

Let the meatloaf cool in the pan for about 5 minutes before slicing.

Serve with roasted sweet potatoes or steamed green beans.

Slow Cooker Chicken and Vegetable Stew

Yield: 6 servings   **Preparation Time:** 15 minutes   **Cooking Time:** 6-7 hours

Calories: 220 kcal | Carbohydrates: 20g | Total Fat: 4g | Saturated Fat: 0.5g | Cholesterol: 45mg | Protein: 23g | Sodium: 310mg
(per serving)

Ingredients:

- 1 lb (450g) boneless, skinless chicken breasts, diced
- 4 cups (960 ml) low-sodium chicken broth
- 1 cup carrots, sliced
- 1 cup celery, sliced
- 1 medium onion, diced
- 2 cloves garlic, minced
- 1 medium zucchini, sliced
- 1 medium red bell pepper, diced
- 1 medium yellow potato, diced
- 1 cup (125g) green beans, trimmed and halved
- ½ tsp (0.5g) dried thyme
- ½ tsp (0.5g) dried rosemary
- ½ tsp (1.5g) paprika
- ¼ tsp (0.5g) black pepper
- ¼ tsp (1.5g) salt (optional)
- 1 tbsp (4g) fresh parsley, chopped (optional garnish)

Instructions:

Dice the chicken breast and chop all the vegetables as instructed above.

In a slow cooker, add the chicken, chicken broth, carrots, celery, onion, garlic, zucchini, bell pepper, potato, green beans, thyme, rosemary, paprika, black pepper, and salt (if using).

Cover and simmer on low for 6–7 hours or high for 3–4 hours or until the chicken is cooked and the veggies are soft.

Stir the stew gently before serving, and garnish with chopped fresh parsley if desired.

For added fiber, serve with a piece of whole-grain bread.

Pair with a side of brown rice or quinoa to increase whole grains and make it more filling.

Lean Beef Stir-Fry with Broccoli

Yield: 4 servings	**Preparation Time:** 10 minutes	**Cooking Time:** 15 minutes

Calories: 280 kcal | Carbohydrates: 12g | Total Fat: 12g | Saturated Fat: 3g | Cholesterol: 50mg | Protein: 26g | Sodium: 320mg
(per serving)

Ingredients:

- 1 lb (450g) lean beef sirloin or flank steak, sliced thinly against the grain
- 2 cups (180g) broccoli florets
- 1 medium red bell pepper, sliced
- 1 small carrot, thinly sliced
- 3 green onions, sliced
- 3 cloves garlic, minced
- 1 tbsp (7g) fresh ginger, grated
- 2 tbsp (30 ml) low-sodium soy sauce
- 1 tbsp (15 ml) olive oil or avocado oil
- ½ tbsp (7 ml) sesame oil (optional for flavor)
- 1 tbsp (15 ml) rice vinegar
- ¼ tsp (0.5g) black pepper
- ¼ tsp (0.5g) red pepper flakes
- 1 tsp (3g) sesame seeds for garnish

Instructions:

Thinly slice the lean beef against the grain for tenderness. Set aside.

Slice the bell pepper, carrot, and green onions (white and green parts separated). Trim broccoli florets into bite-size pieces.

Heat 1 tablespoon olive oil over medium-high heat in a large skillet or wok.

Add broccoli, bell pepper, carrot, and the white parts of the green onions. Sauté for 4-5 minutes until vegetables are tender-crisp. Remove from skillet and set aside.

Add sliced beef, garlic, and ginger to the same skillet. Sear on high heat for 3-4 minutes until the beef is browned but still tender.

Reduce the heat to medium and add the low-sodium soy sauce, rice vinegar, black pepper, and red pepper flakes. Stir well to coat the beef.

Return the vegetables to the skillet and toss everything together. Cook for 2-3 more minutes until all ingredients are heated through.

Sprinkle sesame seeds on top and add the green portions of the green onions.

Add extra steamed green vegetables like snap peas or green beans for variety.

Spiced Turkey Meatballs with Marinara Sauce

Yield: 4 servings	**Preparation Time:** 15 minutes	**Cooking Time:** 30 minutes

Calories: 250 kcal | Carbohydrates: 10g | Total Fat: 10g | Saturated Fat: 2g | Cholesterol: 65mg | Protein: 24g | Sodium: 560mg
(per serving)

Ingredients:

Meatballs:
- 1 lb (450g) lean ground turkey
- ¼ cup (15g) whole-grain breadcrumbs
- 1 large egg, beaten (or 1 tbsp (7g) ground flaxseed + 3 tbsp (45 ml) water as an egg substitute)
- ¼ cup onion, finely chopped
- 2 cloves garlic, minced
- ¼ cup (40g) parsley, chopped
- ½ tsp (1g) ground cumin
- ½ tsp (1g) paprika
- ¼ tsp (0.5g) cayenne pepper (optional for spice)
- ¼ tsp (1.5g) salt (optional)
- ¼ tsp (0.5g) black pepper

Marinara Sauce:
- 2 cups (480 ml) low-sodium marinara sauce
- 1 tsp (5 ml) olive oil
- 1 clove garlic, minced
- ¼ tsp (0.5g) red pepper flakes (optional)
- 1 tbsp (3g) fresh basil

Instructions:

Preheat your oven to 400°F (200°C). Line a baking sheet with parchment paper.

In a big bowl, combine ground turkey, breadcrumbs, beaten egg (or flaxseed mixture), onion, garlic, parsley, cumin, paprika, cayenne pepper (if using), salt, and black pepper. To avoid overmixing, mix just until combined.

After the baking sheet is ready, roll the mixture into 1-inch meatballs and put them on it.

Bake for 20 minutes or until the meatballs are golden brown and fully cooked, reaching an internal temperature of 165°F (74°C).

While the meatballs are baking, heat 1 teaspoon of olive oil in a saucepan over medium heat. Sauté the red pepper flakes and minced garlic for 1-2 minutes or until fragrant.

Pour in the marinara sauce, add basil, and stir. Simmer for 5–10 minutes on low heat.

Once the meatballs are baked, transfer them to the saucepan with the marinara sauce. Simmer for 5 minutes more to let the flavors blend.

If desired, warmly serve the meatballs and sauce, garnished with fresh parsley or basil.

Serve over whole-grain spaghetti or zucchini noodles.

Pair with steamed broccoli or a green salad with a light vinaigrette for extra fiber and nutrients.

Grilled Flank Steak with Chimichurri

Yield: 4 servings   **Preparation Time:** 15 minutes   **Cooking Time:** 45 minutes

Calories: 280 kcal | Carbohydrates: 2g | Total Fat: 18g | Saturated Fat: 3g | Cholesterol: 65mg | Protein: 25g | Sodium: 200mg
(per serving)

Ingredients:

For the Steak:
- 1 lb (450g) flank steak, trimmed of any visible fat
- 1 tbsp (15 ml) olive oil
- ½ tsp (3g) salt (optional)
- ½ tsp (1g) black pepper

For the Chimichurri Sauce:
- 1 cup (30g) fresh parsley, finely chopped
- ¼ cup (8g) fresh cilantro (optional), finely chopped
- 3 cloves garlic, minced
- ¼ cup (60 ml) red wine vinegar
- ¼ cup (60 ml) olive oil
- ½ tsp (1g) red pepper flakes
- ¼ tsp (0.5g) black pepper

Instructions:

Mix olive oil, salt, and black pepper in a small bowl. Evenly rub the flank steak on both sides with this mixture. For added flavor and tenderness, the steak can be left at room temperature for 30 minutes or chilled for up to 2 hours.

Set your grill's temperature to high, between 400°F and 450°F.

Mix parsley, cilantro (if using), garlic, red wine vinegar, olive oil, red pepper flakes, and black pepper in a medium bowl. Stir well to combine. Set aside.

Place the flank steak on the preheated grill. For medium-rare, grill for 4–6 minutes on each side or until done to your liking.

To preserve its juices, move the steak to a cutting board and leave it for five minutes.

To preserve the flank steak's tenderness, cut it thinly against the grain.

Serve the steak with chimichurri sauce on the side or drizzle it over the cut steak.

Serve with whole-grain quinoa or brown rice for added fiber and heart health.

Pair with grilled vegetables such as zucchini, bell peppers, or asparagus.

Balsamic Glazed Chicken Chops with Apples

Yield: 4 servings   **Preparation Time:** 10 minutes   **Cooking Time:** 20 minutes

Calories: 280 kcal | Carbohydrates: 18g | Total Fat: 10g | Saturated Fat: 2g | Cholesterol: 65mg | Protein: 26g | Sodium: 200mg
(per serving)

Ingredients:
- 4 boneless, skinless chicken breast chops (about 1 lb/450g)
- 1 tbsp (15 ml) olive oil
- ½ tsp (3g) salt (optional)
- ½ tsp (1g) black pepper
- 1 tsp (1g) dried rosemary or thyme
- ½ cup (120 ml) balsamic vinegar
- 1 tbsp (15 ml) honey or maple syrup as a natural sweetener
- 2 medium apples, cored and sliced thinly (Honeycrisp or Gala recommended)

Instructions:

Season chicken breast chops with salt (optional), black pepper, and rosemary or thyme on both sides.

Heat 1 tablespoon of olive oil in a large skillet over medium-high heat.

Place the seasoned chicken chops in the skillet. Cook until golden brown and thoroughly cooked, 4–5 minutes per side (internal temperature should reach 165°F/74°C). Remove the chicken from the pan and place it on a platter.

In the same skillet, add the balsamic vinegar and honey. Stir and let it simmer for about 2-3 minutes until it reduces slightly and thickens to a glaze.

Add the sliced apples to the skillet with the balsamic glaze, stirring to coat them. Sauté for about 3-4 minutes until tender but still slightly crisp.

Place the chicken back into the skillet with the apples and spoon the balsamic glaze over the chicken chops to coat them.

Transfer the chicken and apples to plates, drizzling any remaining glaze over the top.

Serve with steamed green beans or roasted Brussels sprouts for additional fiber and nutrients.

Stuffed Zucchini Boats with Ground Turkey and Quinoa

Yield: 4 servings   **Preparation Time:** 15 minutes   **Cooking Time:** 35 minutes

Calories: 180 kcal | Carbohydrates: 15g | Total Fat: 5g | Saturated Fat: 1g | Cholesterol: 30mg | Protein: 18g | Sodium: 140mg
(per serving)

Ingredients:

- 4 large zucchinis
- ½ lb (225g) ground turkey (93% lean)
- ½ cup (90g) cooked quinoa
- ½ cup (60g) onion, diced
- ½ cup (75g) bell pepper, diced (any color)
- 2 cloves garlic, minced
- 1 tsp (5 ml) olive oil
- ½ tsp (3g) salt (optional)
- ¼ tsp (0.5g) black pepper
- ½ tsp (1g) dried Italian herbs (oregano, basil, thyme)
- ¼ cup (60 ml) marinara sauce (low sodium)
- ¼ cup (50g) cherry tomatoes, halved
- 2 tbsp (8g) fresh parsley or basil, chopped (for garnish)

Instructions:

Preheat the oven to 375°F (190°C).

Split each zucchini in half lengthwise, then use a spoon to remove the flesh, leaving a thin border around the edges. Set the scooped-out zucchini flesh aside for later.

Arrange the zucchini boats, face up, on a baking sheet lined with parchment paper.

In a big skillet, heat olive oil over medium heat. Add the diced onion and bell pepper, and sauté for 3-4 minutes until softening. Add the garlic and cook for one more minute.

Cook the ground turkey in the skillet, breaking it up with a spoon, until it is no longer pink, which should take 5-7 minutes.

Stir in the cooked quinoa, reserved zucchini flesh, salt (if using), black pepper, Italian herbs, and marinara sauce. Mix well and cook for another 2-3 minutes.

Using a spoon, evenly fill each zucchini boat with the turkey and quinoa mixture. Top with cherry tomato halves.

After preheating the oven, put the baking sheet in and bake for 20 to 25 minutes, or until the filling is thoroughly heated and the zucchini is soft.

Take the stuffed zucchini out of the oven and top it with fresh basil or parsley.

Pair with a mixed green salad with a light vinaigrette for a complete meal.

Garnish with a tiny sprinkle of Parmesan cheese or additional fresh herbs if desired.

Savory Meatloaf with Oats and Vegetables

Yield: 6 servings   **Preparation Time:** 15 minutes   **Cooking Time:** 60 minutes

Calories: 180 kcal | Carbohydrates: 11g | Total Fat: 5g | Saturated Fat: 1g | Cholesterol: 30mg | Protein: 21g | Sodium: 180mg
(per serving)

Ingredients:

- 1 lb (450g) lean ground turkey (93% lean)
- ½ cup (40g) rolled oats (whole grain)
- ½ cup (60g) finely chopped onion
- ½ cup (60 ml) grated carrot
- ½ cup (75g) finely chopped bell pepper (any color)
- ¼ cup (30g) grated zucchini (optional for moisture)
- 1 clove garlic, minced
- 1 large egg white
- ¼ cup (60 ml) low-sodium tomato sauce or unsalted tomato puree
- 1 tbsp (15 ml) Worcestershire sauce (optional for flavor)
- 1 tsp (1g) Italian seasoning
- ¼ tsp (1.5g) salt (optional)
- ¼ tsp (0.5g) black pepper

Topping (optional)

- 2 tbsp (30 ml) low-sugar ketchup or tomato paste

Instructions:

Preheat the oven to 350°F (175°C). Lightly coat a loaf pan with cooking spray or parchment paper.

In a big mixing bowl, combine the ground turkey, oats, onion, bell pepper, carrot, zucchini, and garlic. Mix well.

Add egg white, tomato sauce, Worcestershire sauce (if using), Italian seasoning, salt (optional), and pepper. Mix everything together gently until just combined.

Transfer the mixture to the prepared loaf pan. Press the mixture evenly to make a smooth surface.

Spread the ketchup or tomato paste evenly over the meatloaf if desired.

After preheating the oven, bake the loaf pan for 50 to 60 minutes or until the internal temperature reaches 165°F (74°C).

Before slicing, let the meatloaf rest for 5 to 10 minutes to help it maintain its shape.

Serve with steamed green beans or roasted sweet.

This meatloaf also pairs well with a simple side salad or brown rice.

Beef and Vegetable Stir-Fry with Brown Rice

Yield: 4 servings   **Preparation Time:** 15 minutes   **Cooking Time:** 20 minutes

Calories: 390 kcal | Carbohydrates: 15g | Total Fat: 5g | Saturated Fat: 1g | Cholesterol: 50mg | Protein: 18g | Sodium: 140mg
(per serving)

Ingredients:
For the Stir-Fry
- 1 lb (450g) lean beef sirloin, thinly sliced
- 2 cups (180g) broccoli florets
- 1 red bell pepper, sliced
- 1 yellow bell pepper, sliced
- 1 medium zucchini, sliced
- 1 medium carrot, julienned
- ½ cup (60g) snap peas
- 1 tbsp (15 ml) olive oil or sesame oil
- 3 cloves garlic, minced
- 1-inch piece of fresh ginger (5g), minced
- 3 green onions, chopped (optional garnish)

For the Sauce
- 3 tbsp (45 ml) low-sodium soy sauce
- 1 tbsp (15 ml) rice vinegar
- 1 tbsp (15 ml) honey or maple syrup
- 1 tsp (4g) cornstarch mixed with 1 tbsp (15 ml) water (optional for thickening)

For the Brown Rice
- 1 cup (190g) brown rice, uncooked
- 2 cups (480 ml) water or low-sodium vegetable broth

Instructions:
In a saucepan, combine brown rice and water (or broth). Bring to a boil, lower the heat, cover, and simmer until the rice is tender, about 35 to 40 minutes. After cooking, use a fork to fluff and set aside.

In a small bowl, whisk together soy sauce, rice vinegar, and honey. To make a thicker sauce, mix in the cornstarch and water and set aside.

Heat ½ tbsp oil over medium-high heat in a large skillet or wok. Add garlic and ginger, stir-frying for about 30 seconds until fragrant.

Add broccoli, bell peppers, zucchini, carrot, and snap peas. After 5-7 minutes of stirring, the vegetables should be crisp-tender. Place the veggies on a platter and leave them there.

Add the remaining ½ tbsp oil to the same skillet and stir-fry the beef strips for 3-5 minutes until browned and cooked.

Return the vegetables to the skillet with the beef, pour the sauce over the mixture, and stir well to coat. Allow to cook for one to two minutes or until everything is thoroughly heated and the sauce slightly thickens.

Spoon the brown rice onto plates and top with the beef and vegetable stir-fry. Garnish with green onions if desired.

Grilled Chicken Sausages with Peppers

Yield: 4 servings   **Preparation Time:** 10 minutes   **Cooking Time:** 20 minutes

Calories: 240 kcal | Carbohydrates: 12g | Total Fat: 12g | Saturated Fat: 2g | Cholesterol: 60mg | Protein: 21g | Sodium: 450mg
(per serving)

Ingredients:
- 4 lean chicken sausages (400g), preferably low-sodium, low-fat
- 1 tbsp (15 ml) olive oil
- 1 red bell pepper, sliced
- 1 yellow bell pepper, sliced
- 1 green bell pepper, sliced
- 1 medium red onion, sliced
- 1 tsp (1g) dried Italian herbs (basil, oregano, thyme mix)
- ¼ tsp (0.5g) black pepper
- ¼ tsp (0.5g) garlic powder
- 1 tbsp (3g) fresh parsley, chopped (for garnish)
- Whole-grain mustard (optional for serving)

Instructions:
Preheat an outdoor grill to medium-high heat (or preheat an indoor grill pan if cooking indoors).

Place sliced peppers and onion in a large mixing bowl. Sprinkle with garlic powder, black pepper, and Italian herbs after drizzling with olive oil. Toss to coat evenly.

Place the chicken sausages on the preheated grill and cook for 10-12 minutes, turning occasionally, until they are browned and cooked through. Remove from grill and keep warm.

While the sausages are cooking, place the pepper and onion mixture in a grilling basket or directly on the grill (use a grill mat if necessary). Grill for about 8-10 minutes, stirring occasionally, until the vegetables are slightly charred and tender.

Arrange the grilled sausages on a platter, topped with the grilled peppers and onions. If preferred, serve with a side of whole-grain mustard and garnish with chopped parsley.

Enjoy this dish with a side of mixed greens dressed in balsamic vinegar or a whole-grain roll for a satisfying, heart-healthy meal.

Herb-Roasted Turkey Breast with Cranberry Relish

Yield: 6 servings | **Preparation Time:** 15 minutes | **Cooking Time:** 60 minutes

Calories: 180 kcal | Carbohydrates: 15g | Total Fat: 5g | Saturated Fat: 1g | Cholesterol: 30mg | Protein: 18g | Sodium: 140mg
(per serving)

Ingredients:

Turkey Breast
- 2 lb (900g) boneless, skinless turkey breast
- 1 tbsp (15 ml) olive oil
- 1 tsp (3g) garlic powder
- 1 tsp (1g) dried rosemary
- 1 tsp (1g) dried thyme
- ½ tsp (1g) black pepper
- ½ tsp (3g) salt

Cranberry Relish
- 1 cup (100g) fresh cranberries
- 1 medium orange, peeled and segmented
- 1 tbsp (15 ml) maple syrup or honey
- ¼ tsp (0.5g) cinnamon
- 1 tbsp (3g) fresh mint, finely chopped (optional for garnish)

Instructions:

Preheat the oven to 375°F (190°C).

In a small bowl, mix olive oil, garlic powder, rosemary, thyme, black pepper, and salt to create an herb rub.

Line a baking sheet with parchment paper and place the turkey breast on it. Rub the herb mixture evenly over the turkey breast, covering all sides.

The turkey breast should be cooked for 45 to 60 minutes or until the internal temperature reaches 165°F (74°C). Remove from oven and let it rest for 10 minutes before slicing.

Make the cranberry relish while the turkey roasts. Add fresh cranberries, orange segments, maple syrup, and cinnamon to a food processor. Pulse until roughly chopped, creating a slightly chunky consistency.

Move to a bowl, keep it covered, and chill it until it is time to serve. Garnish with fresh mint if desired.

Slice the turkey breast and serve with a spoonful of cranberry relish on top or on the side. If desired, garnish with extra rosemary or thyme.

Beef Tacos with Fresh Salsa and Avocado

Yield: 4 servings | **Preparation Time:** 20 minutes | **Cooking Time:** 10 minutes

Calories: 270 kcal | Carbohydrates: 26g | Total Fat: 11g | Saturated Fat: 2g | Cholesterol: 40mg | Protein: 17g | Sodium: 210mg
(per serving)

Ingredients:

For the Tacos:
- ½ lb (225g) lean ground beef (90% lean or higher)
- ¼ cup (50g) onion, finely chopped
- 1 clove garlic, minced
- ¼ tsp (0.5g) ground cumin
- ¼ tsp (0.5g) smoked paprika
- Salt and pepper, to taste
- 8 small whole wheat tortillas

For the Fresh Salsa:
- 1 cup (150g) cherry tomatoes, diced
- ¼ cup (50g) red onion, finely chopped
- ¼ cup (8g) cilantro, chopped
- Juice of 1 lime
- Salt and pepper, to taste

For Garnish:
- 1 medium avocado, sliced
- Fresh lime wedges (optional)
- Fresh chopped cilantro (optional)

Instructions:

Mix the diced tomatoes, red onion, cilantro, lime juice, salt, and pepper in a medium bowl.

Stir well and set aside to let the flavors meld.

Cook the ground beef in a nonstick skillet over medium heat for 5 to 7 minutes or until browned. Drain any excess fat.

Add onion, garlic, cumin, smoked paprika, salt, and pepper. Stir well and cook until onions are softened, about 3-4 minutes. Remove from heat.

Warm the whole wheat tortillas in a pan or microwave until pliable.

Evenly distribute the beef mixture over each tortilla.

Top each taco with a spoonful of fresh salsa and a few slices of avocado, and garnish with lime wedges or extra cilantro if desired.

Serve right now, along with mixed greens or another vegetable of your choosing.

Vegetable Recipes

Roasted Brussels Sprouts with Balsamic Glaze

Yield: 4 servings | **Preparation Time:** 10 minutes | **Cooking Time:** 25 minutes

Calories: 90 kcal | Carbohydrates: 10g | Total Fat: 4g | Saturated Fat: 0.5g | Cholesterol: 0mg | Protein: 3g | Sodium: 35mg (per serving)

Ingredients:

- 1 lb (450 g) Brussels sprouts, trimmed and halved
- 1 tbsp (15 ml) extra-virgin olive oil
- Salt and pepper, to taste
- 2 tbsp (30 ml) balsamic vinegar
- 1 tsp (5 ml) honey (optional for added sweetness)

Optional Garnishes:

- 1 tbsp (10g) toasted almonds or walnuts, chopped
- Fresh parsley, chopped

Instructions:

Set the oven's temperature to 400°F (200°C).

Rinse and trim the Brussels sprouts, cutting each one in half.

Place the Brussels sprouts on a baking sheet. Season with salt, pepper, and olive oil. Toss to coat evenly.

Arrange the Brussels sprouts in a uniform layer on the baking sheet, leaving room between them to ensure even roasting.

Roast in the preheated oven for 20-25 minutes, or until they are golden brown and tender, turning them halfway through for even cooking.

Put the honey and balsamic vinegar in a small saucepan over medium heat while the Brussels sprouts roast.

Let it simmer for 3-5 minutes until it reduces by half and becomes a thicker glaze. Remove from heat and set aside.

After removing the Brussels sprouts from the oven, cover them with the balsamic glaze.

Gently toss to coat, then move to a platter for serving.

Garnish with optional toasted nuts and fresh parsley if desired.

Serve these Brussels sprouts as a filling side dish or with lean protein like grilled fish or chicken.

Grilled Vegetable Platter with Pesto

Yield: 4 servings | **Preparation Time:** 15 minutes | **Cooking Time:** 15 minutes

Calories: 180 kcal | Carbohydrates: 8g | Total Fat: 16g | Saturated Fat: 2g | Cholesterol: 0mg | Protein: 3g | Sodium: 50mg (per serving)

Ingredients:

Grilled Vegetables:

- 1 medium zucchini, sliced into rounds
- 1 medium yellow squash, sliced into rounds
- 1 red bell pepper, sliced into strips
- 1 yellow bell pepper, sliced into strips
- 1 small eggplant, sliced into rounds
- 8 oz (225g) asparagus, trimmed
- 1 tbsp (15 ml) extra-virgin olive oil
- Salt and black pepper, to taste

Pesto Sauce:

- 1 cup (30g) fresh basil leaves
- 2 tbsp (15g) walnuts or almonds, lightly toasted
- 1 clove garlic, minced
- 1 tbsp (15 ml) fresh lemon juice
- ¼ cup (60 ml) extra-virgin olive oil
- Salt and black pepper, to taste

Optional Garnishes:

- Fresh cherry tomatoes, halved
- Sprinkling of pine nuts or walnuts
- Fresh basil leaves

Instructions:

Preheat your grill to medium-high heat.

Place the sliced zucchini, yellow squash, bell peppers, eggplant, and asparagus in a large bowl. Season with salt and black pepper and drizzle with one tablespoon of olive oil. Toss to coat evenly.

Place the vegetables on the grill and cook each side for 3-5 minutes or until tender with excellent grill marks. Remove from the grill and set aside on a platter.

Combine the basil leaves, walnuts or almonds, garlic, and lemon juice in a food processor or blender. Pulse until finely chopped.

Add the olive oil gradually while blending until the pesto is smooth. Add black pepper and salt to taste.

Place the grilled veggies on a sizable platter for serving.

Drizzle the pesto sauce over the vegetables or serve on the side as a dip.

Garnish with halved cherry tomatoes, additional nuts, or fresh basil leaves if desired.

Serve this platter as a main dish with a side of whole-grain bread or brown rice, or enjoy it as a colorful appetizer.

Cauliflower Steaks with Chimichurri Sauce

Yield: 4 servings	Preparation Time: 10 minutes	Cooking Time: 15 minutes

Calories: 180 kcal | Carbohydrates: 15g | Total Fat: 5g | Saturated Fat: 1g | Cholesterol: 30mg | Protein: 18g | Sodium: 140mg
(per serving)

Ingredients:

Cauliflower Steaks:

- 1 large head of cauliflower
- 2 tbsp (30 ml) olive oil
- Salt and black pepper, to taste
- ½ tsp (1g) smoked paprika (optional for added flavor)

Chimichurri Sauce:

- 1 cup (30g) fresh parsley, chopped
- ½ cup (15g) fresh cilantro, chopped
- 2 cloves garlic, minced
- ¼ cup (60 ml) olive oil
- 2 tbsp (30 ml) red wine vinegar
- 1 tbsp (15 ml) fresh lemon juice
- ¼ tsp (0.5g) red pepper flakes (optional)
- Salt and black pepper, to taste

Optional Garnishes:

- Lemon wedges
- Fresh parsley leaves

Instructions:

Preheat the oven to 400°F (200°C), and line a baking sheet with parchment paper.

Trim the cauliflower's stem, keeping the center whole, and remove the outer leaves.

Cut the cauliflower into 1-inch thick slices. A large cauliflower should yield about 4 "steaks."

Place the cauliflower steaks on the prepared baking sheet, brush with olive oil, and season with salt, black pepper, and smoked paprika (if using).

Bake the cauliflower for 20 minutes in a preheated oven, turning it halfway through until it is soft and golden brown.

While the cauliflower is roasting, combine the chopped parsley, red pepper flakes, cilantro, lemon juice, minced garlic, olive oil, red wine vinegar, salt, and black pepper in a bowl.

Stir well and adjust the seasoning to taste. Set aside.

After taking the cauliflower steaks out of the oven, arrange them on a platter for serving.

Drizzle each steak with chimichurri sauce and garnish with lemon wedges or fresh parsley, if desired.

For a full meal, serve these cauliflower steaks as a main course with quinoa, brown rice, or a crisp green salad.

You can also serve them as a hearty vegetable side to complement other heart-healthy dishes.

Sautéed Greens with Garlic and Olive Oil

Yield: 4 servings	Preparation Time: 5 minutes	Cooking Time: 10 minutes

Calories: 60 kcal | Carbohydrates: 5g | Total Fat: 4.5g | Saturated Fat: 0.5g | Cholesterol: 0mg | Protein: 2g | Sodium: 150mg
(per serving)

Ingredients:

- 1 tbsp (15 ml) extra-virgin olive oil
- 2 cloves garlic, thinly sliced
- 6 cups (180g) mixed greens (e.g., spinach, kale, Swiss chard)
- ¼ tsp (1.5g) salt
- ¼ tsp (0.5g) black pepper
- 1 tbsp (15 ml) lemon juice

Optional garnishes:

- Red pepper flakes for heat
- Freshly grated lemon zest
- Toasted sesame seeds

Instructions:

Rinse the greens thoroughly and pat them dry with paper towels or a salad spinner. Chop the leaves coarsely and remove the stems. Set aside.

In a big skillet, heat the olive oil over medium heat. Add the sliced garlic and cook for 1-2 minutes or until golden. Keep in mind that burning the garlic will turn it bitter.

Add the mixed greens and garlic to the skillet. Toss frequently for 4–5 minutes or until the greens are just wilted and tender.

Season the greens with salt, pepper, and lemon juice. Toss everything together for another 1–2 minutes to blend the flavors.

Transfer the sautéed greens to a serving platter. Add optional garnishes, if desired, and enjoy while warm.

Serve alongside lean proteins like grilled chicken or fish, or incorporate them into grain bowls with quinoa or brown rice.

Spicy Roasted Carrots with Honey and Cumin

Yield: 4 servings **Preparation Time:** 10 minutes **Cooking Time:** 30 minutes

Calories: 90 kcal | Carbohydrates: 12g | Total Fat: 3.5g | Saturated Fat: 0g | Cholesterol: 0mg | Protein: 1g | Sodium: 150mg
(per serving)

Ingredients:

- 1 lb (450g) carrots
- 1 tbsp (15 ml) extra-virgin olive oil
- 1 tbsp (15 ml) honey or maple syrup
- 1 tsp (2g) ground cumin
- ½ tsp (1g) smoked paprika
- ¼ tsp (0.5g) cayenne pepper
- ¼ tsp (1.5g) salt
- ¼ tsp (0.5g) black pepper

Optional Garnishes:

- 1 tbsp (4g) fresh parsley or cilantro, chopped

Instructions:

Preheat the oven to 400°F (200°C). Line a baking sheet with parchment paper or oil it a little to prevent it from sticking.

In a big mixing bowl, combine olive oil, honey, cumin, smoked paprika, cayenne pepper, salt, and black pepper. Whisk until well blended.

Cut carrots into sticks or rounds after peeling.

Add the carrots to the bowl and toss to coat them evenly in the spice mixture.

Arrange the carrots on the prepared baking sheet in a single layer. After 25 to 30 minutes of roasting in a preheated oven, carrots should be soft and caramelized; turn them halfway through to ensure even roasting.

After taking the carrots out of the oven, move them to a platter. Sprinkle with chopped parsley or cilantro for added color and freshness.

Serve these spicy roasted carrots alongside a lean protein, such as grilled fish or chicken. This dish also makes a fantastic side for holiday meals.

Creamy Pumpkin and Cauliflower Mash

Yield: 4 servings **Preparation Time:** 10 minutes **Cooking Time:** 20 minutes

Calories: 90 kcal | Carbohydrates: 12g | Total Fat: 3g | Saturated Fat: 0g | Cholesterol: 0mg | Protein: 2g | Sodium: 20mg
(per serving)

Ingredients:

- 2 cups (240g) pumpkin peeled and diced
- 2 cups (180g) cauliflower florets
- ¼ cup (60 ml) unsweetened almond milk
- 1 tbsp (15 ml) olive oil
- ½ tsp (1.5g) garlic powder
- ¼ tsp (0.5g) nutmeg (optional, for warmth and depth of flavor)
- Salt and pepper to taste

Optional garnishes:

- Fresh chives, chopped
- A sprinkle of smoked paprika
- Toasted pumpkin seeds for crunch

Instructions:

Place the diced pumpkin and cauliflower florets in a steamer basket over boiling water. Cover and steam for 15-20 minutes until both vegetables are tender and easily pierced with a fork.

Transfer the steamed pumpkin and cauliflower to a large mixing bowl. Blend until smooth using a potato masher or immersion blender.

Stir in the almond milk, olive oil, garlic powder, nutmeg, salt, and pepper. Blend until creamy and well combined, adding more almond milk if needed for a smoother consistency.

Taste and adjust seasonings, adding more salt, pepper, or garlic powder as desired.

Spoon the mash into a serving bowl and garnish with chopped chives, a sprinkle of smoked paprika, or toasted pumpkin seeds for added texture and flavor.

Stuffed Acorn Squash with Wild Rice and Nuts

Yield: 4 servings	Preparation Time: 15 minutes	Cooking Time: 50 minutes

Calories: 280 kcal | Carbohydrates: 40g | Total Fat: 12g | Saturated Fat: 1g | Cholesterol: 0mg | Protein: 5g | Sodium: 100mg
(per serving)

Ingredients:

- 2 medium acorn squashes
- 1 tbsp (15 ml) olive oil
- Salt and black pepper to taste
- 1 cup (190g) cooked wild rice
- ½ cup (80g) finely chopped onions
- ½ cup (50g) diced celery
- ½ cup (75g) diced apple (e.g., Granny Smith or Honeycrisp)
- ¼ cup (40g) dried cranberries
- ¼ cup (30g) chopped walnuts or pecans
- 1 tsp (1g) dried thyme
- 1 tsp (1g) dried sage
- ¼ tsp (0.5g) ground cinnamon
- ¼ cup (60 ml) vegetable broth or water

Optional Garnishes:

- Fresh parsley or thyme for garnish
- A sprinkle of pomegranate seeds for color and flavor

Instructions:

Preheat the oven to 400°F (200°C). Halve acorn squash and remove seeds. Place the acorn squash halves, cut side up, on a baking sheet. Drizzle with olive oil, and season with salt and black pepper. Roast until the squash is tender and has a hint of caramel on the edges, 30-35 minutes.

Add a small amount of olive oil to a medium skillet over medium heat. Sauté the onions and celery until softened, about 5 minutes. Add the diced apple, dried cranberries, walnuts or pecans, thyme, sage, and cinnamon. Sauté for an additional 3-4 minutes until fragrant.

Pour the cooked wild rice into the skillet and mix everything together. Add the vegetable broth or water and stir. Cook the mixture for 2-3 minutes to let the flavors combine. Add black pepper and salt to taste.

Once the squash halves are tender, remove them from the oven. Divide the wild rice mixture evenly among the four squash halves, spooning it into the hollowed centers.

Put the stuffed squash back in the oven and bake it for 10-15 minutes, or until the filling is hot and the flavors have blended together.

Garnish with fresh parsley or thyme and optional pomegranate seeds for a festive touch. Serve warm.

Pair with a green salad or roasted vegetables for a balanced meal.

Creamy Spinach and Artichoke Dip

Yield: 6 servings	Preparation Time: 10 minutes	Cooking Time: 20 minutes

Calories: 140 kcal | Carbohydrates: 14g | Total Fat: 9g | Saturated Fat: 0g | Cholesterol: 0mg | Protein: 2g | Sodium: 120mg
(per serving)

Ingredients:

- 1 tbsp (15 ml) olive oil
- 1 small onion, finely chopped
- 2 cloves garlic, minced
- 1 (14-ounce/400g) can artichoke hearts, drained and chopped
- 5 ounces (140g) fresh spinach, chopped (or 1 cup (150g) frozen, thawed and drained)
- ½ cup (120 ml) Greek yogurt
- ½ cup (120g) low-fat cottage cheese
- ¼ cup (25g) grated Parmesan cheese
- ¼ cup (30g) part-skim mozzarella cheese, shredded
- ¼ tsp (1.5g) salt
- ¼ tsp (0.5g) black pepper
- ¼ tsp (0.5g) red pepper flakes (optional, for a slight kick)

Optional garnishes:

- Chopped fresh parsley
- Extra sprinkle of Parmesan

Instructions:

Preheat the oven to 375°F (190°C).

Heat a medium skillet over medium heat and add the olive oil. Add the garlic and onions and cook for approximately three minutes, or until the onions are transparent and soft.

Add the chopped spinach and artichokes to the skillet. Cook until everything is well combined and the spinach has wilted, about 3 to 5 minutes. Remove from heat.

Blend the Greek yogurt and cottage cheese in a blender or food processor until smooth. Pour this mixture into a mixing bowl.

Add the cooked spinach and artichoke mixture, Parmesan, and mozzarella to the bowl with the yogurt mixture. Season with salt, black pepper, and, if using, red pepper flakes. Stir to combine.

Spoon the dip mixture into a small baking dish and spread it evenly.

Bake for 15-20 minutes or until the dip is hot and bubbly and has a slightly golden top.

If desired, top with additional Parmesan and fresh parsley. Serve warm.

This dip makes a heart-healthy snack or appetizer when served with whole-grain crackers, fresh vegetable sticks (like celery, cucumber, and bell pepper), or whole-grain pita wedges.

Vegetable Medley Stir-Fry with Soy Sauce

Yield: 4 servings   **Preparation Time:** 10 minutes   **Cooking Time:** 15 minutes

Calories: 95 kcal | Carbohydrates: 12g | Total Fat: 4g | Saturated Fat: 0g | Cholesterol: 0mg | Protein: 3g | Sodium: 200mg
(per serving)

Ingredients:
- 1 tbsp (15 ml) olive oil or avocado oil
- 1 small onion, sliced
- 2 cloves garlic, minced
- 1 cup (90g) broccoli florets
- 1 red bell pepper, sliced
- 1 yellow bell pepper, sliced
- 1 medium zucchini, sliced
- 1 medium carrot, thinly sliced
- 1 cup snap peas
- ¼ cup (60 ml) low-sodium soy sauce
- 1 tbsp (15 ml) rice vinegar
- 1 tsp (5 ml) sesame oil (optional for flavor)
- ¼ tsp (0.5g) black pepper
- ¼ tsp (0.5g) red pepper flakes

Optional Garnishes:
- Sesame seeds
- Sliced green onions
- Fresh cilantro or parsley

Instructions:

Whisk together the low-sodium soy sauce, rice vinegar, sesame oil (if using), and black pepper. Put aside.

In a big skillet or wok, heat olive oil over medium-high heat.

After adding the onion and garlic, cook for 1-2 minutes or until fragrant and just beginning to soften.

Add the broccoli, carrots, and snap peas to the skillet. Stir-fry until they begin to soften, about 3 minutes.

Add the bell peppers and zucchini. Continue to stir-fry for an additional 4-5 minutes until all vegetables are tender-crisp.

Pour the prepared sauce over the vegetables, stirring to coat them evenly. Allow the sauce to heat through and slightly reduce by cooking it for 1-2 minutes.

If you like spicy food, sprinkle it with red pepper flakes. Transfer to a serving dish and garnish with sesame seeds, sliced green onions, or fresh herbs if desired.

Serve this stir-fry over brown rice, quinoa, or alongside whole-grain noodles for added fiber and nutrients. This dish can also be paired with a lean protein like grilled chicken or tofu.

Roasted Sweet Potatoes with Cinnamon

Yield: 4 servings   **Preparation Time:** 10 minutes   **Cooking Time:** 35 minutes

Calories: 120 kcal | Carbohydrates: 18g | Total Fat: 4g | Saturated Fat: 0g | Cholesterol: 0mg | Protein: 3g | Sodium: 300mg
(per serving)

Ingredients:
- 2 large sweet potatoes (about 1 lb)
- 1 tbsp (15 ml) olive oil or avocado oil
- 1 tsp (2g) ground cinnamon
- ¼ tsp (0.5g) ground nutmeg (optional for extra warmth)
- ¼ tsp (1.5g) salt (optional)
- ¼ tsp (0.5g) black pepper

Optional garnishes:
- Fresh thyme or rosemary sprigs
- Toasted pecans or walnuts (for crunch)

Instructions:

Line a baking sheet with parchment paper and heat the oven to 400°F (200°C).

In a mixing bowl, combine the peeled and cubed sweet potatoes with olive oil, ground cinnamon, nutmeg (if using), salt, and black pepper. Toss the sweet potatoes evenly to coat them.

Arrange the seasoned sweet potatoes on the prepared baking sheet in a single layer to guarantee even roasting.

After preheating the oven, put the baking sheet in and roast the sweet potatoes for 30 to 35 minutes, turning them halfway through, until they are soft and have a hint of caramel on the edges.

Remove from the oven and transfer to a serving dish. Garnish with toasted nuts or fresh herbs for more taste and texture.

Grilled Corn Salad with Cilantro and Lime

Yield: 4 servings	Preparation Time: 10 minutes	Cooking Time: 15 minutes

Calories: 120 kcal | Carbohydrates: 18g | Total Fat: 4g | Saturated Fat: 0g | Cholesterol: 0mg | Protein: 3g | Sodium: 40mg
(per serving)

Ingredients:
- 4 ears of corn, husked
- 1 tbsp (15 ml) olive oil
- ¼ cup (8g) fresh cilantro, chopped
- ½ cup (80g) cherry tomatoes, halved
- ¼ cup (50g) red onion, finely diced
- ½ red bell pepper, diced
- Juice of 1 lime
- Zest of 1 lime
- Salt and pepper to taste

Optional Garnishes:
- ¼ cup (30g) crumbled feta cheese (optional)
- 1 avocado, diced (for extra creaminess)
- Additional lime wedges for serving

Instructions:

Set your grill temperature to medium-high. To keep corn from sticking, lightly coat each ear with olive oil.

Place the corn on the grill, turning every few minutes until it's slightly charred on all sides (about 10-15 minutes total). Once grilled, remove from heat and allow to cool for a few minutes.

To remove the kernels from each corn ear, hold it upright on a cutting board and carefully cut down along the sides. Then, put the kernels in a big bowl and mix them.

Add the cherry tomatoes, red onion, red bell pepper, cilantro, lime juice, and lime zest to the bowl with the corn. Toss until all ingredients are combined.

Add salt and pepper to taste. If desired, add crumbled feta or diced avocado for extra flavor and texture.

Move to a platter and, if you would like, top with additional cilantro or lime wedges.

This refreshing grilled corn salad is an excellent side dish for lean proteins like grilled chicken or fish. It also works well as a topping for tacos or alongside whole-grain options like quinoa or brown rice to create a balanced, heart-healthy meal.

Curried Cauliflower and Chickpeas

Yield: 4 servings	Preparation Time: 10 minutes	Cooking Time: 25 minutes

Calories: 180 kcal | Carbohydrates: 26g | Total Fat: 5g | Saturated Fat: 0g | Cholesterol: 0mg | Protein: 6g | Sodium: 190mg
(per serving)

Ingredients:
- 1 medium head of cauliflower, cut into florets
- 1 can (15 oz/425g) chickpeas, drained and rinsed
- 1 tbsp (15 ml) olive oil
- 1 medium onion, chopped
- 2 cloves garlic, minced
- 1 tbsp (6g) fresh ginger, minced
- 1 tbsp (6g) curry powder
- ½ tsp (1g) ground turmeric
- ½ tsp (1g) ground cumin
- ½ tsp (1g) ground coriander
- ¼ tsp (0.5g) red chili flakes
- 1 can (14 oz/400g) diced tomatoes
- ½ cup (120 ml) low-sodium vegetable broth
- Salt and pepper to taste

Optional garnishes:
- Fresh cilantro, chopped (for garnish)
- 1 tbsp (5g) unsweetened coconut flakes

Instructions:

Rinse and cut the cauliflower into florets. Drain and rinse the chickpeas.

In a big pan or skillet, heat the olive oil over medium heat. Add the onion and sauté for 3-4 minutes until softened. Add the ginger and garlic for one more minute or until fragrant.

Add the turmeric, cumin, coriander, curry powder, and optional red chili flakes and stir. Sauté for 1-2 minutes to toast the spices and release their flavor.

Coat the chickpeas and cauliflower florets with the spice mixture by adding them to the pan and stirring thoroughly.

Add the vegetable broth and diced tomatoes and stir to mix. Bring the mixture to a simmer.

Cover the pan and let the mixture simmer for 15-20 minutes or until the cauliflower is tender. If the curry gets too thick, add more broth and stir occasionally.

Season to taste with salt and pepper.

For added flavor, top with optional coconut flakes and fresh cilantro after transferring to a serving bowl.

Add a side of steamed spinach or a fresh green salad to complete the dish.

Holiday Recipes

Holiday Vegetable Platter with Dips

Yield: 8 servings	**Preparation Time:** 20 minutes	**Cooking Time:** None

Calories: 100 kcal | Carbohydrates: 16g | Total Fat: 3g | Saturated Fat: 0.5g | Cholesterol: 0mg | Protein: 5g | Sodium: 150mg
(per serving)

Ingredients:

- 1 cup (130g) baby carrots
- 1 cup (100g) cucumber slices
- 1 cup (150g) cherry tomatoes
- 1 cup (90g) red bell pepper strips
- 1 cup (90g) broccoli florets
- 1 cup (90g) cauliflower florets
- 1 cup (100g) celery sticks
- 1 cup (120g) radishes, halve

For the Creamy Herb Dip:

- 1 cup (240 ml) Greek yogurt (non-fat)
- 1 tbsp (2g) fresh dill, finely chopped
- 1 tbsp (2g) fresh chives, finely chopped
- 1 tbsp (4g) fresh parsley, finely chopped
- 1 tsp (3g) garlic powder
- 1 tbsp (15 ml) lemon juice
- Salt and pepper to taste

For the Roasted Red Pepper Hummus:

- 1 cup (160g) canned chickpeas
- ¼ cup (40g) roasted red bell pepper
- 1 tbsp (15g) tahini
- 1 tbsp (15 ml) lemon juice
- 1 garlic clove, minced
- 1 tbsp (15 ml) extra-virgin olive oil
- Salt and pepper to taste

Instructions:

Arrange all prepared vegetables (carrots, cucumber slices, cherry tomatoes, red bell pepper strips, broccoli, cauliflower, celery, and radishes) on a large platter. You can arrange them in sections or in a festive shape, such as a wreath.

Prepare the Creamy Herb Dip: In a small bowl, combine Greek yogurt, dill, chives, parsley, garlic powder, and lemon juice. Mix thoroughly, then add salt and pepper to taste. Put aside after transferring to a serving bowl.

Prepare the Roasted Red Pepper Hummus: In a food processor, combine chickpeas, roasted red pepper, tahini, lemon juice, garlic, and olive oil. Process until smooth, adding a splash of water to achieve a creamy consistency. After adding salt and pepper to taste, move the mixture to a serving bowl.

Place the prepared dips in small bowls on the platter alongside the vegetables.

If desired, add fresh herb sprigs to the platter as a garnish.

This holiday vegetable platter with herb and hummus dips is a great gathering appetizer. As an optional addition, serve with whole-grain crackers or pita chips. Arrange the vegetables in a creative, colorful pattern to add festive cheer.

Herb-Roasted Turkey Breast with Citrus Glaze

Yield: 6 servings	**Preparation Time:** 15 minutes	**Cooking Time:** 60 minutes

Calories: 220 kcal | Carbohydrates: 7g | Total Fat: 9g | Saturated Fat: 2g | Cholesterol: 60mg | Protein: 28g | Sodium: 180mg
(per serving)

Ingredients:

For the Turkey Breast:

- 2 pounds (900 g) boneless, skinless turkey breast
- 2 tbsp (30 ml) extra-virgin olive oil
- 2 tbsp (3g) fresh rosemary, chopped
- 2 tbsp (3g) fresh thyme, chopped
- 1 tbsp (2g) fresh sage, chopped
- 1 tsp (3g) garlic powder
- Salt and pepper to taste

For the Citrus Glaze:

- Zest and juice of 1 orange
- 2 tbsp (30 ml) honey or agave syrup
- 1 tbsp (15 ml) Dijon mustard
- 1 tbsp (15 ml) apple cider vinegar
- Fresh rosemary sprigs
- Orange slices

Instructions:

Preheat your oven to 350°F (175°C). Line a baking sheet with parchment paper and place the turkey breast on it. Rub the turkey with olive oil, then season with rosemary, thyme, sage, garlic powder, salt, and pepper. Massage the herbs and seasoning evenly over the turkey breast.

Combine the orange zest, orange juice, lemon zest, lemon juice, honey (or agave), Dijon mustard, and apple cider vinegar in a small bowl. Whisk until well mixed.

After preheating the oven, roast the turkey breast for 40 minutes. Remove from the oven, brush with the prepared citrus glaze, and return to the oven for 20-30 minutes or until the internal temperature reaches 165°F (74°C). Brush with additional glaze every 10 minutes for a beautiful, flavorful crust. After taking the turkey breast out of the oven, give it 10 minutes to rest before slicing.

If desired, add orange slices and fresh rosemary sprigs as garnish.

Serve this herb-roasted turkey with roasted Brussels sprouts, steamed green beans, or a mixed greens salad with a simple vinaigrette for a nutrient-rich, heart-healthy meal.

Pomegranate Glazed Salmon with Quinoa

Yield: 4 servings   **Preparation Time:** 15 minutes   **Cooking Time:** 25 minutes

Calories: 360 kcal | Carbohydrates: 38g | Total Fat: 10g | Saturated Fat: 2g | Cholesterol: 60mg | Protein: 30g | Sodium: 150mg
(per serving)

Ingredients:

For the Salmon:
- 4 (4-ounce/450g) salmon fillets, skin removed
- Salt and pepper to taste
- 1 tbsp (15 ml) extra-virgin olive oil

For the Pomegranate Glaze:
- ½ cup (120g) pomegranate juice (100% juice, unsweetened)
- 2 tbsp (30 ml) balsamic vinegar
- 1 tbsp (15 ml) honey or maple syrup
- 1 tsp (5 ml) Dijon mustard
- ¼ tsp (0.5g) ground black pepper

For the Quinoa:
- 1 cup (170g) quinoa, rinsed
- 2 cups (240g) low-sodium vegetable or chicken broth
- ¼ cup (8g) fresh parsley, chopped
- ¼ cup (40g) pomegranate arils (seeds) for garnish

Instructions:

Combine pomegranate juice, balsamic vinegar, honey (or maple syrup), Dijon mustard, and black pepper in a small saucepan.

Bring to a boil over medium heat, then reduce heat to a simmer and cook for about 10-15 minutes or until the mixture thickens to a glaze consistency. Set aside.

Put the broth and quinoa in a medium saucepan. After bringing it to a boil, lower the heat to a simmer, cover, and cook for 15 minutes, or until the quinoa is cooked and the liquid has been absorbed.

Take off the heat, use a fork to fluff it up, and then add the fresh parsley.

Add olive oil to a skillet and heat it over medium-high heat.

Sprinkle the salmon fillets with a little salt and pepper.

Place the salmon in the skillet and cook it for 3–4 minutes on each side or until it is cooked through and has a slightly crispy exterior.

Brush the salmon generously with the pomegranate glaze during the last minute of cooking, allowing it to caramelize.

Plate the quinoa, top with a salmon fillet, and drizzle any remaining pomegranate glaze over the salmon.

Add pomegranate arils and some fresh parsley as garnish.

Maple Glazed Roasted Pumpkin Wedges

Yield: 4 servings   **Preparation Time:** 10 minutes   **Cooking Time:** 25 minutes

Calories: 100 kcal | Carbohydrates: 16g | Total Fat: 4g | Saturated Fat: 0g | Cholesterol: 0mg | Protein: 1g | Sodium: 20mg
(per serving)

Ingredients:
- 1 small pumpkin (about 2 lbs/900g), cut into wedges
- 2 tbsp (30 ml) pure maple syrup
- 1 tbsp (15 ml) olive oil
- ½ tsp (1g) ground cinnamon
- ¼ tsp (0.5g) nutmeg
- Salt and pepper to taste

Optional Garnishes
- Fresh thyme or rosemary sprigs
- Pomegranate seeds for a pop of color
- Chopped pecans or walnuts for crunch

Instructions:

Preheat your oven to 400°F (200°C). Line a baking sheet with parchment paper.

Wash and slice the pumpkin into 1-inch thick wedges, removing any seeds and stringy bits.

Whisk together the maple syrup, olive oil, cinnamon, nutmeg, salt, and pepper.

In a large mixing bowl, pour the maple glaze over the pumpkin wedges, tossing to coat each wedge well.

Arrange the glazed pumpkin wedges on the prepared baking sheet in a single layer. Roast in the preheated oven for 20-25 minutes, flipping halfway through, until the pumpkin is tender and caramelized at the edges.

Move to a serving dish, and garnish with fresh thyme, pomegranate seeds, or nuts if desired. Serve warm.

Grilled Peach Salad with Arugula and Feta

Yield: 4 servings	**Preparation Time:** 10 minutes	**Cooking Time:** 5 minutes

Calories: 220 kcal | Carbohydrates: 18g | Total Fat: 14g | Saturated Fat: 2g | Cholesterol: 15mg | Protein: 5g | Sodium: 170mg
(per serving)

Ingredients:
- 4 fresh peaches, halved and pitted
- 4 cups (120g) arugula
- ½ cup (60g) crumbled feta cheese (low-fat if available)
- ¼ cup (40g) red onion, thinly sliced
- ¼ cup (30g) chopped pecans or walnuts

Dressing:
- 2 tbsp (30 ml) extra-virgin olive oil
- 1 tbsp (15 ml) balsamic vinegar
- 1 tsp (5 ml) honey or maple syrup
- 1 tsp (5 ml) Dijon mustard
- Salt and black pepper to taste

Optional Garnishes:
- Fresh basil or mint leaves
- Additional drizzle of balsamic glaze

Instructions:

Set your grill temperature to medium-high. To prevent the peach halves from sticking, lightly coat them with olive oil.

Put the peaches on the grill, cut side down, and cook for two to three minutes or until grill marks start to show. Flip and grill the other side for 1-2 minutes until slightly softened. Remove the peaches from the grill and let cool slightly before slicing each half into wedges.

Whisk together olive oil, balsamic vinegar, honey, Dijon mustard, salt, and black pepper until well combined.

In a large salad bowl, combine arugula, grilled peach slices, red onion, and crumbled feta. If using, sprinkle with chopped pecans or walnuts.

Drizzle the dressing over the salad and gently toss to combine, ensuring an even coating.

Plate the salad in individual servings and garnish with fresh basil or mint, if desired. For extra flavor, add a final drizzle of balsamic glaze.

Low-Fat Chocolate Hazelnut Tart

Yield: 8 servings	**Preparation Time:** 15 minutes	**Cooking Time:** 2 hours

Calories: 190 kcal | Carbohydrates: 18g | Total Fat: 11g | Saturated Fat: 1g | Cholesterol: 0mg | Protein: 5g | Sodium: 60mg
(per serving)

Ingredients:
Crust:
- 1 cup (90g) oat flour (or ground oats)
- ¼ cup (30g) almond flour
- 2 tbsp (10g) unsweetened cocoa powder
- 2 tbsp (30 ml) maple syrup
- 2 tbsp unsweetened applesauce
- ¼ tsp (1.5g) salt

Filling:
- 1 cup (240 ml) unsweetened almond milk
- ½ cup (90g) dark chocolate chips (70% cocoa or higher)
- 2 tbsp (30g) hazelnut butter (or almond butter)
- 1 tbsp (15 ml) pure vanilla extract
- 1 tbsp (15 ml) maple syrup

Garnish (optional):
- ¼ cup (30g) chopped hazelnuts, toasted
- Fresh raspberries or strawberries
- Dusting of cocoa powder or shaved dark chocolate

Instructions:

Set the oven temperature to 175°C (350°F).

Combine oat flour, almond flour, cocoa powder, maple syrup, applesauce, and salt in a mixing bowl. Stir until a crumbly dough forms.

To create a crust, evenly press the dough into a 9-inch tart pan, pressing it up the sides.

Bake for 12–15 minutes or until firm. Let cool completely.

In a small saucepan, warm almond milk over low heat (do not boil).

Remove the heat and add the chocolate chips. Let them sit for a few minutes, then whisk until smooth and fully melted.

Stir the maple syrup, vanilla extract, and hazelnut butter into the chocolate mixture until smooth.

Spread the chocolate filling evenly over the chilled crust.

Place the tart in the refrigerator for at least 2 hours to set.

Before serving, garnish the tart with chopped hazelnuts, fresh berries, or cocoa powder. Slice and enjoy!

This tart tastes great with a side of fresh fruit, like strawberries or raspberries, which give the rich chocolate a tangy contrast.

Low-Fat Cheesecake with Fresh Berries

Yield: 8 servings	**Preparation Time:** 20 minutes	**Cooking Time:** 50 minutes

Calories: 140 kcal | Carbohydrates: 20g | Total Fat: 4g | Saturated Fat: 1g | Cholesterol: 10mg | Protein: 8g | Sodium: 100mg
(per serving)

Ingredients:

Crust:
- 1 cup (120g) graham cracker crumbs (whole grain if possible)
- 2 tbsp (30g) melted coconut oil or unsweetened applesauce
- 1 tbsp (15 ml) maple syrup or honey

Filling:
- 1 cup (240g) low-fat ricotta cheese
- 1 cup (240 ml) low-fat Greek yogurt
- ¼ cup (60 ml) honey or maple syrup
- 2 tbsp (16g) cornstarch
- 1 tsp (5 ml) pure vanilla extract
- Zest of 1 lemon
- Juice of ½ lemon

Topping:
- 1 cup (150g) fresh berries (such as strawberries, blueberries, and raspberries)

Optional Garnishes:
- Fresh mint leaves
- Lemon zest

Instructions:

Preheat your oven to 350°F (175°C).

In a medium bowl, combine maple syrup, melted coconut oil (or applesauce), and graham cracker crumbs. Stir until the mixture resembles wet sand.

Press the mixture firmly and evenly into the bottom of a 9-inch springform pan.

Bake until lightly golden, 8-10 minutes. Allow the crust to cool.

Combine the ricotta cheese, lemon zest, Greek yogurt, honey, cornstarch, vanilla extract, and lemon juice in a large mixing bowl.

Blend the mixture with a hand mixer (or whisk) until smooth and creamy. Evenly distribute the filling over the chilled crust.

Place the pan in the oven and bake for 45–50 minutes or until the center is set but still slightly jiggly.

Once baked, turn off the oven and leave the cheesecake inside with the door open for about 15 minutes to cool gradually.

After taking it out of the oven, allow it to cool to room temperature and then place it in the refrigerator for at least 3 hours.

Place fresh berries over the cheesecake before serving.

Optionally, garnish with fresh mint leaves or additional lemon zest.

Cranberry-Orange Relish with Walnuts

Yield: 8 servings	**Preparation Time:** 10 minutes	**Cooking Time:** 5 minutes

Calories: 180 kcal | Carbohydrates: 17g | Total Fat: 12g | Saturated Fat: 2g | Cholesterol: 0mg | Protein: 3g | Sodium: 80mg
(per serving)

Ingredients:
- 1 bag (12 oz/340g) fresh cranberries
- 1 large orange, zested and juiced
- ¼ cup (60 ml) freshly squeezed orange juice
- ½ cup (120 ml) honey or maple syrup
- ½ cup (60g) chopped walnuts
- ¼ tsp (0.5g) ground cinnamon

Instructions:

Rinse the cranberries and set aside. Combine cranberries, orange juice, and honey or maple syrup in a medium saucepan over medium heat. Stir well.

Bring the mixture to a simmer, allowing the cranberries to soften and burst for about 5-7 minutes. Stir occasionally, lightly mash some cranberries with a spoon to reach a chunky consistency.

Stir in the orange zest and cinnamon for added flavor. If desired, adjust the sweetness with additional honey or maple syrup.

After turning off the heat, add the chopped walnuts and fold. Let the relish cool to room temperature, allowing flavors to meld.

Transfer the relish to a serving bowl. For garnish, add additional orange zest or a sprinkle of chopped walnuts.

This Cranberry-Orange Relish is perfect as a holiday side for roasted turkey or chicken. It also pairs well with whole-grain dishes, like quinoa or wild rice, or can be spread on whole-wheat toast for a nutritious snack.

Pumpkin Pie with Whole Wheat Crust

Yield: 8 servings   **Preparation Time:** 20 minutes   **Cooking Time:** 1 hour

Calories: 160 kcal | Carbohydrates: 24g | Total Fat: 6g | Saturated Fat: 1g | Cholesterol: 0mg | Protein: 3g | Sodium: 230mg
(per serving)

Ingredients:

Crust:
- 1 cup (120g) whole wheat flour
- ¼ tsp (1.5g) salt
- ¼ cup (60 ml) cold olive oil or avocado oil
- 3-4 tbsp (60 ml) ice-cold water

Pumpkin Filling:
- 1 can (15 oz/400) pumpkin puree
- ½ cup (120 ml/80g) unsweetened almond or oat milk
- ⅓ cup (80 ml) maple syrup or honey
- 2 tbsp (16g) cornstarch
- 1 tsp (5 ml) vanilla extract
- 1 tsp (2g) ground cinnamon
- ½ tsp (1g) ground ginger
- ¼ tsp (0.5g) ground nutmeg
- ¼ tsp (0.5g) ground cloves

Optional Garnishes:
- Fresh berries (e.g., raspberries, blueberries)
- Sprinkle of cinnamon

Instructions:

Place the whole wheat flour in a medium-sized mixing bowl and add the salt. Using a fork, cut the cold oil into the flour until it resembles coarse crumbs.

Gradually add ice-cold water, 1 tablespoon at a time, mixing until the dough just comes together. Avoid over-mixing.

Roll out the dough on a floured surface into a circle about 12 inches across. Gently transfer the circle to a 9-inch pie pan and press it evenly into the sides and bottom.

Preheat the oven to 375°F (190°C). With a fork, poke a few holes in the bottom of the crust. Line the crust with parchment paper, then add pie weights or dried beans to the paper. Bake for 10 minutes. Remove the weights and parchment paper, then bake an additional 5 minutes. Set aside to cool slightly.

In a big mixing bowl, whisk together pumpkin puree, almond milk, maple syrup, cornstarch, vanilla extract, cinnamon, ginger, nutmeg, and cloves until smooth.

Using a spatula, evenly distribute the pumpkin mixture into the prebaked crust.

Place the pie in the oven and bake at 375°F (190°C) for 40-45 minutes or until the filling is set. The center should be slightly jiggly.

Allow the pie to cool for at least two hours at room temperature before serving.

Spiced Pear and Cranberry Galette

Yield: 8 servings   **Preparation Time:** 30 minutes   **Cooking Time:** 40 minutes

Calories: 185 kcal | Carbohydrates: 28g | Total Fat: 8g | Saturated Fat: 0g | Cholesterol: 0mg | Protein: 3g | Sodium: 80mg
(per serving)

Ingredients:

Crust:
- 1 cup (120g) whole wheat flour
- ½ cup (40g) rolled oats
- 2 tbsp (24g) coconut sugar or maple sugar
- ¼ tsp (1.5g) salt
- ⅓ cup (80g) cold coconut oil or vegan butter (cut into small cubes)
- 3-4 tbsp (60 ml) ice-cold water

Filling:
- 3 ripe pears, thinly sliced
- ½ cup (50g) fresh cranberries
- 2 tbsp (15 ml) maple syrup or agave syrup
- 1 tbsp (8g) cornstarch or arrowroot powder
- 1 tsp (2g) ground cinnamon
- ½ tsp (1g) ground ginger
- ¼ tsp (0.5g) ground nutmeg
- Zest of 1 lemon

Optional Garnishes:
- Chopped walnuts for crunch
- Fresh thyme leaves
- A light dusting of cinnamon

Instructions:

Whisk together the whole wheat flour, coconut sugar, powdered oats (blended into a fine powder), and salt in a medium mixing bowl.

Use your fingers or a pastry cutter to cut the cooled coconut oil cubes into the flour until the mixture resembles coarse crumbs.

Gradually add ice water, one tablespoon at a time, mixing until the dough just comes together.

Form the dough into a disk, cover it with plastic wrap, and refrigerate for at least one hour.

Combine the pear slices, fresh cranberries, maple syrup, cornstarch, cinnamon, ginger, nutmeg, and lemon zest in a large bowl. Toss gently to ensure uniform coating, then put aside.

Preheat the oven to 375°F (190°C). Put parchment paper on a baking sheet.

On a lightly floured surface, roll out the cold dough into a rough 12-inch circle approximately ⅛ inch thick.

Transfer the rolled-out dough to the prepared baking sheet.

Leave a 2-inch border around the sides of the dough, and spoon the pear and cranberry mixture into the middle. To give the dish a rustic look, gently fold the dough's edges over the filling, overlapping as necessary.

Bake for 35 to 40 minutes in a preheated oven or until the filling is bubbling and the crust is brown.

Before cutting, let the galette cool a little.

Chocolate Coconut Energy Bites

Yield: 12 bites | **Preparation Time:** 10 minutes | **Cooking Time:** 30 minutes

Calories: 110 kcal | Carbohydrates: 12g | Total Fat: 6g | Saturated Fat: 1g | Cholesterol: 0mg | Protein: 3g | Sodium: 100mg
(per serving)

Ingredients:
- 1 cup (80g) rolled oats
- ½ cup (120g) almond butter (or any nut/seed butter)
- ¼ cup (25g) unsweetened cocoa powder
- ¼ cup (20g) unsweetened shredded coconut, plus extra for rolling
- ¼ cup (30g) ground flaxseed
- 3 tbsp (45 ml) pure maple syrup or honey
- 1 tsp (5 ml) vanilla extract
- 2 tbsp (30g) dark chocolate chips or chopped dark chocolate (optional)

Optional Garnishes:
- Extra shredded coconut
- Crushed nuts or seeds

Instructions:

Combine the rolled oats, almond butter, cocoa powder, shredded coconut, ground flaxseed, maple syrup, and vanilla extract in a large mixing bowl.

Stir the mixture until well combined and sticky. Fold in dark chocolate chips or chopped dark chocolate for an extra hint of chocolate flavor.

Scoop about 1 tablespoon of the mixture and roll it between your hands to form a ball. Repeat with the remaining mixture.

Roll each ball in additional shredded coconut or crushed nuts for extra texture and flavor.

After putting the energy bites in an airtight container, let them set in the refrigerator for at least half an hour.

These energy bites are best served chilled and can be stored in the refrigerator for up to a week.

Almond and Cranberry Biscotti

Yield: 16 biscotti | **Preparation Time:** 15 minutes | **Cooking Time:** 35 minutes

Calories: 80 kcal | Carbohydrates: 12g | Total Fat: 3g | Saturated Fat: 0g | Cholesterol: 0mg | Protein: 2g | Sodium: 60mg
(per serving)

Ingredients:
- 1 cup (120g) whole wheat flour
- ½ cup (50g) almond flour
- ½ cup (60g) dried cranberries (unsweetened, if possible)
- ½ cup (70g) sliced almonds
- ⅓ cup (50g) coconut sugar (or preferred low-glycemic sweetener)
- 1 tsp (4g) baking powder
- ¼ tsp (1.5g) salt
- 2 large egg whites (or ¼ cup (60 ml) unsweetened applesauce for a vegan option)
- 1 tsp (5 ml) vanilla extract
- 1 tsp (5 ml) almond extract

Optional Garnishes:
- 1 tbsp (5g) sliced almonds for topping

Instructions:

Preheat your oven to 350°F (175°C). Line a baking sheet with parchment paper.

Combine whole wheat flour, almond flour, coconut sugar, baking powder, and salt. Mix in the dried cranberries and sliced almonds.

Whisk the egg whites, vanilla extract, and almond extract in a small bowl until well combined. (If you use applesauce as an egg replacement, mix the applesauce directly with the extracts.)

To make a dough, combine the wet and dry ingredients. If it's too crumbly, add a teaspoon of water until it comes together.

After the baking sheet is ready, move the dough to it. Shape it into a long, rectangular log (about 12 inches by 3 inches and ¾-inch thick). Sprinkle additional almond slices on top if desired.

Bake in the oven for 20–25 minutes or until the log is firm and slightly golden.

Allow the baked log to cool for about 10 minutes. Using a serrated knife, cut it into ¾-inch thick slices.

Return the slices to the baking sheet and bake for 10 to 12 minutes on each side or until crisp and golden brown.

Allow biscotti to cool completely on a wire rack. As they cool, they will keep solidifying.

Holiday Fruit and Nut Bread

Yield: 10 slices	Preparation Time: 15 minutes	Cooking Time: 50 minutes

Calories: 190 kcal | Carbohydrates: 27g | Total Fat: 8g | Saturated Fat: 0.5g | Cholesterol: 0mg | Protein: 4g | Sodium: 140mg (per serving)

Ingredients:

- ½ cup (60g) whole wheat flour
- ½ cup (60g) almond flour
- 1 tsp (4g) baking soda
- ½ tsp (3g) salt
- 1 tsp (2g) ground cinnamon
- ¼ tsp (0.5g) ground nutmeg
- ½ cup (120 ml) unsweetened applesauce
- ⅓ cup (80 ml) maple syrup or honey
- 1 large egg or ¼ cup (60 ml) unsweetened applesauce (for egg-free)
- 1 tsp (5 ml) vanilla extract
- ½ cup (60g) dried cranberries
- ½ cup (70g) dried apricots, chopped
- ⅓ cup (40g) chopped walnuts
- ⅓ cup (40g) chopped pecans
- ¼ cup (60 ml) orange juice (freshly squeezed, if possible)
- Zest of 1 orange

Optional Garnishes:
- Sprinkle oats on top for texture
- Additional chopped nuts or dried fruit

Instructions:

Preheat your oven to 350°F (175°C). Line a loaf pan with parchment paper or lightly coat it with olive oil spray.

Mix the whole wheat flour, almond flour, salt, cinnamon, baking soda, and nutmeg in a big bowl. Set aside.

In a separate bowl, whisk the applesauce, maple syrup (or honey), egg (or additional applesauce if vegan), vanilla extract, orange juice, and orange zest until well combined.

Mix the dry and wet ingredients until just combined. Fold in the dried cranberries, chopped apricots, walnuts, and pecans.

After the loaf pan is ready, pour the batter into it. Smooth the top, and sprinkle oats or extra nuts on top for added texture.

A toothpick inserted in the middle should come out clean after 45 to 50 minutes of baking.

After 10 minutes of cooling in the pan, move the bread to a wire rack to finish cooling before slicing.

Roasted Garlic and Herb Flatbread

Yield: 8 slices	Preparation Time: 20 minutes	Cooking Time: 90 minutes

Calories: 140 kcal | Carbohydrates: 16g | Total Fat: 7g | Saturated Fat: 1g | Cholesterol: 0mg | Protein: 3g | Sodium: 180mg (per serving)

Ingredients:

Roasted Garlic:
- 1 head of garlic
- 1 tsp (15 ml) olive oil

Flatbread Dough:
- 1 cup (120g) whole wheat flour
- 1 cup (120g) all-purpose flour
- 1 tsp (5g) salt
- 1 tsp (1g) dried rosemary (or other dried herbs of choice)
- 1 tsp (1g) dried thyme
- 1 tsp (1g) dried oregano
- 1 tbsp (15 ml) olive oil
- ¾ cup (180 ml) warm water (110°F/43°C)

Topping:
- 2 tbsp (30 ml) olive oil, divided
- 2 tsp (2g) fresh parsley, chopped
- 1 tsp (1g) fresh rosemary, chopped
- 1 tsp (1g) fresh thyme, chopped
- Freshly cracked black pepper (optional)

Optional Garnishes:
- Red pepper flakes for a touch of heat
- Fresh basil leaves

Instructions:

Preheat oven to 400°F (200°C).

Cut off the top of the garlic head, drizzle with 1 teaspoon of olive oil, wrap in foil, and roast for 25 minutes or until soft and caramelized. Let cool, and then use a fork to mash the roasted garlic cloves after removing them from their skins.

Mix whole wheat flour, all-purpose flour, salt, rosemary, thyme, and oregano in a large bowl. To make a soft dough, add the olive oil and roasted garlic, then slowly stir in the warm water.

Knead the dough on a floured surface for 5-7 minutes until smooth and elastic. Put the dough in a lightly oiled bowl, cover it, and let it rise for an hour or until it has doubled in size.

Preheat the oven to 450°F (230°C) and place a baking sheet or pizza stone in the oven to heat. Divide the dough into 2 portions and roll each portion out on a lightly floured surface into a thin oval or circle (about ¼-inch thick).

After brushing each flatbread with 1 tablespoon of olive oil, sprinkle it with freshly chopped parsley, rosemary, thyme, and freshly cracked black pepper.

Carefully transfer the flatbreads onto the hot baking sheet or pizza stone. Bake for 8-10 minutes or until the flatbread is golden and crisp around the edges.

Cut the flatbread into pieces and add optional garnishes like fresh basil or red pepper flakes.

Pumpkin Smoothie Bowl with Almond Butter

Yield: 2 servings | **Preparation Time:** 5 minutes | **Cooking Time:** none

Calories: 190 kcal | Carbohydrates: 30g | Total Fat: 7g | Saturated Fat: 0.5g | Cholesterol: 0mg | Protein: 4g | Sodium: 80mg
(per serving)

Ingredients:

- 1 cup (240 ml) pumpkin puree (canned or homemade, unsweetened)
- ½ cup (120 ml) unsweetened almond milk (or any plant-based milk of choice)
- 1 frozen banana
- ½ tsp (1g) pumpkin pie spice
- 1 tbsp (15g) almond butter
- 1 tsp (15 ml) pure maple syrup or honey (optional for added sweetness)

Topping Options (customizable)

- 1 tbsp (10g) granola (low sugar, whole grain)
- 1 tbsp (10g) chia seeds or flaxseeds
- ¼ cup (40g) fresh berries (like blueberries or sliced strawberries)
- 1 tbsp (10g) pumpkin seeds or sliced almonds
- A sprinkle of cinnamon or extra pumpkin pie spice

Instructions:

In a blender, combine the pumpkin puree, almond milk, frozen banana, pumpkin pie spice, almond butter, and maple syrup (if using). Blend until smooth and creamy.

Add a few ice cubes and blend again for a thicker smoothie bowl. Add a little more almond milk until the desired texture is achieved for a thinner consistency.

Pour the smoothie mixture into a bowl. Top with a sprinkle of granola, chia seeds, fresh berries, pumpkin seeds, and a dash of cinnamon or extra pumpkin pie spice.

Serve and enjoy this creamy, flavorful, heart-healthy smoothie bowl immediately.

Roasted Garlic and Herb Flatbread

Yield: 6 servings | **Preparation Time:** 25 minutes | **Cooking Time:** 45 minutes

Calories: 215 kcal | Carbohydrates: 18g | Total Fat: 14g | Saturated Fat: 1g | Cholesterol: 0mg | Protein: 5g | Sodium: 210mg
(per serving)

Ingredients:
Filling:

- 1 tbsp (15 ml) olive oil
- 1 large onion, finely chopped
- 2 garlic cloves, minced
- 1 cup (70g) mushrooms, chopped
- 1 medium carrot, finely diced
- 1 small zucchini, finely diced
- 1 bell pepper, diced
- ½ cup (15g) baby spinach, chopped
- ½ cup (60g) walnuts, chopped
- ½ tsp (0.5g) thyme
- ½ tsp (0.5g) rosemary
- Salt and pepper, to taste

Pastry:

- 1 sheet whole wheat puff pastry (store-bought, thawed)

Glaze:

- 1 tbsp (15 ml) almond milk (unsweetened)
- 1 tsp (5 ml) maple syrup

Optional Garnishes:

- Fresh rosemary or thyme sprigs
- Pomegranate seeds for a festive touch

Instructions:

Preheat your oven to 400°F (200°C). Line a baking sheet with parchment paper.

In a large skillet, heat the olive oil over medium heat.

Add the onions and sauté for 3–4 minutes until softened.

Add garlic and mushrooms, cooking until mushrooms are golden brown, about 5–6 minutes.

Stir in carrot, zucchini, and bell pepper, cooking for an additional 5 minutes until softened.

Add the chopped spinach, walnuts, thyme, and rosemary, cooking for another 2–3 minutes until the spinach is wilted. Season with salt and pepper to taste.

Remove from heat and allow the mixture to cool.

Roll out the puff pastry on a lightly floured surface to about 1/8-inch thick.

Place the vegetable filling along the center of the pastry, leaving about 1-inch of space on all sides.

Fold the pastry over the filling, pinching the edges to seal. Place seam-side down on the prepared baking sheet.

Mix almond milk and maple syrup, then brush over the pastry.

Bake for 40–45 minutes, until golden brown.

Let cool slightly before slicing. For a festive look, garnish with fresh rosemary or thyme and sprinkle pomegranate seeds on top.

45-Day Meal Plan

	Breakfast	Snacks	Lunch	Dinner
Day 1	Berry and Spinach Smoothie Bowl with Chia Seeds	Healthy Carrot Cake Muffins	Grilled Mahi-Mahi with Pineapple Salsa Grilled Vegetable Platter with Pesto	Roasted Cauliflower and Chickpeas with Tahini Sauce
Day 2	Oatmeal with Almond Butter and Fresh Banana	Almond-Crusted Cauliflower Bites	Lemon Herb Grilled Chicken Breasts Brown Rice Stir-Fry with Mixed Vegetables	Vegetable Stir-Fry with Tofu and Brown Rice
Day 3	Creamy Avocado Toast with Tomato and Basil	Fresh Fruit Skewers with Yogurt Dip	Baked Cod with Lemon, Dill, and Garlic Kale Salad with Avocado and Lemon Dressing	Whole Wheat Pasta Primavera with Seasonal Vegetables
Day 4	Fluffy Egg White and Veggie Omelet	Baked Sweet Potato Chips with Sea Salt	Turkey and Quinoa Stuffed Peppers Lentil and Spinach Soup with Herbs	Stuffed Portobello Mushrooms with Spinach and Cheese
Day 5	Chia Seed Pudding with Coconut and Mango	Spicy Guacamole with Whole Grain Tortilla Chips	Shrimp and Veggie Skewers with Chimichurri Bulgur Wheat Salad with Tomatoes and Parsley	Lentil Loaf with Tomato Glaze
Day 6	Whole Wheat Pancakes with Blueberries	Roasted Chickpeas with Paprika and Cumin	Spicy Chicken Stir-Fry with Vegetables Quinoa and Black Bean Pilaf with Cilantro	Herb-Roasted Turkey Breast with Cranberry Relish
Day 7	Fluffy Egg White and Veggie Omelet	Baked Veggie Spring Rolls with Dipping Sauce	Spicy Tuna Salad with Avocado and Cucumber Brown Rice and Lentil Casserole	Zucchini Noodles with Marinara and Turkey Meatballs
Day 8	Fresh Fruit Salad with Lime and Mint	Dark Chocolate Avocado Mousse	Baked Chicken Thighs with Garlic and Rosemary Mediterranean Quinoa Salad with Chickpeas	Herb-Crusted Baked Cod with Steamed Broccoli
Day 9	Whole Wheat Pancakes with Blueberries	Mini Stuffed Peppers with Cream Cheese	Slow-Cooked Beef Stew with Root Vegetables Chickpea Salad with Lemon-Tahini Dressing	Pasta Primavera with Seasonal Vegetables
Day 10	Chia Seed Pudding with Coconut and Mango	Fruit Sorbet with Fresh Mint	Mediterranean Chicken Skewers with Tzatziki Quinoa Salad with Roasted Vegetables and Feta	Ginger Garlic Salmon with Broccoli
Day 11	Greek Yogurt Salad with Berries and Mixed Nuts	Spicy Roasted Carrots with Honey and Cumin	Baked Trout with Almond Crust Cauliflower Rice Stir-Fry with Vegetables	Grilled Lemon Garlic Chicken with Quinoa

Day 12	Savory Quinoa Breakfast Bowl with Spinach and Feta	Savory Oatmeal Energy Bites	Herb-Roasted Chicken with Root Vegetables Black Bean and Corn Salad with Avocado	Ratatouille with Fresh Herbs and Olive Oil
Day 13	Overnight Oats with Apples and Cinnamon	Edamame with Sea Salt and Lemon	Sautéed Scallops with Lemon and Spinach Coconut Rice with Mango and Lime	Turkey Meatloaf with Vegetables
Day 14	Banana-Walnut Muffins with Whole Grain Flour	Lemon Sorbet with Fresh Herbs	Honey Mustard Chicken with Brussels Sprouts Barley Risotto with Mushrooms and Peas	Turkey and Quinoa Stuffed Peppers
Day 15	Tofu Scramble with Bell Peppers and Onions	Oatmeal Raisin Cookies with Almond Flour	Ginger Garlic Salmon with Broccoli Chickpea and Avocado Salad with Lime Dressing	Whole Wheat Pasta Primavera with Seasonal Vegetables
Day 16	Caprese Salad with Fresh Mozzarella and Basil	Healthy Carrot Cake Muffins	Chicken and Vegetable Curry with Coconut Milk Wild Rice with Cranberries and Pecans	Spicy Thai Green Curry with Vegetables
Day 17	Overnight Oats with Apples and Cinnamon	Coconut Chia Seed Pudding with Pineapple	Turkey Meatloaf with Vegetables Sweet Potato and Black Bean Tacos	Herb-Crusted Baked Cod with Steamed Broccoli
Day 18	Spaghetti Squash with Marinara Sauce	Roasted Chickpeas with Paprika and Cumin	BBQ Chicken Quinoa Bowl Broccoli Salad with Almonds and Cranberries	Baked Lemon Herb Salmon with Asparagus
Day 19	Whole Wheat Pancakes with Blueberries	Baked Veggie Spring Rolls with Dipping Sauce	Fish Cakes with Quinoa and Veggies Mixed Greens with Grapes and Pecans	Herb-Roasted Turkey Breast with Seasonal Vegetables
Day 20	Creamy Avocado Toast with Tomato and Basil	Herb and Garlic Popcorn	Asian Glazed Chicken Thighs with Sesame Vegetable Sushi Rolls with Brown Rice	Grilled Veggie Sandwich on Whole Grain Bread
Day 21	Vegetable Sushi Rolls with Brown Rice	Frozen Yogurt Bark with Mixed Berries	Lean Beef Stir-Fry with Broccoli Quinoa and Black Bean Pilaf with Cilantro	Zucchini Noodles with Marinara and Turkey Meatballs
Day 22	Tofu Scramble with Bell Peppers and Onions	Zucchini Fritters with Greek Yogurt Dip	Slow Cooker Chicken and Vegetable Stew Whole Wheat Pasta with Garlic, Olive Oil and Spinach	Grilled Mahi-Mahi with Pineapple Salsa
Day 23	Zucchini and Feta Breakfast Casserole	Almond and Cranberry Biscotti	Roasted Salmon with Honey Mustard Glaze Farro Salad with Roasted Vegetables and Feta	Stuffed Acorn Squash with Wild Rice and Nuts

Day 24	Fluffy Egg White and Veggie Omelet	Dark Chocolate Avocado Mousse	Balsamic Glazed Chicken Chops with Apples Cauliflower Rice with Herbs and Lemon Zest	Fish Cakes with Quinoa and Veggies
Day 25	Almond Flour Pancakes with Maple Syrup	Spicy Roasted Carrots with Honey and Cumin	Spiced Turkey Meatballs with Marinara Sauce Couscous Salad with Chickpeas and Cucumbers	Barley Risotto with Mushrooms and Peas
Day 26	Quinoa and Berry Breakfast Bake	Almond Flour Brownies with Dark Chocolate	Grilled Chicken Sausages with Peppers Chickpea Salad with Lemon-Tahini Dressing	Vegetable Stir-Fry with Tofu and Brown Rice
Day 27	Greek Yogurt Salad with Berries and Mixed Nuts	Baked Apples with Oats and Cinnamon	Spaghetti with Clams and Garlic Olive Oil Cabbage and Carrot Slaw with Apple Cider Dressing	Baked Trout with Almond Crust
Day 28	Chickpea and Avocado Salad with Lime Dressing	No-Bake Chocolate Peanut Butter Bars	Stuffed Zucchini Boats with Ground Turkey and Quinoa Caprese Salad with Fresh Mozzarella and Basil	Spaghetti with Clams and Garlic Olive Oil
Day 29	Bulgur Wheat Salad with Tomatoes and Parsley	Baked Veggie Spring Rolls with Dipping Sauce	Grilled Flank Steak with Chimichurri Spaghetti Squash with Marinara Sauce	Shredded Chicken Tacos with Fresh Salsa
Day 30	Berry and Spinach Smoothie Bowl with Chia Seeds	Coconut Chia Seed Pudding with Pineapple	Pasta Primavera with Seasonal Vegetables Citrus Salad with Pomegranate Seeds and Mint	Honey Mustard Chicken with Brussels Sprouts
Day 31	Fresh Fruit Salad with Lime and Mint	Greek Yogurt Salad with Berries and Mixed Nuts	Seafood Paella with Brown Rice Cranberry Walnut Salad with Citrus Vinaigrette	Stuffed Zucchini Boats with Ground Turkey and Quinoa
Day 32	Grilled Veggie Sandwich on Whole Grain Bread	Spiced Apple Chips with Cinnamon	Turkey and Quinoa Stuffed Peppers Roasted Beet and Goat Cheese Salad	Farro Salad with Roasted Vegetables and Feta
Day 33	Wild Rice with Cranberries and Pecans	Fresh Fruit Skewers with Yogurt Dip	Savory Meatloaf with Oats and Vegetables Spinach and Strawberry Salad with Balsamic Vinaigrette and Chickpeas	Herb-Roasted Turkey Breast with Seasonal Vegetables
Day 34	Banana-Walnut Muffins with Whole Grain Flour	Cucumber Slices with Avocado Hummus	Spicy Chicken Stir-Fry with Vegetables Lentil Salad with Cherry Tomatoes and Feta	Stuffed Portobello Mushrooms with Spinach and Cheese
Day 35	Bulgur Wheat Salad with Tomatoes and Parsley	Zucchini Fritters with Greek Yogurt Dip	Miso-Glazed Cod with Bok Choy Cauliflower Rice Stir-Fry with Vegetables	Slow-Cooked Beef Stew with Root Vegetables

Day 36	Almond Flour Pancakes with Maple Syrup	Lemon Sorbet with Fresh Herbs	Balsamic Glazed Chicken Chops with Apples Spinach and Ricotta Stuffed Shells with Marinara	Couscous Salad with Chickpeas and Cucumbers
Day 37	Brown Rice and Lentil Casserole	Coconut Chia Seed Pudding with Pineapple	Beef and Vegetable Stir-Fry with Brown Rice Carrot and Raisin Salad with Greek Yogurt Dressing	Baked Cod with Lemon, Dill, and Garlic
Day 38	Overnight Oats with Apples and Cinnamon	Savory Oatmeal Energy Bites	Slow-Cooked Beef Stew with Root Vegetables Edamame and Quinoa Salad with Sesame Dressing	Spicy Thai Green Curry with Vegetables
Day 39	Quinoa Salad with Roasted Vegetables and Feta	Fresh Fruit Skewers with Yogurt Dip	Mediterranean Shrimp with Tomatoes and Olives Whole Wheat Wraps with Hummus and Fresh Veggies	Grilled Lemon Garlic Chicken with Quinoa
Day 40	Coconut Rice with Mango and Lime	Roasted Chickpeas with Paprika and Cumin	Herb-Roasted Turkey Breast with Cranberry Relish Curried Cauliflower and Chickpeas	Beef and Vegetable Stir-Fry with Brown Rice
Day 41	Oatmeal with Almond Butter and Fresh Banana	Oatmeal Raisin Cookies with Almond Flour	Spinach and Feta Quiche with Whole Wheat Crust Zucchini Noodles with Pesto and Cherry Tomatoes	Baked Lemon Herb Salmon with Asparagus
Day 42	Ratatouille with Fresh Herbs and Olive Oil	Almond-Crusted Cauliflower Bites	Baked Chicken Thighs with Garlic and Rosemary Roasted Vegetable Salad with Tahini Dressing	Herb-Roasted Turkey Breast with Seasonal Vegetables
Day 43	Tofu Scramble with Bell Peppers and Onions	Spicy Guacamole with Whole Grain Tortilla Chips	Beef Tacos with Fresh Salsa and Avocado Asian-Inspired Cabbage Salad with Peanut Dressing	Grilled Chicken with Quinoa and Spinach Salad
Day 44	Savory Quinoa Breakfast Bowl with Spinach and Feta	Fruit Sorbet with Fresh Mint	Stuffed Bell Peppers with Brown Rice and Herbs Tropical Mango Salad with Black Beans and Lime Dressing	Grilled Shrimp Tacos with Cabbage Slaw
Day 45	Chia Seed Pudding with Coconut and Mango	Baked Apples with Oats and Cinnamon	Cilantro Lime Fish Tacos with Slaw Arugula Salad with Pears and Gorgonzola	Spinach and Ricotta Stuffed Shells with Marinara

Cooking Conversion Charts

Oven Temperatures

°C	°F	Oven
90	220	Very Cool
110	225	Cool
120	250	Cool
140	275	Cool – Moderate
150	300	Warm Moderate
160	325	Medium
180	350	Moderate
190	375	Moderate – Hot
200	400	Fairly Hot
215	425	Hot
230	450	Very Hot
250	475	Very Hot
260	500	Very Hot

Dry Weights

CUP	TBSP	TSP	GRAM	OUNCE
1 C	16 tbsp	48 tsp	227 g	8 oz
3/4 C	12 tbsp	36 tsp	171 g	6 oz
2/3 C	10 tbsp	32 tsp	152 g	5 oz
1/2 C	8 tbsp	24 tsp	115 g	4 oz
1/3 C	6 tbsp	16 tsp	85 g	3 oz
1/4 C	4 tbsp	12 tsp	57 g	2 oz
1/8 C	2 tbsp	6 tsp	28 g	1 oz
1/16 C	1 tbsp	3 tsp	15 g	1/2 oz

Liquid Volumes

CUP	OUNCE	TBSP	TSP	ML
1/8 C	1 oz	2 tbsp	6 tsp	30 ml
1/4 C	2 oz	4 tbsp	12 tsp	60 ml
1/3 C	3 oz	5 tbsp	16 tsp	80 ml
1/2 C	4 oz	8 tbsp	24 tsp	120 ml
2/3 C	5 oz	11 tbsp	32 tsp	160 ml
3/4 C	6 oz	12 tbsp	36 tsp	177 ml
1 C	8 oz	16 tbsp	48 tsp	240 ml
2 C	16 oz	32 tbsp	96 tsp	470 ml

Index recipes

Spinach and Strawberry Salad with Balsamic Vinaigrette and Chickpeas 43
Chickpea and Avocado Salad with Lime Dressing 46
Couscous Salad with Chickpeas and Cucumbers 59
Curried Cauliflower and Chickpeas 88
Mediterranean Quinoa Salad with Chickpeas 43

clams
Spaghetti with Clams and Garlic Olive Oil 68

cod
Herb-Crusted Baked Cod with Steamed Broccoli 33
Baked Cod with Lemon, Dill, and Garlic 63
Cilantro Lime Fish Tacos with Slaw 65
Fish Cakes with Quinoa and Veggies 67
Miso-Glazed Cod with Bok Choy 69

corn tortillas
Sweet Potato and Black Bean Tacos 26
Grilled Shrimp Tacos with Cabbage Slaw 34

cranberries
Cranberry Walnut Salad with Citrus Vinaigrette 45
Broccoli Salad with Almonds and Cranberries 48
Arugula Salad with Pears and Gorgonzola 48
Wild Rice with Cranberries and Pecans 58
Herb-Roasted Turkey Breast with Cranberry Relish 82
Stuffed Acorn Squash with Wild Rice and Nuts 86
Cranberry-Orange Relish with Walnuts 92
Spiced Pear and Cranberry Galette 93
Holiday Fruit and Nut Bread 95
Almond and Cranberry Biscotti 94

cream cheese
Mini Stuffed Peppers with Cream Cheese 41

cucumber
Savory Quinoa Breakfast Bowl with Spinach and Feta 16
Chickpea Salad with Lemon-Tahini Dressing 22
Whole Wheat Wraps with Hummus and Fresh Veggies 22
Edamame and Quinoa Salad with Sesame Dressing 25
Vegetable Sushi Rolls with Brown Rice 28
Chickpea and Avocado Salad with Lime Dressing 46
Lentil Salad with Cherry Tomatoes and Feta 47
Couscous Salad with Chickpeas and Cucumbers 59
Spicy Tuna Salad with Avocado and Cucumber 64
Holiday Vegetable Platter with Dips 89
Cucumber Slices with Avocado Hummus 36

E

edamame
Edamame and Quinoa Salad with Sesame Dressing 25
Edamame with Sea Salt and Lemon 40
Brown Rice Stir-Fry with Mixed Vegetables 56

egg
Savory Quinoa Breakfast Bowl with Spinach and Feta 16
Poached Eggs with Sweet Potato and Kale Hash 17
Banana-Walnut Muffins with Whole Grain Flour 18
Whole Wheat Pancakes with Blueberries 15
Quinoa and Berry Breakfast Bake 19
Almond Flour Pancakes with Maple Syrup 19
Healthy Banana Bread with Walnuts 51
Oatmeal Raisin Cookies with Almond Flour 52
Almond Flour Brownies with Dark Chocolate 53
Healthy Carrot Cake Muffins 54
Fish Cakes with Quinoa and Veggies 67
Turkey Meatloaf with Vegetables 77

Spiced Turkey Meatballs with Marinara Sauce 78
Almond and Cranberry Biscotti 94
Holiday Fruit and Nut Bread 95
Fluffy Egg White and Veggie Omelet 14
Zucchini and Feta Breakfast Casserole 20

eggplant
Grilled Veggie Sandwich on Whole Grain Bread 23
Ratatouille with Fresh Herbs and Olive Oil 32
Spicy Thai Green Curry with Vegetables 35

F

feta
Chickpea Salad with Lemon-Tahini Dressing 22
Black Bean and Corn Salad with Avocado 23
Grilled Veggie Sandwich on Whole Grain Bread 23
Stuffed Bell Peppers with Brown Rice and Herbs 24
Spinach and Feta Quiche with Whole Wheat Crust 27
Spinach and Strawberry Salad with Balsamic Vinaigrette and Chickpeas 43
Kale Salad with Avocado and Lemon Dressing 44
Cranberry Walnut Salad with Citrus Vinaigrette 45
Mixed Greens with Grapes and Pecans 45
Citrus Salad with Pomegranate Seeds and Mint 46
Lentil Salad with Cherry Tomatoes and Feta 47
Farro Salad with Roasted Vegetables and Feta 58
Couscous Salad with Chickpeas and Cucumbers 59
Bulgur Wheat Salad with Tomatoes and Parsley 60
Mediterranean Shrimp with Tomatoes and Olives 67
Grilled Corn Salad with Cilantro and Lime 88
Grilled Peach Salad with Arugula and Feta 91
Fluffy Egg White and Veggie Omelet 14
Savory Quinoa Breakfast Bowl with Spinach and Feta 16
Zucchini and Feta Breakfast Casserole 20
Quinoa Salad with Roasted Vegetables and Feta 21
Mediterranean Quinoa Salad with Chickpeas 43

flank steak
Grilled Flank Steak with Chimichurri 79

G

grapefruit
Citrus Salad with Pomegranate Seeds and Mint 46

grapes
Fresh Fruit Skewers with Yogurt Dip 38
Mixed Greens with Grapes and Pecans 45

green onion
Black Bean and Corn Salad with Avocado 23
Vegetable Stir-Fry with Tofu and Brown Rice 30
Cauliflower Rice Stir-Fry with Vegetables 26
Roasted Salmon with Honey Mustard Glaze 68
Spicy Chicken Stir-Fry with Vegetables 71
Brown Rice and Lentil Casserole 61

greens
Cranberry Walnut Salad with Citrus Vinaigrette 45
Mixed Greens with Grapes and Pecans 45
Roasted Vegetable Salad with Tahini Dressing 47
Sautéed Greens with Garlic and Olive Oil 84

H

hummus
Whole Wheat Wraps with Hummus and Fresh Veggies 22
Grilled Veggie Sandwich on Whole Grain Bread 23

J

jalapeño
Black Bean and Corn Salad with Avocado 23
Sweet Potato and Black Bean Tacos 26
Grilled Shrimp Tacos with Cabbage Slaw 34
Spicy Guacamole with Whole Grain Tortilla Chips 38
Grilled Mahi-Mahi with Pineapple Salsa 63
Shredded Chicken Tacos with Fresh Salsa 74
jasmine rice
Coconut Rice with Mango and Lime 61

K
kale
Poached Eggs with Sweet Potato and Kale Hash 17
Kale Salad with Avocado and Lemon Dressing 44
kiwi
Fresh Fruit Salad with Lime and Mint 20
Fresh Fruit Skewers with Yogurt Dip 38

L
lean beef
Lean Beef Stir-Fry with Broccoli 78
Beef and Vegetable Stir-Fry with Brown Rice 81
Beef Tacos with Fresh Salsa and Avocado 82
lentils
Lentil and Spinach Soup with Herbs 21
Lentil Loaf with Tomato Glaze 34
Lentil Salad with Cherry Tomatoes and Feta 47
Brown Rice and Lentil Casserole 61
lettuce
Shredded Chicken Tacos with Fresh Salsa 74

M
mango
Chia Seed Pudding with Coconut and Mango 15
Fresh Fruit Salad with Lime and Mint 20
Vegetable Sushi Rolls with Brown Rice 28
Tropical Mango Salad with Black Beans and Lime Dressing 49
Coconut Rice with Mango and Lime 61
mozzarella cheese
Caprese Salad with Fresh Mozzarella and Basil 25
Creamy Spinach and Artichoke Dip 86
Turkey and Quinoa Stuffed Peppers 70
mushrooms
Stuffed Portobello Mushrooms with Spinach and Cheese 30
Fluffy Egg White and Veggie Omelet 14
Zucchini and Feta Breakfast Casserole 20
Spinach and Feta Quiche with Whole Wheat Crust 27
Barley Risotto with Mushrooms and Peas 57
mussels
Seafood Paella with Brown Rice 69

O
oat
Greek Yogurt Salad with Berries and Mixed Nuts 16
Overnight Oats with Apples and Cinnamon 17
Lentil Loaf with Tomato Glaze 34
Savory Oatmeal Energy Bites 42
Baked Apples with Oats and Cinnamon 51
Oatmeal Raisin Cookies with Almond Flour 52
No-Bake Chocolate Peanut Butter Bars 55
Turkey Meatloaf with Vegetables 77
Savory Meatloaf with Oats and Vegetables 80
Low-Fat Chocolate Hazelnut Tart 91

Spiced Pear and Cranberry Galette 93
Chocolate Coconut Energy Bites 94
Oatmeal with Almond Butter and Fresh Banana 14
olives
Fluffy Egg White and Veggie Omelet 14
Whole Wheat Wraps with Hummus and Fresh Veggies 22
Mediterranean Shrimp with Tomatoes and Olives 67
orange
Fresh Fruit Salad with Lime and Mint 20
Roasted Beet and Goat Cheese Salad 27
Citrus Salad with Pomegranate Seeds and Mint 46
Herb-Roasted Turkey Breast with Cranberry Relish 82

P
Parmesan cheese
Stuffed Portobello Mushrooms with Spinach and Cheese 30
 Mini Stuffed Peppers with Cream Cheese 41
Barley Risotto with Mushrooms and Peas 57
Creamy Spinach and Artichoke Dip 86
Whole Wheat Pasta Primavera with Seasonal Vegetables 31
Zucchini Noodles with Marinara and Turkey Meatballs 32
Whole Wheat Pasta with Garlic, Olive Oil and Spinach 57
Brown Rice and Lentil Casserole 61
Pasta Primavera with Seasonal Vegetables 62
Spinach and Ricotta Stuffed Shells with Marinara 62
peaches
Grilled Peach Salad with Arugula and Feta 91
peanut butter
Asian-Inspired Cabbage Salad with Peanut Dressing 28
No-Bake Chocolate Peanut Butter Bars 55
pearl barley
Barley Risotto with Mushrooms and Peas 57
pears
Fresh Fruit Salad with Lime and Mint 20
Arugula Salad with Pears and Gorgonzola 48
Spiced Pear and Cranberry Galette 93
Cauliflower Rice Stir-Fry with Vegetables 26
Barley Risotto with Mushrooms and Peas 57
Vegetable Medley Stir-Fry with Soy Sauce 87
pineapple
Fresh Fruit Salad with Lime and Mint 20
Fresh Fruit Skewers with Yogurt Dip 38
Coconut Chia Seed Pudding with Pineapple 50
Grilled Mahi-Mahi with Pineapple Salsa 63
pomegranate
Pomegranate Glazed Salmon with Quinoa 90
Pomegranate Glazed Salmon with Quinoa 90
Fresh Fruit Salad with Lime and Mint 20
Stuffed Acorn Squash with Wild Rice and Nuts 86
Maple Glazed Roasted Pumpkin Wedges 90
Roasted Red Pepper and Walnut Dip 41
pumpkin
Creamy Pumpkin and Cauliflower Mash 85
Maple Glazed Roasted Pumpkin Wedges 90
Pumpkin Pie with Whole Wheat Crust 93

Q
quinoa
Savory Quinoa Breakfast Bowl with Spinach and Feta 16
Quinoa and Berry Breakfast Bake 19
Quinoa Salad with Roasted Vegetables and Feta 21
Edamame and Quinoa Salad with Sesame Dressing 25

Grilled Chicken with Quinoa and Spinach Salad 29
Grilled Lemon Garlic Chicken with Quinoa 33
Mediterranean Quinoa Salad with Chickpeas 43
Quinoa and Black Bean Pilaf with Cilantro 56
Fish Cakes with Quinoa and Veggies 67
Fish Cakes with Quinoa and Veggies 67
Turkey and Quinoa Stuffed Peppers 70
BBQ Chicken Quinoa Bowl 75
Stuffed Zucchini Boats with Ground Turkey and Quinoa 80
Pomegranate Glazed Salmon with Quinoa 90

R

radishes
Holiday Vegetable Platter with Dips 89
Overnight Oats with Apples and Cinnamon 17
Banana-Walnut Muffins with Whole Grain Flour 18
Carrot and Raisin Salad with Greek Yogurt Dressing 49
Baked Apples with Oats and Cinnamon 51
Oatmeal Raisin Cookies with Almond Flour 52
Healthy Carrot Cake Muffins 54

red onion
Quinoa Salad with Roasted Vegetables and Feta 21
Poached Eggs with Sweet Potato and Kale Hash 17
Chickpea Salad with Lemon-Tahini Dressing 22
Whole Wheat Wraps with Hummus and Fresh Veggies 22
Black Bean and Corn Salad with Avocado 23
Grilled Veggie Sandwich on Whole Grain Bread 23
Sweet Potato and Black Bean Tacos 26
Grilled Chicken with Quinoa and Spinach Salad 29
Spicy Guacamole with Whole Grain Tortilla Chips 38
Spinach and Strawberry Salad with Balsamic Vinaigrette and Chickpeas 43
Kale Salad with Avocado and Lemon Dressing 44
Mixed Greens with Grapes and Pecans 45
Chickpea and Avocado Salad with Lime Dressing 46
Roasted Vegetable Salad with Tahini Dressing 47
Lentil Salad with Cherry Tomatoes and Feta 47
Broccoli Salad with Almonds and Cranberries 48
Arugula Salad with Pears and Gorgonzola 48
Farro Salad with Roasted Vegetables and Feta 58
Couscous Salad with Chickpeas and Cucumbers 59
Bulgur Wheat Salad with Tomatoes and Parsley 60
Shrimp and Veggie Skewers with Chimichurri 64
Cilantro Lime Fish Tacos with Slaw 65
 Grilled Chicken Sausages with Peppers 81
Beef Tacos with Fresh Salsa and Avocado 82
Grilled Corn Salad with Cilantro and Lime 88
Grilled Peach Salad with Arugula and Feta 91

ricotta cheese
Stuffed Portobello Mushrooms with Spinach and Cheese 30
Spinach and Ricotta Stuffed Shells with Marinara 62
Low-Fat Cheesecake with Fresh Berries 92

S

salmon
Baked Lemon Herb Salmon with Asparagus 29
Ginger Garlic Salmon with Broccoli 66
Roasted Salmon with Honey Mustard Glaze 68
Pomegranate Glazed Salmon with Quinoa 90

sea scallops
Sautéed Scallops with Lemon and Spinach 66

shrimp

Grilled Shrimp Tacos with Cabbage Slaw 34
Shrimp and Veggie Skewers with Chimichurri 64
Mediterranean Shrimp with Tomatoes and Olives 67
Seafood Paella with Brown Rice 69

spinach
Berry and Spinach Smoothie Bowl with Chia Seeds 13
Fluffy Egg White and Veggie Omelet 14
Savory Quinoa Breakfast Bowl with Spinach and Feta 16
Lentil and Spinach Soup with Herbs 21
Spinach and Feta Quiche with Whole Wheat Crust 27
Grilled Chicken with Quinoa and Spinach Salad 29
Stuffed Portobello Mushrooms with Spinach and Cheese 30
Whole Wheat Pasta with Garlic, Olive Oil and Spinach 57
Spinach and Ricotta Stuffed Shells with Marinara 62
Sautéed Scallops with Lemon and Spinach 66
Creamy Spinach and Artichoke Dip 86

squash
Whole Wheat Pasta Primavera with Seasonal Vegetables 31
Spaghetti Squash with Marinara Sauce 59
Ratatouille with Fresh Herbs and Olive Oil 32
Pasta Primavera with Seasonal Vegetables 62
Grilled Vegetable Platter with Pesto 83

strawberries
Fresh Fruit Salad with Lime and Mint 20
Fresh Fruit Skewers with Yogurt Dip 38
Spinach and Strawberry Salad with Balsamic Vinaigrette and Chickpeas 43
Chocolate-Dipped Strawberries 55

sweet potato
Poached Eggs with Sweet Potato and Kale Hash 17
Herb-Roasted Turkey Breast with Seasonal Vegetables 35
Baked Sweet Potato Chips with Sea Salt 37
Herb-Roasted Chicken with Root Vegetables 73
Sweet Potato and Black Bean Tacos 26
Slow-Cooked Beef Stew with Root Vegetables 72
Roasted Sweet Potatoes with Cinnamon 87

T

tofu
Tofu Scramble with Bell Peppers and Onions 18
Vegetable Sushi Rolls with Brown Rice 28
Vegetable Stir-Fry with Tofu and Brown Rice 30

tomatoes
Creamy Avocado Toast with Tomato and Basil 13
Tofu Scramble with Bell Peppers and Onions 18
Grilled Veggie Sandwich on Whole Grain Bread 23
Caprese Salad with Fresh Mozzarella and Basil 25
Ratatouille with Fresh Herbs and Olive Oil 32
Spicy Guacamole with Whole Grain Tortilla Chips 38
Bulgur Wheat Salad with Tomatoes and Parsley 60
Spaghetti Squash with Marinara Sauce 59
Mediterranean Shrimp with Tomatoes and Olives 67

trout
Baked Trout with Almond Crust 65

tuna
Spicy Tuna Salad with Avocado and Cucumber 64

turkey
Zucchini Noodles with Marinara and Turkey Meatballs 32
Turkey and Quinoa Stuffed Peppers 70
Turkey Meatloaf with Vegetables 77
Spiced Turkey Meatballs with Marinara Sauce 78

Stuffed Zucchini Boats with Ground Turkey and Quinoa 80
Savory Meatloaf with Oats and Vegetables 80
Herb-Roasted Turkey Breast with Cranberry Relish 82
Herb-Roasted Turkey Breast with Seasonal Vegetables 35
Herb-Roasted Turkey Breast with Citrus Glaze 89

W

whole wheat flour
Whole Wheat Pancakes with Blueberries 15
Banana-Walnut Muffins with Whole Grain Flour 18
Spinach and Feta Quiche with Whole Wheat Crust 27
Almond-Crusted Cauliflower Bites 37
Healthy Carrot Cake Muffins 54
Chicken Piccata with Capers and Lemon 75
Pumpkin Pie with Whole Wheat Crust 93
Spiced Pear and Cranberry Galette 93
Almond and Cranberry Biscotti 94
Holiday Fruit and Nut Bread 95
Roasted Garlic and Herb Flatbread 95
Zucchini Fritters with Greek Yogurt Dip 39
Healthy Banana Bread with Walnuts 51
whole grain bread
Creamy Avocado Toast with Tomato and Basil 13
Lentil and Spinach Soup with Herbs 21
Grilled Veggie Sandwich on Whole Grain Bread 23
whole grain toast
Tofu Scramble with Bell Peppers and Onions 18

whole grain tortillas
Spicy Guacamole with Whole Grain Tortilla Chips 38
whole wheat bread crumbs
Zucchini and Feta Breakfast Casserole 20
Zucchini Noodles with Marinara and Turkey Meatballs 32
Herb-Crusted Baked Cod with Steamed Broccoli 33
whole wheat pasta
Whole Wheat Pasta Primavera with Seasonal Vegetables 31
Whole Wheat Pasta with Garlic, Olive Oil and Spinach 57
Pasta Primavera with Seasonal Vegetables 62
Spinach and Ricotta Stuffed Shells with Marinara 62
Spaghetti with Clams and Garlic Olive Oil 68
wild rice
Wild Rice with Cranberries and Pecans 58
Stuffed Acorn Squash with Wild Rice and Nuts 86
zucchini
Zucchini and Feta Breakfast Casserole 20
Grilled Veggie Sandwich on Whole Grain Bread 23
Vegetable Stir-Fry with Tofu and Brown Rice 30
Whole Wheat Pasta Primavera with Seasonal Vegetables 31
Zucchini Noodles with Marinara and Turkey Meatballs 32
Pasta Primavera with Seasonal Vegetables 62
Fish Cakes with Quinoa and Veggies 67
Beef and Vegetable Stir-Fry with Brown Rice 81
Grilled Vegetable Platter with Pesto 83
Zucchini Fritters with Greek Yogurt Dip 39
Stuffed Zucchini Boats with Ground Turkey and Quinoa 80

Your Journey to Better Health

Congratulations on reaching the end of the Low Cholesterol Diet Cookbook! You've taken a significant step toward improving your heart health, and that decision alone is a considerable achievement. Throughout these pages, you've learned the essentials of a diet designed to lower cholesterol, prevent heart disease, and boost your overall well-being. But more importantly, you've been empowered to make informed, sustainable choices that will positively impact your life in the long term.

As you continue on this journey, use this cookbook as a resource, but don't be afraid to get creative in the kitchen. Experiment with different ingredients, adapt recipes to your tastes and explore new cuisines that align with the Low Cholesterol Diet principles. The goal is to create an enjoyable, sustainable, and effective diet and lifestyle for your personal health goals.

Beyond the diet, embrace the holistic elements of a heart-healthy lifestyle, such as regular exercise, stress management, and self-care. Combined with a nutritious diet, these practices will enhance your physical and mental well-being, helping you live your best, healthiest life.

With the knowledge and recipes provided in this cookbook, you can make positive, lasting changes to your health. Here's to a future filled with heart-healthy meals, vibrant energy, and confidence from knowing you're doing something incredible for your body and mind.

A Final Word from the Author

Dear Reader,

Thank you for joining me on this journey toward better heart health with the **Low Cholesterol Diet Cookbook for Beginners**. I am truly grateful that you've taken the time to read this book, and I hope it has provided you with valuable insights and delicious recipes to support your wellness goals.

My passion for nutrition began with my own personal struggles. Just a few years ago, I was facing high cholesterol and dealing with excess weight that seemed impossible to shed. These challenges motivated me to delve deep into the world of nutrition. Over the past four years, I've dedicated myself to studying and understanding how our foods impact our bodies, particularly our heart health.

Writing this cookbook has been a labor of love and a culmination of my personal and professional experiences. I aimed to create a resource that is informative, practical, and enjoyable. I believe that healthy eating doesn't have to be a chore—it can be a delightful and fulfilling part of your life.

If you found this book helpful, I kindly ask you to share your experience by leaving a review on Amazon. Your feedback is incredibly valuable to me and helps other readers discover tools that might assist them on their own health journeys.

Remember, every small step you take makes a significant difference. Stay committed, keep exploring new flavors, and most importantly, enjoy the process of nurturing your body.

Wishing you health and happiness,

Olivia Robbins

Made in the USA
Monee, IL
11 April 2025

15571557R20063